Designing Neuroinclusive Workplaces

KAY SARGENT

Designing Neuroinclusive Workplaces

Advancing **Sensory Processing**
and **Cognitive Well-Being**
in the **Built Environment**

WILEY

Library of Congress Cataloging-in-Publication Data is Available:

ISBN 9781394309337 (Cloth)
ISBN 9781394309344 (ePub)
ISBN 9781394309351 (ePDF)

Cover Design: Paul Mccarthy
Cover Art: HOK Group, Inc.

SKY10096970_012325

To all the individuals who contributed to this effort by lending your voices and sharing your stories: you are truly inspirational.

To my children—Katie, Kevin, Eric, Kyle, and Karly—who inspire me daily to try to make the world a better place and to lead with empathy and understanding. Love you!

To the leadership at HOK for enabling us to forge ahead on topics that need to be addressed and for your support and encouragement. And to my colleagues at HOK who grabbed the baton and ran with it. It is wonderful to see this research reaching into so many sectors—academia, healthcare, sports and entertainment, transportation, justice, and science and technology. Stay tuned as our teams continue expanding our research on inclusion.

Contents

Foreword

We are witnessing an extraordinary societal shift toward inclusivity, one that acknowledges and celebrates the diverse ways in which individuals experience and interact with the world. This transformation is not merely a reflection of evolving societal values but a necessary response to the historical exclusion and challenges faced by neurodiverse individuals in the workplace. Advances in research, increased media representation, and expanded advocacy efforts have significantly contributed to this movement. More important, there is a growing recognition of the value that neurodiverse employees bring to the workplace, moving away from stigmatization and toward appreciation of their unique perspectives and skills.

As we embrace this change, there is an urgent need for new strategies and guidelines to design workplaces where neurodiverse employees can truly thrive, embracing a design ethos that goes beyond the traditional one-size-fits-all approach. This book, *Designing Neuroinclusive Workplaces: Advancing Sensory Processing and Cognitive Well-Being in the Built Environment*, arrives as a crucial resource, offering valuable insights and practical solutions for creating work environments that accommodate and empower neurodiverse employees.

My personal connection with this topic has evolved in many ways. Throughout my early research and development of the adaptive thermal comfort model and my research group's work on personal comfort systems at the Center for the Built Environment, I have long championed the importance of individual agency in controlling one's own environment. My recent work, a book called *Experiential Design Schemas*, co-authored with Mark DeKay, addresses broader sensory systems and explores how nature-connected spaces can bring delight and help everybody thrive. Our schemas can be used to create varying experiential intensities, and we argue that sensory diversity should be recognized as a new civil right, similar to accessibility.

More directly related to this work, I have had the privilege of attending presentations by Kay Sargent and other HOK team members at various conferences, where their work has consistently garnered enthusiastic support from audiences. However, it was in a more intimate setting—when Kay spoke with my students in my Sensory Space class at UC Berkeley—that the depth and impact of her work truly stood out. Kay discussed the neurodiversity spectrum and the importance of designing spaces that cater to both lower and higher sensory needs. Her reference to the World Health Organization's quote, "Physical, cognitive and social exclusion can occur at the point of interaction between the individual and the environment when there is a misalignment between them," was particularly powerful. Kay's message was clear: while designers cannot change an individual's sensory or cognitive profile, they have a profound responsibility to create environments that accommodate diverse needs. This perspective resonated deeply with my students, many of whom felt a newfound confidence to share their own experiences. This engagement was not only eye-opening for the students but also directly connected to the work we were doing in the class with *Experiential Design Schemas*. The students eagerly linked Kay's presentation to our efforts to document existing spaces and design new ones that offer varying intensities for different sensory systems.

One exciting outcome of Kay's engagement with my class is seen in the work of two student teams who participated in the Academy of Neuroscience for Architecture (ANFA) Student Design Competition, created to spotlight the transformative potential of combining neuroscience and design to enhance emotional and mental well-being. Students were invited to conceptualize a community center inspired by the iconic Salk Institute campus designed by Louis Kahn in La Jolla, California. Drawing inspiration from the Schemas and HOK's neurodiversity guidelines, one team created a Center for Neuro-Architecture that incorporated sensory zoning to address various sensitivities. Another team focused on designing a memory-enhancing environment for Alzheimer's patients. Both projects demonstrated how neuroscience can inform architectural design to improve cognitive function and well-being. These teams excelled in the competition, winning first and second place, highlighting the importance of integrating neurodiversity with architectural and workplace design.

Over the past decade, HOK has emerged as a leader in developing guidelines for neurodiverse workplaces, part of their broader commitment to inclusive and human-centered design. The significance of HOK's pioneering work is reflected in the many other admirable design firms also making advances in this field, such as Gensler, HDR, M Moser Associates, and Perkins&Will, among others. HOK stands out not only in that they are advancing their own research and guidelines but are also dedicated to fostering a collaborative community within the design profession to make everyone stronger. Their contributions include making reports freely available, co-hosting workshops, and including diverse voices from the field in this book's Spotlights. HOK's dedication to sharing knowledge and building community reflects a genuine commitment to advancing inclusive design.

Designing Neuroinclusive Workplaces serves as a comprehensive and invaluable resource on a complex and multifaceted topic. It offers a holistic description of neurodiversity, its attributes, and the language used to discuss it—emphasizing the significance of "words matter." The focus on sensory processing is particularly relevant, given designers' ability to influence indoor environmental qualities that can significantly impact human response. Beyond providing design guidelines, the book addresses the process of designing for inclusivity and the potential effects on a firm's organization and culture.

Creating supportive, neuroinclusive work environments is a collective responsibility, extending beyond designers and consultants to include workplace managers, HR professionals, educators, students, and neurodivergent individuals themselves. This book empowers all stakeholders to advocate for and address diverse needs within their environments.

From my own experience, I value the varied ways that applied research can impact the design profession, from flexible design tools and guidelines to various forms of policies—green building rating systems, standards, and enforceable building codes. I see this book as an essential resource for fostering systemic, transformative change. Its comprehensive guidelines can stand on their own, or can serve as a foundation for other applications, whether firm-specific, regional, or culturally adapted. The book's detailed approach and practical insights make it a vital tool for advancing inclusive design.

I am enthusiastic about this book not only for its depth of information but also for its forward-thinking and inspiring tone. It reframes the design conversation in positive terms, focusing on creative opportunities that enable all individuals to thrive. By emphasizing the importance of designing for individuality rather than an abstract average, the book advocates for environments that offer choice and control. It celebrates the value of variability and the experiential richness it brings, challenging the monotony of static and uniform environments.

Ultimately, recognizing that everyone falls somewhere on the neurodiversity spectrum and has varying sensory needs is a powerful step toward creating more inclusive environments. I encourage readers to embrace the insights and guidelines offered in this book and take meaningful action toward more inclusive design. This book is a fantastic resource for anyone committed to advancing inclusive practices, and I am confident it will inspire meaningful actions across the design community and beyond.

—Gail Brager
Professor of Architecture
Director, Center for the Built Environment
University of California, Berkeley

Preface

We welcome the move to a neuroaffirming society, which
recognizes the range of neurodivergent conditions in addition
to autism and learning disabiity.
            —Alison Clarke, chair of the task and finish group that
                    developed the British Psychological Society's
                                    Neurodiversity Manager's Guide

HOK's team began exploring the topic of neurodiversity in 2016. At the
time, many people were not familiar with the term. When a client asked
about it, we had an answer, but we wanted to know more. So, we started to
research the topic. What we found were a drought of information on how
the built environment could be designed to support neuroinclusion. We saw
an opportunity to rectify that and our team started to conduct research on
the topic. In this book, we share what we have learned so far.

Key Terms

Words matter, and language is ever-evolving. While we understand that different groups prefer different terminology, we have strived to use the most
accepted nonableist and neuroinclusive terminology. The majority of neurodivergents and their advocates we talked to during this process said they
prefer identity-first language, such as "autistic person," "ADHDer," or "dyslexic person," so we have followed that preference. These definitions reflect

commonly accepted terminology synthesized from various authoritative sources in this evolving field as of 2024.

These are key terms used in the book:

- **Neurodiversity**: The breadth of human cognitive functioning, including both typical and atypical cognition
- **Neurotypical**: Individuals whose neurological development and functioning are consistent with what is perceived to be the predominant societal standard
- **Neurotype or neurodistinct**: A collection of traits common to people with similar neurological structures
- **Neurodivergent individuals** or **neurominorities**: People whose neurocognitive functioning differs from the predominant societal standards
- **Neurodivergence**: A naturally occurring variation in neurocognitive functioning that differs from the predominant neurotype

Personally, I dislike the reference to "typical" and "divergence." We all function differently, so is there really any "typical" or "average" way to think or function? I would suggest that "neuropredictable" is a better term to use than "neurotypical." But since these are the words most commonly used today, we will use them until we collectively make our language more inclusive.

Individual preferences vary. When interacting with someone directly, we can simply ask about their preferred terminology. Consider asking whether they prefer person-first language, like "person with autism," or identity-first language, such as "autistic person," and how they would like to be addressed.

Setting the Stage

Kai steps off the packed elevator into the lobby of his new office. His heart is pounding. Sounds assault him from all sides. Conversations echo off hard floors, phones ring nonstop, and the fluorescent light feels like it is pulsing through his body. He searches in vain for refuge among countless rows of identical gray desks. There is no landmark to guide him.

Zara is still struggling in the new open office. She flinches every time someone passes behind her workstation. The enormous company logos plastered across the walls flash in her peripheral vision and conversations between her coworkers on calls

are overwhelming. She turns up the music playing through her headphones and won-
ders how she is supposed to focus.

Jamie gazes at the blank white walls of the meeting room, trying to concentrate
on a colleague's presentation. Bright overhead lights make the text on their laptop
screen almost illegible. The sterile room lacks plants or art, and there is no visual con-
nection to the outdoors. The seats around the table are tightly packed, and there is no
space to stand, move, or fidget without impacting others.

Does any of this seem familiar? These issues afflict millions of employees every day—some more severely than others. The unfortunate reality is
that most of today's offices fail to accommodate the spectrum of people's
diverse sensory needs.

This book describes how we can close this divide and use neuroinclusive design to create workplace environments where everyone can thrive.

Research and Objectives

Much of the current body of research focuses on single neurotypes, such
as autism, obsessive-compulsive disorder (OCD), or attention-deficit/
hyperactivity disorder (ADHD). Our goal is to take a more holistic
approach and address the environmental impact, needs, and strategies of
various neurotypes that fall under the neurodiversity umbrella. This more
accurately reflects the dynamics one is likely to encounter in a general
office population.

Current studies indicating that at least 20 percent of people identify as
neurodivergent, but our most research studies indicate that 20 percent might
be conservative. And in sectors like life sciences and technology, that percentage can be much higher. Yet neurominorities often suffer from "ableism,"
a form of discrimination where neurodivergents are seen as lesser and negatively impacted by prejudice and lack of access or accommodation. To us,
addressing the needs of a diverse population is an inclusion imperative and
what good design should be about—empowering people. So, we decided to
leverage our skills and develop material that addresses the needs of various
neurotypes in workplace settings.

When you consider that:

- Hearing loss or severe auditory impairment affects 6.2 percent of
  U.S. adults[1]

- Even with corrective lenses, 5.5 percent of American adults experience significant visual impairment or blindness[2]
- Mobility challenges or difficulty walking affect 6.8 percent of U.S. adults[3]

These physical disabilities affect 18.5 percent of the population, and we have rightly adapted how we design buildings to meet their needs. Yet while at least 20 percent of people are neurodivergent—and that is on the conservative side—relatively little has been done to address their needs in the built environment. That needs to change.

Article 23 of the Universal Declaration of Human Rights addresses workers' rights, recognizing the opportunity for gainful employment free of discrimination. This includes the right to "just and favorable conditions of work," ensuring that employees are treated fairly and provided with suitable working conditions that uphold their dignity.[4] As designers and architects, we have a responsibility to create inclusive work environments that support these fundamental rights.

HOK's Mission and Commitment

As a firm, HOK wants to be a leader on topics impacting people in the built environment. We are always working to provide clients with more human-centric, evidence-based solutions. Our mission is clear: "HOK is a collective of future-forward thinkers and designers who are driven to face the critical challenges of our time. We are dedicated to improving people's lives, serving our clients, and healing the planet."

Early in our research on addressing neuroinclusion in the built environment, we shared the material around the firm for feedback and vetting. One colleague was so excited about the potential that she declared, "We're going to own this topic!" We quickly clarified that this was not our intention. No one is going to "own" this topic because it is too vast and important to control. Instead, our intention is to design the most inclusive environments possible, while sharing what we learn to help advance the entire profession.

Collaboration and Industry Progress

The research on designing for neuroinclusion is constantly growing and improving. From the outset, we committed to leading on neurodiversity while openly sharing our findings. Though I know this was the right decision, there were times when I questioned it. The design profession is competitive, and sharing proprietary research is not common, but this topic is different. I recall a pivotal discussion with HOK's then chief executive officer, Bill Hellmuth, where we agreed that some topics transcend competitive advantage and become a moral imperative. This is one of those topics.

We appreciate all the others who have waded in to help expand this knowledge. We need the industry to come together around neuroinclusion, set aside attempts to own the subject, and collaborate however we can. The last thing we need is 10 different neurodiversity checklists. Instead, we need one comprehensive resource that everyone can use. What if every design firm had created its own version of the Americans with Disabilities Act (ADA) in 1990? That would have been chaos, and we would never have made the progress that we have to date on designing for physical inclusion.

Going far together was our goal when we began collaborating with the International WELL Building Institute (IWBI) on this topic in 2022. We co-hosted several workshops that brought together members of the design community, neurodivergent individuals, neuroinclusion advocates, environmental and organizational psychologists, and HR professionals—a good start but still just the beginning. We will keep sharing what we learn and pushing toward true collaboration.

The Need for Systemic Changes

What is the corporate real estate and facility industry doing with this relatively newfound awareness of the imperative to design for neuroinclusion? Are we making systemic changes to create more inclusive and welcoming environments? The urgency becomes clearer every day as the number of neurodivergents in the workplace continues to grow.

Helping neurodivergent employees overcome barriers and facilitating the adjustments they need is crucial. We appreciate the importance of collaborating with our clients' HR teams as they address their own onboarding, training, and operational process, but we can't stop there. We need to address the environment as well. These challenges motivate our research and drove us to write this book. They fuel our desire to continue expanding our research into new sectors of the built environment, beyond the workplace, so people with a wide range of abilities can experience all types of spaces that meet their needs.

Who This Book Is For

This topic touches many people, and we hope it will be a valuable resource for a diverse audience. We wrote this book to help:

- Designers and architects create inclusive spaces
- Organizations build neurodivergent-friendly environments
- Human resource (HR) professionals put in place more inclusive practices
- Neurodiversity consultants hone their advocacy skills
- Neurodivergents better understand their environmental needs
- Academics and students learn more about neuroinclusive design

Throughout the book, we have incorporated diverse perspectives, including client stories in sidebars, spotlights on people who have influenced us, interviews with inclusion experts and thought leaders, and profiles of well-known innovators and creators. We also share personal insights from our team that show why we are so passionate about this topic.

1

Framing the Issue

What's a necessity for some should be open to all.
—Maureen Dunne, author of *The Neurodiversity Edge*

My journey into neuroinclusion and designing inclusive spaces is a deeply personal one, sparked by a client's question about designing for ADHD and shaped by my experiences raising five children with diverse cognitive profiles. It turns out that I had been living in my own case study long before I realized it.

Origin Story

This conversation started for me in 2016 when a client asked, "How do you design space for someone with ADHD?" As both a mother and a designer of various educational facilities, I had ideas. I shared a few thoughts about providing options, flexibility, and ways to reduce sensory stimulation, but I sensed my answer was insufficient.

I left that room with my curiosity sparked. My HOK colleagues and I started by reviewing existing neurodiversity research but found that, despite there being plenty of material related to hiring diverse individuals, there was almost none about how to design environments conducive to their success. We began to fill this gap, which took us down a path leading to where we are today.

A colleague with two autistic children with high-support needs embraced the idea of expanding our research beyond what already existed, much of which focused on adolescent boys and educational facilities. We have heard similar suggestions from employers awakening to neuroinclusion issues and from parents wanting to ensure their neurodivergent children can be active participants in the business world once they come of age. My HOK colleagues were excited about the potential to show how evidence-based design could create better and more inclusive spaces.

My thoughts about neuroinclusion began to form long before our clients ever asked about it. When my five children were growing up, there were signs that they each had their own set of specific behavioral traits and they processed information in unique ways. But neurodivergent awareness and diagnoses were far less common in the 1990s, before our understanding of neurodevelopmental variations evolved.

Figure 1.1   Sargent Family - Katie, Kevin, Kay, Kyle, Karly, and Eric

Kevin's Story

I remember when Kevin came home at the end of second grade with a piece of paper that said he had been selected for the Gifted and Talented program. I had always hated that some kids were deemed "gifted" just because they thought differently and excelled at specific tasks. I knew Kevin was smart but always chalked it up to his natural curiosity, intense interest in certain subjects, and ability to think outside the box. There were times I was not sure he even knew where the box was.

At that time, Kevin was in the Spanish immersion program, so 50 percent of his school day, specifically math and science, was taught in Spanish. I loved that the program exposed kids to another language so early, and I embraced how it helped them see things differently as they relied more on their senses to aid in learning. They had to pay attention because they needed every clue to help them understand what was being taught and said.

Kevin's teacher shared that, of all her students, only two truly understood what she was saying most of the time during the immersive part of the day: Kevin and a native speaker. I expressed the desire to keep him in the program, but she encouraged me to shift him into the Gifted and Talented program, giving an example. She had assigned the class to create a Father's Day card using as many adjectives as possible. Kevin asked if they could also use adverbs, noting that when two adjectives are together, one becomes an adverb, so you could use only one adjective unless also using adverbs. She did not see his question as a challenge, but many other teachers would have deemed him a smart-ass and penalized him. She explained that teachers in the Gifted and Talented program were trained to deal with students who see things differently and challenge the norm.

The Gifted and Talented students excelled in many areas, were often challenged in others, were overly energetic, and were always a handful. They were given more complex assignments over extended periods because they were deemed "smart." This often posed a challenge because "smart" does not always equate to "organized," and many struggled with daily tasks and complex assignments.

Kevin was never diagnosed as neurodivergent, but there were clear parallels between his cognitive traits and those of neurodivergent individuals. Many people have things in common with those who have official diagnoses. We do not want that to diminish the experience of individuals who are genuinely struggling or oversimplify their situations. Yet many more people than we realize are impacted by complex neuro and cognitive profiles. Addressing the needs of the neurodivergent community will positively impact not only those individuals but most of us to a far greater extent than we imagine.

A few years later, I was called in to meet with Kevin's sixth-grade teacher, who was concerned that Kevin was doodling elaborate cartoons across the top of all his papers. The quizzes all had something else in common: they were all marked with an "A+" grade. I asked what the problem was since he clearly understood the material. For Kevin, doodling was a coping mechanism to channel his pent-up energy and enable him to listen. I suggested she use this to her advantage by challenging him to draw the assignments. She grudgingly agreed. By the end of the year, it had proved so successful that she gave all students the option to draw or write their assignments.

To this day, Kevin is an unconventional thinker who sees things from a unique perspective. He is unconcerned about how others perceive him, which can be both a strength and a challenge. When interested in something, he goes all in—from teaching himself Japanese in a few weeks so he could watch anime without dubbing or subtitles to solving complex problems quickly. But if Kevin doesn't care about something, he will not engage. For example, at 30 he recently asked me how to address an envelope.

Kyle's Story

Kyle, Kevin's younger brother, faces a different situation. He is very intelligent but also incredibly stubborn and more concerned with social norms and others' opinions. Don't get me wrong, he has strong opinions and freely shares them. But from a purely social aspect, he seeks to belong. His intelligence allowed him to power through elementary school, but when assignments became more complex, he struggled. By nature, he is a procrastinator with a specific way of addressing problems and daily life. At age 13, I had him tested for ADHD.

At the time, the ADHD test was a parent-completed form that seemed like a checklist for a serial killer. "Do they hurt animals?" "Do they set fires?" After completing that form, I was horrified by both the process and the general outlook. The assessment concluded Kyle had slight ADHD and OCD, but he has now come to believe that he was misdiagnosed and more likely has OCD with prominent symmetry and ordering symptoms.

Based on his initial diagnosis, his school developed an individualized education program (IEP) to allow him more time for assignments and presenting them in ways aligned with his processing needs. This should have given him access to tools meant to help him, but teachers often ignored the IEP. Ultimately, he realized IEP requests caused a negative bias against him, so he was better off forgoing them. Clearly, that is something we need to address in our education system.

Kyle was prescribed medication intended to help him focus, but it simply exacerbated his compulsive tendencies, which hindered his ability to complete assignments. As a result, he chose not to take it. Nor did he want to identify as different, so he rarely asked for accommodations if they were not offered.

In high school, Kyle started failing math, even though he was getting the correct answers. The teacher explained that there was a particular way she wanted students to answer, and although he was getting the right answer, he was not doing it *her* way. I pointed out that different people have different learning styles, which they often cannot change, but educators can change how they teach. If material is shared in only one way, teachers will likely miss connecting with many learners. The principal agreed and recognized that if educators were not accommodating, it would not bode well for Kyle and, frankly, many others in the class.

Many believe that standardized testing is an issue for neurodivergents. For Kyle, however, it was the arbitrary work leading up to exams that he had issues with. Ultimately, despite the difficulties of time restrictions on standardized testing, Kyle excelled on these exams and was always among the top scorers. He was one of only 12 students in a class of more than 500 who successfully graduated with an international baccalaureate diploma.

Kyle is wired to do things in a specific order, and if something got out of order, it would derail the entire process and even prevent him from completing the task. If he left his book at school, he could not do the assignment— even if we already had the same book from one of his older siblings readily on hand. He is a very linear thinker, and things had to happen in a specific order, as intended. Accepting alternatives is not an option. This created challenges in college, too. If he missed a class and fell behind, he felt he could not attend the next class because it was not in sequence. This created a domino effect and a self-fulfilling prophecy of defeat. Kyle had to learn, sometimes the hard way, that workarounds are often necessary.

After Kyle's initial assessment, we met with a psychologist who specializes in working with ADHD/OCD individuals. This was the first time I heard Kyle openly talk about his experience in detail. He described feeling like there was a string tied to his back that he feared would get tangled if he was not careful. He shared how he always retraced his steps and would exit the same way he entered to avoid his "string" getting tangled. He had to force himself to overcome that feeling in high school because it became unmanageable. Kyle was so good at masking his repetitive habits that I never noticed his self-regulating behaviors in our chaotic world. But these insights gave me a deeper understanding of who Kyle was and how he navigated the world.

Eric's Story

My third son, Eric, joined our family when he was 13. He came from a situation where education was not actively supported and was already challenged in school. But he rose to the occasion, graduated, and went to college. He earned his associate's degree and started his bachelor's, but after a year determined it was not for him. A great reader, philosopher, and activist with the biggest heart, Eric began working and was a dedicated, reliable employee. He quickly rose to be a manager and now oversees several locations. His dedication and empathy make him a great leader. In his mid-20s, he decided to finish his degree and signed up for classes. But he soon realized that, although he had mastered the material, taking tests and writing papers were challenging. He struggled to stay focused while working full-time. In his late 20s, Eric decided to get tested and was diagnosed with ADHD. Medication has helped him stay on point, and he is thriving.

Reflections

Understanding my boys helped me guide them toward opportunities where their talents will shine, and they have pursued careers that value their strengths. Kevin needs variety and challenges; he works as a project manager with organizations during times of transition. Kyle needs structure, the opportunity to be creative, and hands-on experiences with shorter assignments and marked milestones. Today, he works as an art conservator. Eric needs to leverage his empathy and people skills while being actively engaged; a desk job is not a good fit. He works as a general manager for a series of shops in a college town.

Neither of my daughters has shown similar signs of atypical processing needs. Both have strengths and talents and fall into more predictable ranges than my sons. This could mean they are neurotypical or better at camouflaging, or perhaps it is because we know less about how cognitive diversity presents itself in women.

I didn't initially make a connection between what I did for a living and my children's situation. Once my curiosity was piqued, however, I began to find evidence in our family of how space impacts individuals. As professionals, my colleagues and I often discuss our obligation to leverage our talents and expertise to benefit our clients, but it is bigger than that. We have an opportunity to make a positive impact on neurodivergents and neurotypicals alike.

The Pitfalls of Well-Intentioned Design

Early in our research into designing neuroinclusive space, a colleague asked, "Isn't this just good design?" In the end, yes, but not everyone practices good design, let alone evidence-based design that aids in creating the best solutions. Designers have the education and intuition to understand how space impacts individuals. However, without applying evidence-based principles, it is easy to get it wrong. Designers must apply both the science and art of design. The Montreal Design Declaration issued at the 2017 Montreal World Design Summit states, "Design is the application of intent."

For example, most people understand that sensory stimulation can be overwhelming. Hence, many organizations have created quiet spaces, phone rooms, or pods to provide options for focused work. But often, in an attempt to make those spaces inviting, designers use bright colors or creative wall graphics. This undermines the purpose of the space by putting users in a confined space near design elements they may find distressing.

This is a prime example of why it is not enough to grasp the type of spaces needed for inclusivity. We must understand how the elements and principles of design impact occupants. And we need to apply this knowledge with intent and purpose.

Case in point: One day, I was having a conversation with a colleague of mine while sitting in a small phone booth for privacy. The booth was bright red, with a bold graphic on the wall and no window to the space. As we talked, he was becoming increasingly agitated. He finally blurted out that he needed to get out of the room. This was a vivid example of how space can impact mood and behavior and why we, as designers, need to deepen our understanding of how the spaces we design impact individuals.

Understanding Neurodiversity

We live in a time of increased awareness about neurodivergence, which is a naturally occurring variation in neurocognitive functioning. The unique ways they think, process, feel, and act differ from the predominant neurotype. Neurodivergents simply work on a different operating system.

Today, approximately 20 percent of the population is considered neurodivergent. According to the Centers for Disease Control and Prevention (CDC), 28.7 percent of adults in the United States have at least one disability.[1] For about 10 percent, that disability is invisible, or nonapparent.[2] Many of these individuals are neurodivergent, yet those individuals (also known as *neurominorities*) remain one of the most underrepresented populations in the workplace.[3]

Our brains have more than 86 billion cells connecting in various ways, so it is no wonder there are naturally occurring variances in how they function.[4] The brains of neurotypical individuals tend to function within a set of typical parameters and societal norms, resulting in broadly similar cognitive functioning. In contrast, the brains of neurodivergents tend to fall outside of these parameters, leading to differences in how they process information. These neurological variations can make communication and self-expression challenging for them.

Challenges Faced by Neurodivergents

- 36 percent of adults with ADHD may not know they have it.[5]
- Adults with unmanaged ADHD may experience an annual productivity loss of 22 days per year.[6]
- Employees with ADHD face a 66 percent higher risk of being fired and a 200 percent higher risk of quitting.[7]
- Depression affects a high percentage of neurodivergents.[8]
- Nearly half of employed autistic adults work in positions they are overqualified for.[9]
- The jobless rate for neurodivergent adults in the United States is 30–40 percent, which is triple the unemployment rate for individuals with physical disabilities and eight times higher than the rate for those without disabilities.[10]

- The National Autistic Society in the United Kingdom reports that despite 77 percent of autistic individuals in the United Kingdom wanting to work, only 16 percent of adults with autism work, as opposed to 47 percent of other disabled people.[11]
- A survey of 102 U.S. entrepreneurs found that 35 percent of them had at least four dyslexic traits.[12]
- Underestimating and "othering" neurodivergents often leads to their isolation and feelings of being misunderstood. This marginalization can extend into both personal and professional lives, often resulting in workplace discrimination and underemployment.

Famous Innovators and Creators

Thomas Edison

Thomas Edison was an inventor who loved patterns and experimenting. He constantly questioned things, had an aggressive approach to learning, and was home-schooled. As a child, Edison recited phrases to himself over and over. He read the entire public library collection in the exact order they appeared on the bookshelf.[13] Having never earned a diploma, he may be considered unemployable today. Yet, by the end of his life, Edison had more than 1,000 U.S. patents to his name. In modern terms, he likely would be considered to either be autistic, ADHD, or perhaps both.

The Opportunities

Neurodivergents have been responsible for a huge number of innovations. Even so, a large percentage of this talent pool remains untapped, underemployed, or unemployed. One explanation for this discrepancy could be ill-informed bias and a lack of understanding about how to set neurodivergents up for success—something we hope to help dispel in this book.

In 1998, American journalist and neurodiversity advocate Harvey Blume published an essay in *The Atlantic* magazine titled "Neurodiversity: On the Neurological Underpinnings of Geekdom."[14] The piece highlighted the positive elements of neurodiversity. In that spirit, instead of focusing on the challenges, we prefer a strength-based approach that takes advantage of the positive attributes of neurodivergents. These include:

- ADHDers often exhibit strong imaginative abilities and typically achieve higher scores on creativity tests than non-ADHD people. ADHDers can hyperfocus as well as experience attention deficit.[15]
- The vast majority of dyslexics—84 percent—demonstrate above-average capabilities when it comes to logical reasoning, recognizing patterns, evaluating scenarios, and making decisions.[16]
- Autistic individuals can solve analytical problems 42 percent faster than non-autistic.[17]
- Autistic people tend to rely more on rational and logical reasoning and decision-making, making them less influenced by misinformation and emotions.[18]
- Autistic people have shown superior abilities in identifying patterns and working with systems.[19]
- ADHD brains typically generate more Theta waves, which are associated with a profoundly relaxed state. This may help them excel at out-of-the-box, creative thinking.[20]
- Dyslexic leaders consider themselves as better communicators and are more willing to take risks than non-dyslexic entrepreneurs.[21]
- Neurodivergent employees often display cognitive advantages such as increased efficiency, creativity, focus, and memory, as well as possessing traits like honesty and dedication.[22]

The contributions of neurominorities to cognitive diversity in the workplace include bringing varied perspectives and approaches to knowledge processing.

Neurodivergents often are out-of-the-box thinkers, creators, and innovators. Research conducted by Simon Baron-Cohen, director of Cambridge University's Autism Research Centre, and his team discovered that "modern-day inventors and autistic people share some traits to an elevated degree, and both have minds that are drawn to hyper-systemize, for partly genetic reasons." The study showed that autistic people were far more likely to be on the extreme hyper-systemizing end and that individuals working in science, technology, engineering, or math (STEM) fields also had more autistic traits than those who do not work in STEM.[23] This connection is significant, as the U.S. Bureau of Labor and Statistics has shown a growing need for skilled workers in STEM sectors.[24] Researchers have identified specific skill sets common among neurodivergents that may benefit these fields, including increased focus, more deliberative decision-making, visual acuity, logical thinking, and an affinity for technology.[25]

A Growing Awareness

Typical does not mean better. If you describe something as typical or average, it is rarely a compliment.

The intense pressure people feel to fit in can unconsciously trigger a need for neurotypical-passing, which includes behaviors like masking or camouflaging.[26] Neurodivergent individuals might be suffering through a stressful meeting, or autistic people might force themselves to make uncomfortable eye contact or prepare for social interactions that are difficult for them. Research shows that camouflaging is unsustainable and can be harmful to the individual.[27] "It can result in autistic burnout, illness, and job loss."[28]

The barriers for the neurodivergent community are often invisible. Unlike physical barriers, sensory barriers are not always obvious and often go unaddressed. Social inclusion and our ability to manage sensory and cognitive distractions in the workplace impact our level of engagement. Though this is a nascent movement for many, there is a growing awareness of how sensory stimulation in the built environment affects our cognitive well-being.

What might be merely annoying to neurotypicals could be debilitating to neurodivergents. This aligns with a concept articulated by autism blogger Kirsten Lindsmith: "Autistic people are canaries in the coal mine: our needs aren't actually different from typical people's, just more intense and specific."[29]

Autistic people, for example, are likely to struggle with eye contact, viewing themselves on virtual calls, and higher cognitive loads, while ADHDers may face challenges due to a lack of options for physical movement. Just as we routinely provide adjustments like corrective eyewear, ramps for easier access, and height-adjustable furniture, addressing these needs often reveals important insights about what might negatively impact others as well.

Given that people worldwide spend 85–90 percent of their lives indoors,[30] designing spaces to address the needs of a much broader population, including neurodivergents, is critical.

Spotlight

Angelita Scott's Journey Championing Neurodiversity in Design and Wellness

Angelita Scott, PhD, is a director and community concept lead for the WELL Building Standard and WELL Equity Lead at the International Well Building Institute (IWBI). In her work on the WELL Equity Rating, she creates strategies to support neurodivergent people.

How did your journey into neurodiversity begin?

Angelita: I have a son on the autism spectrum. I started seeing signs associated with autism when he was 2 years old but never wanted to talk about it. He's now 17. There wasn't a lot of information back then, so I did my own research. I found that some were having success with nutrition, so I took him off dairy and gluten and found a practitioner who supported that. We gave him supplements specifically made for his body's deficiencies, and he started seeing a speech therapist. The effect was like night and day. He was able to communicate better, and his eye contact improved.

How did this personal experience influence your professional work?

I always felt that when the time was right, I would use my work to advocate for him and other kids. I had a residential design business focused on principles of well-being and started to incorporate the Sensory Intelligence® assessment into my business because we all process differently. When I joined the IWBI and we started working on the WELL Equity Rating, I wanted to give a voice to marginalized populations. This included creating strategies to support neurodivergent people.

What current initiatives are you involved in regarding neurodiversity in design?

We've partnered with HOK to form a working group to convene interior designers and other related professionals to explore the issues and identify existing research. Our first workshop in

New York felt magical—like we were really on to something. At subsequent follow-up sessions, including one we held at the WELL Summit, so many people wanted to participate that it was standing-room only. We didn't anticipate that, but it's exciting that everyone wants to be involved in this work.

What are your thoughts on the future of neuroinclusive design?

I'm encouraged because we're moving in the right direction. Interior design has the power to change people's lives, either negatively or positively. This is going to impact people positively on a great scale.

HOK's Research on Designing for Inclusion

Since beginning our research on designing for neurodiversity in 2016, HOK has expanded that to include sensory processing and cognitive well-being. Our initial literature review identified a significant gap in existing research and publications on the benefits of designing neuroinclusive spaces and how best to do it, particularly in workplace environments. Next, our team explored the topic more comprehensively. We have conducted more than 300 literary reviews, numerous surveys, and focus groups, as well as developing the initial business case, call to action, and design considerations. We have partnered with various experts including environmental psychologists, social scientists, leading developers of scientific spaces, human resources specialists, academics, the neurodivergent community, and advocates for inclusion.

We have expanded our research into how to design environments that address many of the challenges people face in built spaces—acoustic, visual, tactile, or olfactory. Our objective is to further explore the influence of the physical setting and how we design environments from their inception to be more welcoming and inclusive.

The Value of Neuroinclusive Design

People are the chief currency and greatest asset of any business. With up to 80 percent of a company's expenses going toward staff costs, the workforce must be productive, engaged, and empowered. Yet according to the latest edition of Gallup's annual global engagement survey, 77 percent of workers are disengaged.[31]

Along with just being the right thing to do, there is a compelling business case for greater inclusion. Designing for neurodiversity and inclusion can unleash new opportunities and be good business. Today's spaces need to reflect the diverse makeup of organizations to set everyone up for success. By designing to accommodate a variety of work styles, personality types, and abilities, we can create environments where the vast majority can find settings that meet their needs in the workplace. If we focus on these factors, we can start creating the types of environments we all want to experience.

Consider all we do to accommodate neurodivergent students while they are in school. Their needs do not disappear upon entering the workforce. Incorporating inclusive design practices in workplace environments enables everyone to thrive.

Studies have shown that individuals tend to be more successful in inclusive workplaces and are more likely to innovate, enjoy their jobs, work harder,[32] and, ultimately, stay longer with their employers.[33] As noted in the International Healthy Building Accord, "by adopting inclusive design strategies, equitable access to healthy spaces, and research-based design strategies, we can reduce health disparities and ensure the advantages of healthy buildings reach our most vulnerable and marginalized populations."[34]

The Golden Rule suggests treating others as we want to be treated. That's admirable, but a less self-centric approach would be to embrace the Platinum Rule, which advocates that we "treat others as they wish to be treated." This approach acknowledges our differences and individual perspectives while encouraging us to address the needs of many individuals, not just one.

As design professionals, we have expertise in how spatial conditions and elements can provide different experiences and address the needs of the individuals who occupy the built environment. Currently, most research on human-environment interaction has been conducted by human resources specialists or environmental psychologists who focus on the psychological aspects of space and adjustments that can be made to accommodate various user needs. There is also growing advocacy from many in the neurodiverse community.

We need to hear more from the neurodivergent community and embrace a "nothing about us, without us" philosophy, but also keep in mind that neurodivergents tend to be experts on their own situations. That does not necessarily mean they are experts on the subject—or other people's needs—any more than having cancer makes one a cancer expert.

Occupational and environmental psychologists, human resource professionals, and academics bring essential perspectives. We also need to incorporate insights from design experts who are trained to understand the way the built environment impacts individuals and ways to adjust it. Their diverse input will help us develop a balanced approach that acknowledges the important role each plays in crafting environments that address the needs of a community with a vast range of considerations.

2 | Defining Neurotypes

> In order to support our differences, you must first understand them.
>
> —Lyric Rivera, author of *Workplace NeuroDiversity Rising 2.0*

The human brain is made up of approximately 86 billion neurons with 100 trillion connections, each of which influences how we think, feel, and experience the world.[1] We all process information differently because our brain functions are unique. But while the functioning of neurotypical individuals falls within set norms and expectations, neurodivergent people, or neurominorities, tend to fall outside those parameters.

There is increased awareness around neurodiversity, and studies estimate that neurodivergent individuals make up 15–20 percent of the global adult population, with an estimated 17 percent of the workforce being neurodivergent professionals.[2] Considering that more than 25 percent of the U.S. population lives with some type of disability,[3] we are long overdue for meaningful improvements in how we design inclusive spaces and build workplace cultures that support all individuals, regardless of their neurological or physical differences.

A group of autistic scholars of autism and neurodiversity noted in a 2024 letter to the editor of the journal *Autism* that autistic activists on the Independent Living email list first used the term *neurodiversity* in 1996. Sociologist Judy Singer began to popularize the term in 1998, elevating our collective awareness.[4]

Types of Neurodivergence

Nancy Doyle identified two subtypes of developmental neurominorities,[5] and other experts have suggested a third category[6]:

- **Applied:** Relates to applied and functional skills such as reading or motor control. Present at birth but not considered a health condition. Examples include dyslexia, dyspraxia, dyscalculia, and dysgraphia.
- **Clinical:** Relates to behavioral skills such as self-control, communication, or attention span. Present at birth and considered a health condition. Examples include ADHD, autism, and Tourette syndrome.
- **Acquired:** Developed in response to a health condition, trauma, or injury. Examples include temporary mental health conditions, neurological illnesses, and brain injuries.

The estimate that 17 percent of the workforce is neurodivergent is likely conservative, given that many individuals' conditions remain undiagnosed. The World Health Organization noted that the prevalence of neurological conditions is one of the greatest threats to public health: "There are several gaps in understanding the many issues related to neurological disorders, but we already know enough about their nature and treatment to be able to shape effective policy responses to some of the most prevalent among them."[7]

Understanding Neurodevelopmental Disorders

In medicine, a disorder signals a need for treatment. Traditionally, we look for one of four red flags: distress, dysfunction, deviance, or danger. Neurodevelopmental disorders arise during the developmental period, impacting behavior and cognition. They can affect cognitive functions, motor and linguistic skills, and social interactions. One note on terminology: Many prefer the term *condition* over *disorder,* so we will use that language where applicable.

Neurodistinctions manifest differently, even for people who share the same neurotype. Cognitive profiles, or unique traits, can vary and cover a wide range of functioning and abilities. As neurodivergent inclusivity advocate Stephen Shore once noted, "If you've met one individual with autism, you've met one individual with autism."[8]

Not only is neurodivergence cognitive, but it also affects individuals on physical and emotional levels. In the United States, 61 million people live with some kind of disability. Of these, 73 percent do not require assistive devices, making their challenges less noticeable to others.[9] This means we may not realize how many people we are surrounded by daily are dealing with invisible impairments.

While some disabilities are temporary and others situational, most neurodivergents are born with a neurological difference that typically remains for their entire life. A 1977 study was the first to show that autism was largely genetic.[10] Today, scientists estimate that DNA is the root factor for 80 percent of autism and ADHD diagnoses.[11] These conditions tend to be neurodevelopmental outcomes of how the brain was formed in the womb or early childhood. But in some cases, neurodivergence occurs after an injury or trauma.

Specific Neurotypes

It is important to note that different neurotypes impact individuals and their functions, behaviors, and responses to their interactions and environments in unique ways.

Attention-Deficit Hyperactivity Disorder   Attention-deficit hyperactivity disorder is a brain-based condition typically characterized by a persistent pattern of inattention or hyperactivity and impulsivity due to under-stimulation of the brain. ADHD has three different subtypes: predominantly inattentive, predominantly hyperactive-impulsive, or a combination.

ADHD often coexists with other conditions, such as obsessive-compulsive disorder, anxiety, depression, and oppositional defiance disorder (ODD).[12] ADHDers can experience hyperfocus and be easily distracted. It is important to note that ADHD exists on a spectrum, with individuals experiencing mild, moderate, or severe symptoms.

Prevalence and Subtypes   ADHD starts in childhood and persists into adulthood for approximately 60 percent of those diagnosed,[13] though its manifestation can change over time. The prevalence rate is 4.4 percent,[14] and according to a 2022 CDC survey, ADHD has been diagnosed in 11.4

percent of American children between the ages of 3 and 17,[15] which is 1 million more than in 2016. This means that about one in 10 children in the United States live with an ADHD diagnosis.

ADHD Presentation in Different Groups   For girls, ADHD can present as follows:[16]

- Low self-esteem
- Anxiety
- Academic challenges
- Inattentiveness
- Trouble listening
- Difficulties with executive functioning

For boys, ADHD traits commonly include the following:[17]

- Impulsiveness
- Aggressive behavior
- Difficulty sitting still
- Excessive talking
- Interrupting others

ADHD can be harder to diagnose in adults, as the traits may vary from those of childhood presentations, and adults are likely better at masking their conditions. The condition in adults is often misattributed to depression, anxiety, or even menopause.

Untreated ADHD in adults can lead to issues including the following:[18]

- Impulsiveness
- Disorganization and problems prioritizing
- Poor time management skills
- Problems focusing on a task
- Trouble multitasking
- Excessive activity or restlessness
- Poor planning
- Low frustration tolerance
- Frequent mood swings

- Problems following through and completing tasks
- Hot temper
- Trouble coping with stress

Brain Differences and Neuroscience   Martine Hoogman conducted a study of more than 3,000 individuals between the ages of 4 and 63, using MRI scans of the brains of individuals with and without ADHD. The results showed that people with ADHD have distinct differences. Hoogman noted significant differences in the prefrontal cortex, which is responsible for focus and awareness, mood regulation, and planning and behavioral controls.[19]

The amygdala is the portion of the brain that plays a big role in processing emotions, memory, and decision-making. People with ADHD tend to have smaller amygdala volumes than people without ADHD, which can make it difficult to cheer up or calm down.[20]

Traits and Challenges   ADHDers can be susceptible to sensory inputs like sights, sounds, and smells. With a heightened sensitivity to smells, they are often the first to detect odors, making them the canaries in the coal mine.[21] They can also experience challenges within social and work settings.

Contrary to popular belief, ADHDers can also have hyperfocus and get into an extended flow state.[22] They can become so completely absorbed in their tasks that they tune out everything else. They typically score high on intelligence tests and have been shown to have more original and highly creative ideas.[23] Many may need additional stimulation, as they tend to be risk seekers. They may also enjoy spaces that allow spontaneous engagement or intriguing scenarios.

Many ADHDers have lower levels of dopamine, which is a neurotransmitter in the brain associated with pleasure, reward, motivation, and motor control. This can result in low levels of stimulation and lead many to seek high-stimulation engagements.[24] Many self-stimulate by chewing, fidgeting, doodling, or engaging in some form of movement. Many are kinesthetic learners and need to physically engage to process things. Some people have a lot of excess energy and need to move and fidget. Though people do not outgrow that, they may learn to suppress it.

There is a growing movement to refer to these characteristics as traits, not symptoms, since symptoms imply that there is something wrong and far more stigma is associated with that term. ADHD is just a different way of processing information.

The *Diagnostic and Statistical Manual of Mental Disorders (DSM)* revised the definition in the third edition, issued in 1980, to "ADD (Attention Deficit Disorder) with or without hyperactivity." In 1987, the ADD (Attention Deficit Disorder) label was further refined to "ADHD (Attention-Deficit Hyperactivity Disorder)." ADHD and ADD are often used interchangeably but the accepted term today is ADHD.[25]

"ADHD is worse than any single other life expectancy risk factor that we are concerned about as a population—diabetes, smoking, obesity, alcohol use, and so on. ADHD is worse than all of them," said Russell Barkley. ADHDers often have a higher rate of impulsive behavior, substance abuse, and co-occurring mental health conditions like anxiety and depression that can lead to an increased risk of accidents. Those with untreated ADHD also have a lower rate of preventive healthcare that contributes to shorten life expectancy.[26]

Autism   Autism is a neurological condition that affects how a person acts and interacts with others, communicates socially, learns, and processes sensory information. The prevalence rate is 2.2 percent.[27] An allistic individual is a person not affected by autism. As of the fifth edition of the *Diagnostic and Statistical Manual of Mental Disorders (DSM-5)*, issued in 2013, Asperger's syndrome was reclassified within the broader autism umbrella and is no longer a distinct diagnosis. Because some still use this term, however, it is included here.

Initially, Asperger's was considered to be high-functioning autism since it does not cause learning difficulties, while autistic individuals were classified as low-functioning. However, many believe that to be an oversimplification and a disservice to both, as high-functioning individuals are often ignored since they are considered closer to "normal," and low-functioning individuals are often written off due to their challenges. As Kyler Shumway and Daniel Wendler point out in their lecture series, "Neurodiversity and the Myth of Normal,"[28] both need support. Changes in the *DSM-5* resulted in all levels of function falling under the autism spectrum. The current categories are not based on a person's level of functioning, but on the level of support they need.[29]

- Level 1: Need support
- Level 2: Need substantial support
- Level 3: Need very substantial support

This enables all to have their specific needs addressed at the appropriate level of care. Along with being different from neurotypicals, neurodivergents are distinct from each other. It is best to consider autism on a case-by-case basis and embrace the differences that define each individual.

Neurological Differences The brains of autistic people tend to have more neural connections and density, which can result in different sensations and responses to stimuli than those in the neuromajority.[30]

Autistic people often have a larger hippocampus—the part of the brain most responsible for memory formation and recall.[31] This is where the notion of neurodivergents having "superpowers" or being savants comes from. But not all experience the same abilities. Some excel in specific areas, while others may not have exceptional skills and could resent the pressure to exhibit "superpowers."

MRI studies show that autistic children have smaller cerebellar vermis volume compared with typically developing children, which results in reduced control of body movement, dexterity, and coordination.[32]

Key Traits and Special Interests Three key traits of autism have been identified: obsessive interests, difficulty in social relationships, and problems communicating.[33] Obsessive interests, often referred to as special interests, go beyond typical hobbies and can border on passion leaning toward obsession. These special interests help autistic individuals manage stress levels and regulate moods. They also can foster connections with groups that share their interest, helping form social bonds.[34]

Autistic people are often more direct and authentic in their communication, partly because they are not as adept at understanding social cues. They often have a strong sense of justice and ethical principles. Their logical mindset usually equates to being more objective, rational, and less swayed by groupthink or pressure to conform. Autistic people typically think more spatially and exhibit strong attention to detail.[35]

Many autistic people also may find it challenging to interpret nonverbal communication, such as body language and social cues. They often prefer straightforward conversation, as they tend to interpret language literally.[36] This can result in awkward social exchanges. Another form of coping with social interaction for autistic individuals is echolalia, copying someone else's speech.[37] While this can be perceived as mocking someone, for an autistic individual it can just be a way of trying to fit in and relate to others.

In Western cultures, direct eye contact is considered a sign of trustworthiness. Neurotypicals often perceive the avoidance of eye contact as evasiveness or inattention. For many people with autism, however, eye contact can be problematic and even cause sensory overload. They often prefer to look at the edges of a face instead of the center or eyes.[38] This could lead them to avoid video calls, go off camera, or seek asymmetrical communication methods.

Sensory Processing   Most autistic individuals can be hyper- or hyposensitive to stimulation. Hypersensitive individuals may be extremely distracted by certain sensory inputs, finding it impossible to concentrate unless they are removed from the environment.[39] Hyposensitive people have less of a response to stimuli, which can lead them to seek out more stimulation, perhaps by constantly touching textures or seeking sounds.[40] Autistic inertia refers to challenges in initiating, changing, or transitioning from one activity to the next.[41] It is often associated with a feeling of being stuck or unable to resume something after being interrupted.

People with autism also often show heightened abilities to recognize, generate, and process patterns,[42] but they have difficulty with habituation.

Famous Innovators and Creators: Alan Turing

Alan Turing is widely recognized as the father of theoretical computer science and artificial intelligence. Turing was also essential in breaking the code of the German Enigma cipher device in World War II and was celebrated for his contributions. It was reported that, based on descriptions from associates and anecdotes from his life, Turing met the criteria for Asperger's syndrome and today would be diagnosed as autistic.[43]

Dyslexia, Dysgraphia, Dyscalculia, and Dyspraxia Dyslexia is a neurological condition that involves problems identifying speech sounds and learning how they relate to letters and words. It affects about 3–7 percent[44] of the population. Dyslexics often score high on intelligence and have been shown to have more original ideas, enhanced creativity, and be more creative than non-dyslexics.[45] They also have an aptitude for linking and connecting disparate concepts and finding commonalities often overlooked by others, making them skilled problem solvers.[46]

Dysgraphia, which affects 10–30 percent of people,[47] is a neurological condition that impairs a person's ability to write and turn their thoughts into written language. It primarily affects handwriting, challenging the movement and sequencing of the finger muscles required for writing. Dysgraphia also can affect the coherence of written expression.[48]

Dyscalculia is a neurological condition that affects a person's ability to understand number-based information and math.[49] Between 3 and 7 percent of people are affected by dyscalculia.[50]

Dyspraxia, sometimes called developmental coordination disorder (DCD), is a complex neurological condition affecting movement and coordination. It involves multiple brain functions governing muscle coordination and perception and may also affect language and thought.[51] Dyspraxia has a prevalence rate of 10 percent.[52]

People with these neurodivergent conditions often discover strengths including increased creativity and innovative thinking, with an ability to strategically apply these traits to solving complex problems.

Tourette Syndrome Tourette syndrome is a complex neurological condition that is genetically inherited and has a prevalence rate of 0.5–0.6 percent.[53] Common involuntary and uncontrollable manifestations of Tourette syndrome include tics, which can be physical (from minor movements to more major body motions) and verbal expressions (which can include laughing, talking, and coughing).[54]

Obsessive-Compulsive Disorder Obsessive-compulsive disorder is a condition characterized by obsessive and compulsive behaviors.[55] Obsessions are typically unwanted, intrusive thoughts or urges that trigger distressing feelings. Compulsions are behaviors that a person engages in to counteract the obsession. Some repetitive behaviors are more like "rituals" that are often a positive, functional part of one's daily activities that bring comfort.

On a Personal Note: Creature of Habit

In my house, everybody always sits in the same place at the dinner table, and Lord forbid you sit in someone else's seat. I remember when my oldest daughter went to college. For months, no one would sit in her place, even though she was hundreds of miles away. For some people, it is just easier when they don't have to sweat the small stuff. But for others, especially those with OCD, routine can be essential. The more consistent they can make their day, the more comfortably they can navigate it.

A few years ago, all my kids came home for dinner with their assorted friends in tow. One had the audacity to sit in my son Kyle's chair. When he arrived at the table to see that his seat was occupied, he was almost paralyzed; he didn't know what to do. His brother, knowing full well what was happening, told him to take any seat, and reluctantly, he did. I noticed that although Kyle was moving his food around, he was not eating it. I promptly announced that anyone who had finished was required to get up and leave the table. That came as a shock to my kids because the rule in our house was that no one left the table until everyone was done. That night was an exception.

My older son Kevin and his friend left the table. Kyle promptly picked up his plate, moved to his spot, sat down, and began to eat his meal, which at that point was ice cold. That did not matter to him. Routine and consistency did.

I apply the same logic to assigned versus unassigned seats in the workplace. For many employees, having options and choices is critical and enables them to find the right space that fits their needs. But it can be equally important for some to have a space that is predictable, reliable, and one less thing to worry about during the day. We need to provide assigned and unassigned options to enable all to thrive.

Synesthesia Synesthesia is a perceptual phenomenon in which one's senses get mixed, and the stimulation of one sensory or cognitive pathway leads to involuntary experiences in another.[56] Research suggests that synesthesia affects between 3 and 5 percent of people, with a higher prevalence among females than males.[57] People with synesthesia may see shapes or colors when listening to music or smelling certain scents. Or they may perceive letters or numbers as different colors. Individuals who experience synesthesia are frequently attracted to musical and artistic pursuits. Renowned artist Vincent Van Gogh claimed to have synesthesia.

Neurotype Comorbidity Comorbidity, the coexistence of multiple conditions, affects a large segment of the neurodivergent population. A recent study of comorbidity issues points toward a shared underlying neuropsychological dysfunction that may give rise to both ADHD and comorbid disorders.[58] There is also a debate on whether comorbid conditions simply accentuate the severity of ADHD traits or if they should be classified as a distinct phenotype. More research is needed to determine the connection, but what is known is that over two-thirds of people with ADHD have at least one other condition.[59]

A 2024 CDC report found that nearly 78 percent of children diagnosed with ADHD had at least one other diagnosed condition.[60] Behavioral issues, anxiety, and developmental delays are most common, but autism and depression were also frequently noted. Common comorbid conditions with ADD/ADHD include the following:

- AuDHD: Individuals who have both ADHD and autism (50–70 percent)[61]
- Oppositional defiant disorder (ODD): 50–60 percent; ODD presents as a frequent pattern of anger, irritability, arguing, and defiance toward parents and other authority figures.[62]
- Conduct disorder: 30–45 percent; conduct disorder is an emotional and behavioral disorder that displays as disruptive and violent behavior.[63]
- Anxiety: 25 percent.[64]
- Depression: 19–53 percent.[65]
- Bipolar condition: 73 percent of kids, 43 percent of teens, and 17 percent of adults; formerly known as bipolar disorder and manic depression, bipolar disorder includes mood swings with emotional highs (mania) and lows (depression).[66]
- Tourette syndrome: 35–90 percent of kids.[67]
- Substance misuse issues: 23 percent.[68]

- OCD: 16 percent.[69]
- Tics (sudden, repetitive movements or sounds that can be involuntary): 9–12 percent.[70]

Neurodiversity and Mental Health

Though they are distinct concepts, neurodiversity and mental health often intersect. Compared to those in the neuromajority, neurodivergents—especially those with autism—may be more prone to anxiety and depression. Studies show that up to 50 percent of autistic individuals will go through depression at some point.[71] Additionally, neurodivergents may be more susceptible to the adverse effects of social media and screen addiction, which are common problems in the modern world.[72]

Consider these statistics:

- 21 percent of U.S. adults live with a mental illness.[73]
- Depression and anxiety cost the global economy USD $1 trillion annually in lost productivity.[74]
- Stress is a factor in 60–80 percent of workplace accidents.[75]
- Of U.S. adults with a mental illness, 55 percent go untreated.[76]

Famous Innovators and Creators: Albert Einstein

Simon Baron-Cohen, who heads the Autism Research Centre at Cambridge University, has suggested that Albert Einstein exhibited key markers linked to Asperger's syndrome: "obsessive interests, difficulty in social relationships, and problems communicating."[77] As a child, Einstein was extremely introverted, often repeating phrases obsessively. Though he maintained some friendships, he had difficulty with close, lasting relationships. Despite his genius, Einstein could not be bothered with things he did not believe were important, like dressing appropriately or observing birthdays.

Midlife Diagnosis Crisis

As awareness of neurodiversity grows, so does the number of individuals seeking diagnosis, and not just among adolescents. As children are assessed, many parents are also exploring their own situations, leading to an increasing number of adults being diagnosed as neurodivergent in recent years. These midlife assessments are leading to new levels of consideration and more individuals looking for accommodations in university and work environments.

On a Personal Note: A Midlife ADHD Diagnosis

An HOK colleague who was actively involved in the new design of one of our offices wholeheartedly embraced designing for neuroinclusion. His team volunteered to serve as a pilot project, leveraging our assessments and even tracking their biometrics, all to further our research. When his son was diagnosed with ADHD, this colleague considered he might have it, too. At age 50, he took a test that confirmed what he had suspected: He, too, was neurodivergent. He said that it explained many of his life experiences and that it was reassuring to officially know. He is now part of a community of midlifers embracing their whole selves, armed with a deeper understanding of what makes them who they are.

Gender-Related Diagnosis

In the United Kingdom, 1 in 57 children is on the autism spectrum.[78] Boys are three times more likely to be diagnosed than girls, as assessments are based on presentations more common in males.[79] Recent studies have shown that ADHD is consistently underdiagnosed or undiagnosed in girls and women. Historically, the diagnosis of males has been at least four times more common than for females, though that is starting to shift.[80] The long-term health risks of delayed ADHD diagnosis or misdiagnosis for women are significant.[81]

Women are more likely than men to experience depression and often are misdiagnosed with a mood disorder while the underlying ADHD is missed. Women diagnosed later in life with ADHD often have diminished mental and physical health, poor relationships, and career struggles.[82]

Spotlight

Kate Wardle Champions Neuroinclusion in South Africa

Kate Wardle is part of the Corporate Member Services team at Neurodiversity in Business (NIB) and founder of Include Me Consulting. With more than 20 years of experience in change management, communications, and employee engagement in the United Kingdom and South Africa, Kate harnesses her lived experience as a late-diagnosed ADHDer to drive inclusion in South Africa.

How did you become an advocate for neuroinclusion?

Kate: My journey started about five or six years ago when I lost my job. The woman who let me go said, "I think there's something wrong with you. I think you have ADHD and should go to a psychiatrist." I was devastated and utterly rejected the idea out of hand. I felt humiliated and ashamed.

Shortly after, I started having challenges with my two children. My eldest, Elliott, now 13, is a very anxious child. He was assessed as gifted at age five and had sensory issues with plenty of meltdowns. My son Greg, 10, was unfocused and slow in his development. By the time they reached school age, it was clear neither of them would thrive in mainstream education.

We went through the typical route of getting our children assessed—speaking to multiple people and reading extensively. The information was overwhelming. When an educational psychologist assessed both children at ages 8 and 10, they suggested both of them might be autistic. I was shocked. Then, I started laughing and asked if I should have my husband, who was in a clinic for burnout at the time, come in for a three-for-one deal. They looked at me and said, "Kate, we understand you're laughing as a coping mechanism, but we feel you should possibly be assessed too." I thought, no way! My first instinct was that it couldn't be possible—I have two degrees! It shows how little I knew and how much stigma from society I had internalized.

So, I started researching, as hyper-focused people do, reading everything I could on the topic. A psychologist later assessed me as being both autistic and ADHD.

What challenges did you face in finding support?

There was a lot of information in the parents' space, but it felt scary and polarized. It seemed as if you were either on the side of taking medication or trying things like rescue remedy and cutting out sugar. I didn't fit into either camp.

I started trying to see what support was available and find the right school for both kids. It's a terribly stressful journey for parents. I also began to think about my own journey and where things had gone wrong in my career. Looking at it through this lens, I thought, what are my kids going to do? How will they work in the future? How can we better advocate for them in the workplace?

I found the charity Neurodiversity in Business (NIB) on LinkedIn and decided to get involved as a volunteer. The founder, Dan Harris, encouraged me to volunteer with them and then consider opening a chapter in South Africa.

What has been the most rewarding aspect of your advocacy work?

The best thing about volunteering has been that the more people you speak to, the more you start to understand yourself better. You feel part of a community, part of a tribe, and I felt that I was on the right path. There's something substantial and good about advocating for neuroinclusion. I find it very rewarding because most neurodivergent women are justice-driven and want to make a difference.

What have you learned about neurodiversity through your family's experiences?

There is a whole debate about the strong overlap between different conditions. It's becoming less important that you are labeled

(continued)

(*continued*)

autistic or ADHD and more important to know that your brain is wired differently. The medical model of having a "condition" to be cured or of caveating a "low-" or "high-"functioning state is increasingly rejected in the neurodivergent community.

Research also indicates that if you are neurodivergent, you are far more likely statistically to also identify as a different gender or not to be heterosexual.

What advice would you give to neurodivergent individuals who are struggling?

Many women, in general, don't like to ask for help. I had a child right after I finished my MBA, and he screamed all the time. I got super depressed because I couldn't sleep or function. My father stepped in and told me I needed help. Sometimes, we need that outside perspective. We can't be afraid to ask for help or use the resources or medications that can make things better. I wish I had known then what I know now—how much harder it is to have a newborn if you also have sensory issues and are neurodivergent. And that neurodivergent babies often have reflux or colic. Listening to crying was almost unbearable.

What type of work are you doing today?

My MBA thesis focused on employee engagement and organizational behavior. I love studying how people work in the workplace, and I've done a lot of academic work and lecturing on this. I'm now working with companies to raise awareness and bring about more inclusion.

Often these types of conversations get lumped into HR and wellness, but the discussion should be broader and conducted across an organization at a strategic level. I've worked before in HR, and many teams are resistant to change or making accommodations because there is concern that everyone will want headphones or software. My role is to try to mitigate this fear and bring about change for all employees. Unlocking talent in the workplace through inclusion has a positive impact on a company's bottom line.

Can you tell us about your ALPHA approach?

I have developed a framework called the ALPHA approach, which is named after the next generation but is a useful way to Assess, Listen, Promote, Harness, and Adapt your workplace needs. It draws on change management theory, lived experience, and emerging technology.

We need to have more conversations about inclusion in the workplace and expanding it beyond the legal requirements here in South Africa, which historically have been mainly racial and gender oriented. We have a problem in South Africa where a lot of our talented people between 20 and 40 years old are emigrating. We must address how we are going to plug that gap because our quality of education has deteriorated, and many young people don't have the right skills or experience to step in.

I'm interested in the intersection between AI and the next, younger, generation coming into the workplace. Gen Z works differently and does not have the same motivators as Gen X. Gen Alpha will be even further away from the ways of working that Gen X was brought up with. The skills that most neurodivergent people have—cognitive reasoning, problem-solving, and spatial planning—will become increasingly necessary in this landscape. If you can unlock these skills, the company benefits.

What are your thoughts on creating more inclusive hiring practices?

Many companies don't know where to start. Several are beginning to send questions in advance so candidates can prepare. We should not be trying to trick people in an interview by surprising

(*continued*)

(*continued*)

them with questions. This creates anxiety and does not showcase true skills and ability. Instead, we should be having meaningful conversations. This starts with introducing a candidate to who will be in the interview, checking if they have any additional requirements to attend the interview, and sending them the questions in advance. We want to bring out the best in people, not waste time for both the candidate and the company.

3

Great for Business

There is a lack of understanding from the managers of neurodiverse staff that results in them not being able to provide the right guidance and support. Some people are also afraid to share that they might struggle with certain tasks, where really, they are very gifted and talented but just learn differently.

—Will Wheeler, founder of The Dyslexic Evolution

Visionary companies do more than accommodate neurodivergence—they actually seek it out. That's because they recognize this largely untapped talent pool has many high-energy, out-of-the box thinkers who tend to excel in crises and be bold problem solvers. Once hired, however, neurodivergent employees often face difficulties in the modern workplace. Creating inclusive environments that support them, along with their neurotypical colleagues, is not just the right thing to do—it is great for business.

The Business Case for Neurodiversity

Driven by an aging workforce, pushback against immigration, early retirements, and falling birth rates, many countries face an impending talent shortage. Studies show that 85 percent of autistic individuals in the United States are unemployed, though 69 percent of them want to work.[1] That is an alarming rate that is significantly higher than that of the overall population, which stands at 4.2 percent.[2] Seventy-five percent of global corporations are having trouble recruiting the talent they need.[3] Businesses facing labor shortages have a compelling opportunity to tap into this undervalued labor pool.

Many neurodivergent thinkers possess exceptional abilities in problem-solving, innovation, design thinking, pattern recognition, and coding. Neurodivergents often bring different but invaluable skill sets to an organization. Since 70 percent of disabilities are invisible, many people fear the exposure or stigma associated with openly acknowledging a disability. As a result, only 4 percent of workers today self-identify as being disabled.[4] The good news is we are starting to see progress in neurodivergent employment. In 2023, employed individuals with disabilities rose to a record high of 22.4 percent.[5]

The Birkbeck Neurodiversity at Work 2023 survey[6] noted the strengths reported by neurodivergent people as the following:

- Hyperfocus: 80 percent
- Creativity: 78.1 percent
- Innovative thinking: 75 percent
- Data processing: 71 percent
- Authenticity: 64.4 percent
- Visual reasoning: 58.3 percent
- Long-term memory: 55.3 percent
- Entrepreneurialism: 46 percent

Research supports the Birkbeck survey results. JPMorgan Chase found that professionals in its Autism at Work initiative outperformed their neurotypical peers—making fewer errors, working 48 percent faster, and being 90–140 percent more productive.[7] A report by Deloitte Insights found that organizations with inclusive cultures are twice as likely to meet or exceed financial targets, three times more likely to be high performing, six times more likely to be innovative and agile, and eight times more likely to achieve better business outcomes.[8]

KPMG's Sean Hoffman, who leads the firm's neurodiversity initiatives, is one of a new generation of corporate leaders who views the underemployment of neurodivergent graduates as an opportunity, not a problem. In his spotlight interview in Chapter 8, Hoffman stresses the benefits of harnessing the distinct perspectives and talents of this often-overlooked group.

Designing for neurodiversity, however, can benefit everyone in an organization. Physical and sensory barriers in the workplace are a form of ableist microaggression that negatively impact neurodivergents' ability to successfully carry out their jobs. The talents that neurodivergents bring to the workplace can be realized only if they are set up for success. True inclusion benefits everyone, leading to happy, healthier employees and a positive organizational culture.

A *Forbes* article by Nancy Doyle notes that neurodivergent children are 46 times more likely to experience school distress than their peers.[9] Behind this statistic are countless personal struggles, some of which this book brings to life through our interviews. Not surprisingly, these early challenges often have enduring effects on self-esteem, trust, and teamwork. As these individuals transition from the educational system into the workforce, their experiences can significantly impact their professional lives.

Creating supportive work environments that address these challenges does not just benefit neurodivergent individuals—it helps entire organizations. This aligns with broader diversity and inclusion research showing that inclusive workplaces increase innovation, job satisfaction, and retention.

Famous Innovators and Creators: Sir Richard Branson

In 2021, Sir Richard Branson, who is dyslexic, wrote an article advocating for neurodiversity in the workplace.[10] He opened with a powerful statement: "Many businesses have caught on to the benefits of inclusion, but there are still lots of opportunities for thinking bigger and embracing different ways of thinking. I've always believed a great business is one that values new perspectives, different ideas, and broader ways of thinking." Branson highlights the advantages that neurodivergent individuals often bring to the table, including divergent thinking, pattern-seeking abilities, and other unique traits. He once noted in an interview with the *Independent*, "My dyslexia became my massive advantage: it helped me to think creatively and laterally and see solutions where others saw problems."[11]

Cognitive Diversity: Breaking Down Groupthink

We all inherently believe our way of thinking is "right," which can lead to unconscious bias and the inability to accept varying cognitive functioning in others. As Maureen Dunne points out in her book, *The Neurodiversity*

Edge, groupthink is one of the biggest threats to organizational success.[12] Groupthink is the practice of thinking or making decisions as a group in a way that does not encourage creativity or individual thoughts. People tend to surround themselves with like-minded individuals who closely resemble themselves. Driven by a desire to be accepted and fit in, groups with familiar cohorts also tend to go with the flow without considering alternatives. Unfortunately, groupthink can lead organizations to a common viewpoint that is narrowly focused, unexamined, and unchallenged.

Individuals who readily accept information without pushing back are perceived as being easy to get along with. Neurodivergents tend to think more independently, see things differently, and challenge the norm. They often are more analytical and skeptical, traits that can be misconstrued as difficult. However, their willingness to engage in an open examination of facts can lead to critical thinking and breakthroughs, which, when welcomed by an organization, can challenge groupthink.

Cognitive diversity embraces the power of unique perspectives. It leverages the different ways people think, feel, solve problems, and interpret things to create fresh ideas. This inclusive approach brings together people from different backgrounds, experiences, and ways of thinking to foster more holistic creativity, generating a wider range of ideas and innovations.

Impact on Business Performance

Employers increasingly recognize that accommodating individuals who think differently can provide a huge competitive advantage. A study by Accenture, in collaboration with disability advocacy organizations, found that companies with the most inclusive environments for employees with disabilities significantly outperformed their peers. These top-performing companies saw, on average, 28 percent higher revenue, 30 percent better profit margins, and double the net income compared to others in their industries over a three-year period from 2015 to 2018.[13]

Several companies have reported benefits from neurodiversity initiatives:

- Dell Technologies implemented an Autism Hiring Program with an agile recruitment process, offering multiple career paths including direct hire and paid internships. Dell provides structured onboarding to ensure successful integration and support for these new hires.[14]

- Employees of JPMorgan Chase's Autism at Work program were 48 percent faster and up to 92 percent more productive than their neurotypical peers. Many attribute this success to their strong visual acuity, ability to hyper-focus, and attention to detail.[15]

- In 2013, SAP began its Autism at Work program. Neurodivergent team members helped develop an innovation that led to a technical solution worth approximately $40 million in savings.[16]

- At DXC Technology, employees voluntarily promoted the firm's autism hiring program, representing organizational values in action.[17]

Several high-profile industry leaders have formed the Neurodiversity at Work Employer Roundtable.[18] The list of companies includes Microsoft, SAP, Cintas, Ford, Ernst & Young, JPMorgan Chase, and DXC Technology.

Other leading companies working to attract and retain neurodiverse talent include Hewlett Packard Enterprise, IBM, Google, Walgreens, British Broadcasting Corporation, Deloitte, and UBS.

Company Initiatives

- Microsoft started an Autism Hiring Program in 2013 and hosts an annual "Ability Summit" for employees, outside experts, and governments. In these summits, business and academic leaders discuss the importance of an inclusive culture and explore how technology can empower people with special abilities.[19]

- IBM launched its Neurodiversity@IBM program in 2015 and has continued to evolve it with input from neurodivergent employees.[20]

- EY has established 23 Neurodiverse Centers of Excellence (NCoE) globally, supporting neurodivergent employees in high-level roles across AI, blockchain, data analytics, and more. As part of EY's broader DEI strategy, the initiative provides accommodating environments and tailored professional development for neurodivergent workers, contributing to the company's innovation and talent diversification efforts.[21]

Challenges and Accommodations

Despite their sought-after advantages and specialist skill sets, neurodivergent thinkers face obstacles in getting hired and staying employed. Inclusive workplace practices must address onboarding, recruitment, and hiring initiatives for neurodivergents. While hiring initiatives begin to break down barriers, neurodivergents may not always be able to thrive within existing workplace norms. People with certain kinds of neurodivergence may struggle to concentrate, manage distractions, regulate emotions, recall information, process details quickly, or communicate effectively.

The BBC's Creating a Positive Environment (CAPE) neurodiversity initiative created an immersive video that helps viewers experience the challenges of working in a typical office from a neurodivergent perspective.[22]

Some forward-thinking employers have had success taking actions that make it easier for neurodivergent staff to contribute. These strategies include modifying the interview process, matching neurodivergent employees with in-house mentors, and conducting awareness training for existing staff.

From our observations of other organizations and industry trends, on-the-job accommodations can be as simple as permitting the use of noise canceling headphones, reducing lighting or screen brightness, providing access to supportive software, and allowing breaks for activity or a change of scene.

Employers surveyed by the U.S. Job Accommodation Network (JAN) reported that more than half of the adjustments cost nothing to implement, with the rest typically costing around $300.[23] Considering that the total cost to recruit, onboard, and train a new employee can be three to four times the annual salary for the position,[24] making accommodations is a relatively low-cost investment with potentially high returns. Plus, these workplace adjustments often benefit all employees, not just those who are neurodivergent.

Designing Inclusive Workplaces

Welcoming the neurodiverse population into the workplace has never been more critical or strategic, given the war for talent, labor shortages, and an increased need for innovative thinking. To embrace this more diverse workforce, many employers are developing inclusive policies, programs, and procedures. There is also a growing desire to address how we design workplaces to be welcoming for all. To date, however, most efforts have focused on onboarding, recruiting, and creating operational guidelines for neurodivergence. Going forward, we need to broaden our focus to include the design of physical spaces.

In 2015, world leaders adopted the United Nations resolution making job security for all, including people with disabilities, one of its sustainable development goals. Since then, 121 countries, including the United States, have passed legislation safeguarding education, employment, and human rights for all people with disabilities.[25]

How we design space can profoundly impact the people who occupy and experience it. Based on HOK's work in this area, it is pretty clear that employees are more productive and satisfied when they have access to a variety of workspace types. Well-designed spaces can remove barriers, help improve culture and attitudes, help eliminate or minimize stigmas, and increase choices that can lead to more individual success in the workplace.

Spotlight

Elizabeth Namugenyi Leads Neuroinclusive Change at IFC

Elizabeth (Eliza) Namugenyi is International Finance Corporation's (IFC) director for budget and business administration based in Washington, DC. With approximately 200 globally dispersed staff, she oversees IFC's budget and global real estate and facilities. Before joining IFC in 2006, she built extensive international experience at PricewaterhouseCoopers in Africa and the United Kingdom. A mother of three, Eliza is a qualified chartered certified accountant with an MBA from Warwick Business School (UK).

Why is neuroinclusivity such an important topic for you?

Eliza: Until about two years ago, I knew very little about neurodiversity. Then, my daughters were diagnosed with conditions considered neurodivergent. One was diagnosed as being on the autism spectrum at age 16, which came as a shock. Her twin sister was diagnosed with severe obsessive-compulsive disorder. Since then,

(continued)

(continued)

I've learned a lot about the challenges they face in getting things done, from studying to simply getting through the day.

I've become more empathetic to their struggles and those of others in my community. A therapist described it to me like this: "Everybody wakes up each day with about 10 stones, and everything that takes energy is like spending a stone. By the end of the day, a neurotypical person might have four stones left. But if you're neurodivergent, you might have spent all 10 of your stones by 9 a.m., so the rest of the day is pure agony."

How has understanding your daughters' experiences changed your approach to workplace design?

I've learned that we need to make the workplace more agnostic to accommodate both neurodivergents and neurotypicals. The work I'm doing for our organization focuses on creating diverse spaces so that people don't even have to ask for accommodations. They know that if they want a quiet spot, it's available. If they want to control the lighting, they can do so in rooms located in our Wellness Center. People can find spaces that work for them.

It's about creating those diverse workspaces and being sensitive to variations in needs. We've also launched an internship program for young neurodivergent adults in my department. We're now on our second intern, and it has been a learning experience for everyone. While they may require more supervision and clarity, as an organization we've gained a lot from them, particularly their significant attention to detail and team support.

Many organizations don't know where to start and fear it will be difficult and costly. What advice would you give to those beginning this journey?

Go the way we went. When we initially had the idea, I broached it with some of my superiors. We had no experts in the field and no way of knowing how we would work. I said, "Let's do what we always do. Let's pilot something, almost like a test and learn."

We partnered with an organization that works with the interns. They prepare them, meet with them weekly, and ensure their needs are being met.

As we work on our modernization concepts, we've been very opportunistic working with the team from HOK. We need to take every opportunity we have, even if it's incremental, to move forward. It's an evolution, not a revolution.

As a mother with two daughters who will soon enter the workforce, what message would you give to their future employers?

One of my daughters goes to a college that I think is best-in-class when it comes to dealing with neurodivergent students. They're very intentional about everything from room assignments to support groups where students can share experiences. They provide accommodations like extended time for assignments or the ability to take tests in a separate quiet room.

In contrast, my other daughter is in a school where it has been a constant fight to get any sort of accommodations or understanding. It's almost like they assume she's trying to get an unfair advantage rather than understanding it's a real need to put her on par with her neurotypical peers.

For many organizations, this is a big change. It requires everything that goes with change management, whether that's communication, increased awareness, or educating yourself about the topic. It's about having the humility to acknowledge that we don't know everything and welcoming learning. Otherwise, there will be no progress.

Energy Resources

Similar to the stone concept Eliza describes, American writer Christine Miserandino coined the term *spoon theory*, the notion that we all have a set amount of mental and physical energy to tap into daily.[26] This theory suggests that not everyone has the same number of spoons, or energy, and once it is depleted, they often do not have reserves to tap into. Neurodivergents typically need to conserve their energy to make it through the day. A recent study shows children who exhibit neurodivergent traits are twice as likely to have chronic disabling fatigue by age 18.[27] This amounts to a "disability tax"—people face disproportionate strains on their energy, finances, time, mental health, and resources just to live their daily lives.

4

Human Functioning and Sensory Processing

Our brains need continuous variety of sensory nourishment to develop and then function.
—A. Jean Ayres, PhD, occupational therapist and neuropsychologist

Neurodivergence is a naturally occurring variation in neurocognitive functioning. It is a unique way of thinking, processing, feeling, and acting that is considered different to the predominant neurotype. Human functioning refers to the various physical and mental abilities and processes that enable humans to carry out daily activities and interact with their environment. Individuals can achieve neurological well-being when physical, cognitive, and social processing are supported. Understanding how neurodivergents experience their surroundings enables us to design spaces that help them and their neurotypical colleagues feel better and work more productively.

Three Interconnected Systems

We can understand human functioning through three interconnected sensory, mental, and physiological/behavioral systems.

Sensory System

Our senses feed us information about the world. Employees often report sensory discomfort in the workplace. How often have we heard that a space is too cold, too bright, or too loud? Our modern workplaces can no longer overlook these factors. By creating clear, structured, and predictable environments, we strive to promote sensory wellness for everyone.

Mental System

The mental system is vital for managing everyday challenges and crises. It encompasses psychological, cognitive, and social health. Mental functions are our abilities to perceive and interpret sensory phenomena, feel and regulate emotions, and perform higher-level functions that enable us to learn, reason, and synthesize information.

- Psychological health is the impact of emotions, brain functioning, thought patterns, and life experiences on mood and cognitive abilities. Heredity, past experiences, cultural norms, and social interactions all can shape these responses.[1]
- Cognitive health involves our mental abilities and memory—thinking, reasoning, learning, remembering, and making decisions. Each person's mental functioning varies. For example, some learn by seeing, others do it by hearing. Some tasks require complete focus, while others are more automatic.[2,3]
- Social health relates to our ability to read social cues and interact with other people effectively.[4,5]

Understanding these mental functions is important because they all affect how we process sensory information from our built environment.

Physiological/Behavioral System

People's bodies respond to their environments in physical and behavioral ways. The spaces we inhabit can affect our comfort, fatigue, muscle tension, heart rate, and even hormone levels.[6]

A 2022 study found that neurodivergents—particularly those with autism or ADHD—are twice as likely to have joint hypermobility syndrome, a genetic condition with symptoms including extreme flexibility and pain.[7] Supporting physical comfort in the workplace has the potential to help neurodivergents experience less pain and stress and get more out of their work.

Spiky Profiles

Many neurodivergents have "spiky" profiles,[8] a phenomenon where the disparity between strengths and weaknesses is more pronounced than for most people. Neurodivergents tend to have more pronounced peaks in ability in some areas, while they may struggle more in others. These peaks often include enhanced creativity, reading, and mathematical abilities. These spikes are sometimes referred to as splinter skills.

A person's cognitive profile typically includes these four elements:

- **Visual skill and perceptual reasoning:** How we take in and use visual information to solve problems
- **Verbal skills:** How we understand concepts expressed in words
- **Working memory:** How we store and recall information
- **Processing speed:** How quickly we receive, understand, and respond to information

Other factors are often considered when mapping an individual's profile and identifying their peaks (strengths) and dips (challenges). These may include the following:[9]

- Sensory differences
- Stimulation preferences
- Numerical skills
- Visual skills
- Analytical skills
- Situational/social skills
- Relationship/emotional processing
- Executive functioning, organization, and time management

Spiky profiles track the heightened skills in some areas and the trenches of others. An individual or lateral's profile does not reflect intelligence. It is simply a visual representation of personal and work-related strengths and areas for development.

Linear versus Lateral Thinking

Linear thinking, sometimes referred to as vertical or convergent thinking, is the traditional problem-solving mode that uses logical reasoning, leverages past data, and applies existing solutions. In contrast, lateral thinking, often referred to as horizontal or divergent thinking, is a problem-solving approach that strives for innovative rather than straightforward, predictable answers. Through spontaneous, free-flow ideation and brainstorming, lateral thinkers thrive by exploring multiple options and perspectives, often taking an approach that is not immediately obvious.[10]

In 1967, psychologist Edward de Bono developed this concept of lateral thinking in his book *The Use of Lateral Thinking*. He notes that the human brain has been taught to think inside the box and apply a logical approach that only sometimes generates the best results. He proposed lateral thinking to move beyond our cognitive biases and fuel invention.[11]

ADHDers are more likely to excel in divergent or lateral thinking, which helps them connect seemingly unrelated concepts and generate multiple solutions to a problem.[12] Some may rely on internal visualization and nonlinear methods of problem-solving, which could contribute to creative innovations. While research suggests strengths in divergent thinking, the relationship varies depending on the severity of ADHD symptoms.

Famous Innovators and Creators: Thomas Jefferson

Thomas Jefferson, a founding father of the United States, third U.S. president, and author of the Declaration of Independence, is believed to have been autistic. There are few things in life that Jefferson did not excel at—among his talents were architecture, philosophy, diplomacy, law, and inventing—but he was also known for having difficulty making direct eye contact. Alexander Hamilton believed this was evidence of his "dishonesty," but perhaps it was just a sign of his suspected neurotype.[13]

Sensory Processing: Foundation and Mechanisms

Though we commonly refer to five basic senses, most experts accept that several more senses contribute to how we perceive the world:[14]

1. Visual (sight)
2. Auditory (hearing)
3. Tactile (touch)
4. Olfactory (smell)
5. Gustatory (taste)
6. Interoception: How we perceive internal bodily signals, such as heart rate, breathing, hunger, and temperature
7. Proprioception: How we perceive the position of our body parts in space
8. Vestibular: How we perceive balance and coordination. Equilibrioception, also related to balance, is the combination of visual cues, inner ear signals, and proprioceptive information to keep us steady and prevent falls

Some researchers also include the following:

9. Thermoception: How we perceive temperature changes.[15]
10. Nociception: How we perceive pain.[16]

This book focuses on the five basic senses, along with interoception, proprioception, and vestibular sense. Understanding these senses helps us design workplaces that support diverse sensory needs.

On average, we receive a bombardment of more than 11 million bits of sensory information every second. But humans are capable only of consciously processing a fraction of that—about 50 bits.[17] This results in us all filtering out redundant and irrelevant stimuli and subconsciously "sensory gating" so we can focus our energy.[18] This sensory assault is increasing in a world where we are exposed to growing chaos and a plethora of media devices forcing us to be more multimodal.

Context also impacts how we process sensory input. We can have emotional or learned responses to stimuli based on our life experiences, which

evolve over time. For example, sensory stimuli in our environment can pro-
voke symptoms in the following:

- More than 1 in 5 U.S. adults who have a mental illness[19]
- Nearly 1 in 6 U.S. adults who get migraines[20]
- Nearly 1 in 100 U.S. adults with active epilepsy[21]

Our senses play a part in how we experience and interact with our
environment. We all process sensory stimulation in our own unique ways.

While having a heightened sensitivity and attunement to our sensory
environment was likely advantageous in natural settings, such as detecting a
predator's subtle movements on the savanna, it can be debilitating in the
modern workplace.

Neurodivergents perceive, process, filter, and organize stimuli in the
built environment differently from those who are neurotypical. Neurodivergents often have either over- or under-responsiveness to stimulation and,
in many cases, a combination of both.

Spotlight

Designing for Neurodiversity: Kristi Gaines on
Sensory-Inclusive Environments

Kristi Gaines, PhD, IIDA, IDEC, is an associate dean of the graduate
school and professor in the Department of Design at Texas Tech
University. A nationally recognized leader in designing learning environments for individuals with sensory sensitivities and developmental
disorders, she has more than two decades of professional interior
design and teaching experience. Her book, *Designing for Autism Spectrum Disorders*, has received awards from four leading interior and
environmental design organizations.

How did you become an advocate for neuroinclusion?

Kristi: I have family members who are on the spectrum or have
sensory integration problems. I've seen that the physical environment plays a big role in their comfort, but there wasn't much

information available on this topic. When I decided to pursue my PhD and was asked about my research interests, sensory stimulation in the built environment immediately came to mind.

Can you share a bit about your work and research?

I started with my dissertation, which was exploratory due to the lack of information available. I decided to focus on classroom environments because there was some existing research, and it appeared that early intervention was crucial. I surveyed more than 500 special education teachers who had worked with children with autism about environmental features, with a particular interest in visual and auditory stimulation. I also conducted focus groups to gather insights.

What insights did your research yield, and what were some of the biggest barriers impacting individuals in the classroom or work environment?

While sensory features impact everybody, noise was the biggest contributor, and visual elements were also a significant factor. Tactile elements and smells played important roles as well. Interestingly, 20 years ago, most literature advocated for removing sensory stimulation. However, my study revealed this wasn't a good idea—people actually need sensory stimulation.

I also examined the impact of color on mood and errors and researched gender differences. I discovered that without some visual stimulation, people tend to lose interest and find it harder to pay attention. The lack of stimuli was just as detrimental as too much sensory stimulation.

I collaborated with a colleague in the United Kingdom, and we published a couple of comparative studies.

Which key principles should guide organizations in designing neuroinclusive workspaces?

First and foremost, consider the sensory environment and connect the dots regarding interventions. It's important to understand that

(continued)

(continued)

it's not one-size-fits-all. It's good to have flexibility, different types of spaces, and some private areas. But environments also need to be predictable.

Are you finding that the factors impacting neurodivergents are also affecting neurotypical individuals?

Yes, absolutely. People have different preferences. Some people like to have more light, while others prefer to work in darker environments. There is a wide range of individual differences.

Can you share what you're working on now?

Since 2015, I've been focusing on the importance of nature and naturalized elements in the environment. I was invited by the Texas Department of State Health Services to join a collaborative effort involving various organizations, and I am one of the original designers. There are so many ways to incorporate nature into spaces.

Having access to natural light or full-spectrum light is crucial. Studies show that a view of nature is so important that all hospital rooms, for example, are required to have one. But often that view is of another building, and you can't even see the sky. That's not truly a view of nature. In these cases, we sometimes need to consider a simulated nature view.

Sensory Thresholds and Processing Challenges

One of the most overlooked workplace challenges is sensory processing and our sensitivities to the daily onslaught of sensory stimuli. As humans, we experience our world and the environments we inhabit through our senses. We rely on them to provide us with vital information needed to navigate and interact with our surroundings and the people within them. Surprisingly, while we often complain about sensory impacts—something is "too loud," "too dark," "too cold"—we tend to overlook the importance of creating spaces that address sensory stimuli more comprehensively.

Neurodivergents are more likely to have sensory processing difficulties that affect their communication styles. Many struggle with executive functioning—the cognitive ability to manage oneself and monitor resources to achieve tasks and navigate daily life.[22] Those with auditory processing differences may have trouble processing spoken communication. They may more easily process details through written, graphic, or visual communication styles.

Neurominorities are not the only ones with heightened sensitivity to stimulation and sensory sensations in the built environment. Individuals with post-traumatic stress disorder (PTSD), Alzheimer's, dementia, or those who have had concussions, strokes, hearing or vision loss, or epilepsy often have increased sensitivity to sensory stimulation. Since the pandemic, many people—even neurotypicals—have been more impacted by the elements they encounter in the office,[23] and many have a heightened awareness to sensory stimulation.

Sensory thresholds are like traits often attributed to introvert and extrovert characteristics (Figure 4.1). In a recent survey conducted by Sensory Intelligence Consulting[24] regarding individuals' sensory sensitivities, Annemarie Lombard shared that participants identified as follows:

Sensitivity Type	Neurodivergent	Mixed Neurotype
Hypersensitive or sensory avoiders	47%	40%
Neurotypical or sensory neutral	35%	38%
Hyposensitive or sensory seekers	18%	22%

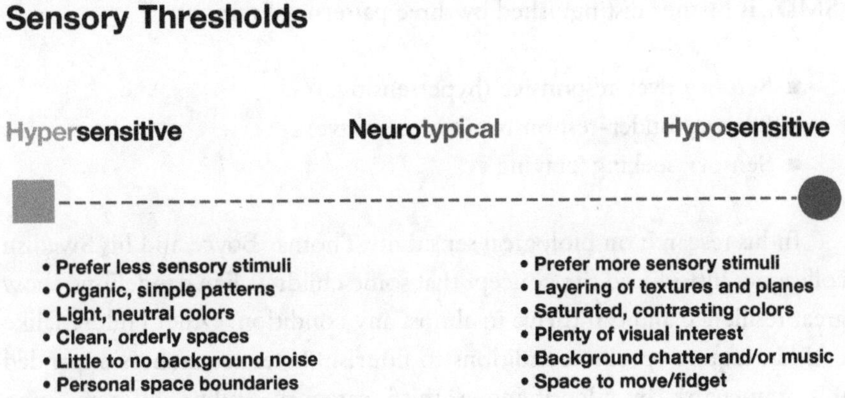

Sensory Thresholds

Hyper**sensitive**   **Neurotypical**   Hypo**sensitive**

- Prefer less sensory stimuli
- Organic, simple patterns
- Light, neutral colors
- Clean, orderly spaces
- Little to no background noise
- Personal space boundaries

- Prefer more sensory stimuli
- Layering of textures and planes
- Saturated, contrasting colors
- Plenty of visual interest
- Background chatter and/or music
- Space to move/fidget

Figure 4.1   Sensory thresholds

Based on these percentages and the principles of additive design, where it is easier to add than reduce stimulation to a space, it is best to start with the needs of those who are hypersensitive and then create areas or zones that provide more sensory stimulation for sensory seekers.

Sensory Processing Challenges

Each individual receives and decodes information differently. Our brain processes and organizes this information to help us understand our surroundings.

In 1972, A. Jean Ayres noted that individuals with deficits in sensory integration cannot process information from several senses at once. As a result, they may exhibit rigid or repetitive behaviors that appear as inappropriate responses. These behaviors are coping mechanisms in response to environmental stimuli.[25] In 2006, Lucy Miller built on Ayres' foundation and coined the term *sensory processing disorder* (SPD).[26] A highly sensitive person (HSP) often has SPD or sensory processing sensitivity (SPS).[27] She described the three parts of SPD:

- Sensory modulation.
- Sensory discrimination.
- Sensory-based motor conditions.

Research shows that the design of the built environment can be modified to support individuals with SPD by adjusting environmental features.

Sensory modulation, formerly known as sensory modulation disorder (SMD), is further distinguished by three patterns of response:[28]

- Sensory over-responsive (hypersensitive)
- Sensory under-responsive (hyposensitive)
- Sensory seeking/craving

In his research on biological sensitivity, Thomas Boyce and his Swedish colleagues introduced the concept that some children, like dandelions, show great resilience and can thrive in almost any condition. Other children, like orchids, require specific conditions to flourish. Later researchers expanded this framework by identifying a third category—tulip children—who display a combination of sensitivity and resilience, falling somewhere between the dandelion and orchid types.[29]

Sensory Over-Responsive/Hypersensitive Sensory over-responsive or hypersensitive individuals tend to prefer predictable environments with less or controlled stimuli. These individuals process sensory details in an overly magnified way and often dislike environments with excessive stimuli such as bright lights, crowds, unfamiliar scents, textures, or temperature fluctuations. Overly active or stimulating spaces may lead people to be sensory avoidant. Unpredictable, chaotic, or confusing spaces with sensory bombardment can present challenges to neurodivergents.[30] These concepts are key to understanding how we should design space to enable individuals to process sensory stimulation at levels optimal for their success.

Sensory Under-Responsive/Hyposensitive Sensory under-responsive or hyposensitive individuals tend to prefer overstimulation or have diminished sensory sensation and need more stimuli to successfully process sensory information. They often have difficulty feeling the acute sensory details in a specific environment.

Sensory Seeking/Craving Sensory seeking, or craving, is a variation of hyposensitivity often manifested by creating or generating sensory encounters, either for gratification or to distract themselves from other objectionable stimuli. Individuals with this trait may find dull spaces unsatisfying, leading them to create their own stimulation.

Sensory Spectrum and Age-Related Changes

We all have reactions to the sensory stimulation that continually comes at us. Everyone is on the sensory spectrum, which ranges from hyper- to hypo-sensitivities. However, neurominorities tend to have more extreme reactions and accentuated or heightened neurological experiences. The needs of children, for example, can vary from those of mature adults. One factor that may impact this difference is the general decline in sensory processing abilities as we age, our sensory processing abilities change, and neurodegeneration is a factor. While children may require more motion to process information effectively, adults tend to experience a decline in sensory and cognitive capacities, which could alter how they interact with their environments.[31,32]

Over time, our sense of taste, equilibrium, hearing, eyesight, and sense of touch tend to diminish to some degree. We need to be acutely aware of that when we are thinking about designing spaces for elder care or spaces that have a higher percentage of older workers. As people live longer and retire later, mature workers are becoming a higher percentage of the general population and workforce, making it imperative to address their needs in workplace environments.

Coping Mechanisms and Perception Variances

Neurodivergents often develop strategies to navigate their environment and process information, which can be understood through their coping mechanisms and distinct perceptual experiences. Understanding sensory processing challenges and coping mechanisms is crucial for creating inclusive environments. By recognizing these issues, we can design spaces that reduce the need for coping mechanisms. By incorporating perception variances into a workplace design, we can create environments that are more structured, ordered, accessible, and comfortable for a diverse range of individuals.

Coping Mechanisms

Many neurominorities have been forced to adjust to environments not designed to respect their needs. Common self-soothing and coping mechanisms are masking, stimming, and echolalia.

Masking   Masking is the involuntary practice of hiding one's true self and attributes, often mirroring others' actions and behaviors. For many, masking is a survival skill to fit in, but it can lead to poor mental health, burnout, depression, stress, anxiety, and a greater risk of suicide.[33]

Stimming   Regardless of whether they are hyper- or hyposensitive, many autistics seek specific kinds of sensory self-stimulation to cope with stress, an act commonly known as *stimming*.[34] Stimming, short for "self-stimulating behaviors," is common among autistics who need an outlet to cope with stress. Stimming can include repetitive motor movements or sounds, such as rocking, fidgeting, pacing, or chewing on a pen. It may also include repetitive movements of the hands (flapping or finger-flicking), feet (pacing or jumping), or body (rocking or spinning), with or without the help of an object (stim toy).[35] Stimming is a natural human impulse, and everyone does it to some extent unconsciously. Most have learned to suppress it to some degree.

Echolalia   Echolalia is the verbal repetition of previously heard sentences or words that help release energy and excessive stimulation.[36] Echolalia is highly common in autistics (many of whom also have ADHD) and occurs in some individuals with Tourette syndrome. It can also appear in aphasia (a language disorder) and nonclinical individuals who are tired, inattentive, or have altered consciousness.

Routine   Simplifying decision-making processes by building habits has been shown to increase productivity. The average adult makes up to 35,000 decisions every day,[37] from simply deciding what to eat and wear to responding to more complex problems. One way many successful people have learned to save time and preserve their brain power is to cut down on the number of decisions they need to make. This can include simply wearing the same outfit every day or sitting in the same spot at work.

Habituation   Often used as a coping mechanism, habituation is a decrease in response to a sensory stimulation after repeated exposure. One can get so used to something in their environment that they stop noticing it. Habituation is part of a multisensory protective system designed to alert us to new information and then push what is not needed to the background.[38]

Many autistic individuals struggle with habituation, which can contribute to persistent hypersensitivities.[39] "People like me who are tactile defensive struggle to habituate," explains Benjamin Jensen, a landscape design professional. "The sensation of my shirt tag, even after I recognize that it's a shirt tag and not a threat, like a spider, does not go away. The layers of sensory input that I fail to habituate, like a vent noise or shirt texture, sometimes leave me emotionally exhausted by the end of the day."

Perception Variances

Autistic individuals often experience visual stimulation distinctly. Research has shown that autistic individuals tend to avoid direct eye contact and prefer looking at the edges of a face rather than the center.[40] This can influence their spatial perception and interactions with their environment and other people.

Visual perception in autism can be complex. The National Autistic Society (UK) describes two main categories:[41]

- Under-sensitive autistics may experience the following:
  - Objects appearing darker or losing features
  - Blurred central vision with sharper peripheral vision
  - Poor depth perception and difficulties with motor tasks
- Over-sensitive autistics may experience the following:
  - Distorted or fragmented vision
  - Preference for focusing on details rather than whole objects
  - Sensitivity to light, affecting sleep

These diverse visual experiences can have a significant impact on how autistic individuals interact with and perceive their surroundings.

The Effects of Monotropism

Monotropism is a cognitive strategy often described figuratively as "tunnel vision," where the brain seems to focus on a single part rather than the whole. Autistic individuals tend to focus on a small number of interests at any given time, often missing things outside this narrow attention tunnel.[42]

Gestalt Principles

Developed by German psychologists, Gestalt principles, also known as Laws of Perception, suggest that structures can be seen as clusters. Humans tend to seek order in disorder, simplify elements, and make connections. Gestalt researchers observed that our brains automatically organize and interpret visual data through grouping.[43] As a result, we perceive things as the sum of their parts, rather than as individual items.

Famous Innovators and Creators: Le Corbusier

Recently, authors and physicians have speculated that Le Corbusier, the Swiss-French architect known as the father of modernism, was autistic and likely suffered from PTSD as a result of World War I. They cite his strained social communication, repetitive behaviors, unusual fascinations (specifically with concrete), and lack of interest in others as rationale for their diagnosis.[44]

Individuals living with ASD literally have too many brain connections, or hyperplasticity, which can overload them and leave them struggling to process and regulate stimulation.[45] As a result, they often struggle with sensory overload, which may be related to nervous system hyperarousal.[46]

If Le Corbusier was indeed autistic, his asymmetric and over-simplified designs may have been a response to his desire to limit stimulation.

Designing for Diverse Functioning

Knowing that we all have different learning and information processing styles, it is important to create environments that enable us to process information and experience space in our own unique ways. Some may be more visual, some auditory, are kinesthetic, or learn in a hands-on environment. We all have varying degrees of sensitivity to sensory stimulation and sensory processing. After all, humans are sensory beings, constantly receiving sensory input. Creating space that addresses sensory processing, sensory stimulation, and cognitive distractions helps all users. For neurodivergents, however, thoughtful design can make the difference between success or failure in that space.

A. Jean Ayres, who developed sensory integration theory, says, "Our brains need continuous variety of sensory nourishment to develop and then function."[47] But our minds also need a sensory diet that we can cope with while balancing hypo- and hypersensitivities.

Spotlight

Katie Gaudion's Insights on Sensory-Inclusive Design and Neurodiversity

Katie Gaudion, PhD, is a design consultant and senior research associate at The Helen Hamlyn Centre for Design, an inclusive design research center at the Royal College of Art in London. Her work focuses on collaborating with neurodivergent individuals to improve

(continued)

(*continued*)

their daily experiences, a journey she navigates daily as a neurodivergent person.

Please share a bit about your personal journey and work around neuroinclusion.

Katie: I'm from a small island called Guernsey, which is in the English Channel near the French coast. My mom is a nurse and worked at the island's only special educational needs school. I remember visiting the school when I was five or six, playing with children my age, and noticing how different they were from me. I have vivid, positive memories from those days. I really enjoyed playing with those children, and perhaps it was my first introduction to practicing empathy, which is such an important skill for an inclusive designer.

Years later, while studying at the Royal College of Art, I got diagnosed with dyslexia and dyspraxia, which has propelled my interest in design and neurodivergence. On reflection, I was very shy and probably masked it quite well. I was really into art, so I just immersed myself in that. Being quite shy and anxious, I probably went unnoticed. It's an invisible condition and very common for girls to go undiagnosed.

How did your interest in neurodivergent design in the environment develop?

My interest came about when I volunteered for a charity in London that had a multisensory environment and van designed to stimulate the senses. As I facilitated sensory sessions with individuals with intellectual disabilities, I observed firsthand the profound impact an environment's sensory qualities can have on people.

Once, when I worked at a kid's holiday camp, an autistic boy was unhappy, and we didn't know why. We called his mom, who asked if he had a paper clip—which he didn't. When we gave him a paper clip, he immediately calmed down and relaxed.

Sometimes, it's the simple things. As a designer, I found it interesting how a paper clip had an alternative use—providing comfort and support for a boy.

Tell us about your work at the Helen Hamlyn Centre for Design.

After receiving my master of philosophy and textiles degree at the Royal College of Art, I spent two years critiquing multisensory environments. I designed a range of sensory props inspired by the individuals I had worked with.

Next, at the Helen Hamlyn Centre for Design, I collaborated with an autism charity called Autism at Kingwood for six years. Inclusive design is key to everything we do at HHCD and during my PhD I became interested in how to authentically and meaningfully co-design with autistic people with intellectual disabilities and limited speech.

Inspired by Winnie Dunn's Sensory Profiling questionnaire, which is often used by occupational therapists, I developed visual sensory preference cards to enable the autistic individuals I was collaborating with to express their likes and dislikes through gesture and eye contact. This became a visual mood board for designing environments and informing person-centered design decisions.

What are some key insights you've gained from your work?

One is knowing that one size does not fit all. In fact, one size fits one. It's important not to generalize or standardize design. We need to keep listening, asking questions, and continually trying to understand how people feel about the space they're in.

An interesting insight from a workplace project I worked on with autistic people was that while the physical environment can be challenging, so too is the social environment and the complexity of workplace social etiquette, which doesn't get the attention it deserves.

(continued)

(continued)

We got a sample of that when I invited you to do that activity at our workshop in London in the spring of 2024. Can you tell us about any innovative tools or methods you've developed?

During that workplace project, the autistic participants developed an activity called "People and Things." This consists of beautifully illustrated cards that depict various elements that could make the workplace more comfortable, such as "I prefer to have my back to the wall" or "I prefer not to shake hands." Interestingly, this card activity is designed for all employees, whether or not they are autistic, because everyone has different sensory preferences that contribute to a comfortable workplace. The activity serves as a starting point for conversations about the workplace environment, helping to understand, empathize, and identify commonalities and differences in our needs, regardless of neurodiversity.

What do you see as the future of neuroinclusive design?

We're just beginning to understand how neurodivergent people experience their environments and how to address neuroinclusion. We're still learning and growing in this field.

I would like to see more exploration into how we can incorporate greater personalization and autonomy into the design of spaces, especially shared public spaces.

I would like to see a shift in focus from the challenges and deficits of neurodivergent individuals to the strengths and opportunities their unique perspectives can bring to the design world. From experience, I know that neurodivergent people offer valuable insights and innovative approaches that enhance creativity and inclusivity in design. This shift in perspective will not only benefit neurodivergent individuals but also enrich the entire design field by incorporating a wider range of experiences and ideas.

It's also crucial to involve more people with intellectual disabilities and limited verbal communication in the design process. By addressing the needs of those at the extremes, the outcomes will benefit everyone.

5 | Sensory Intelligence

> We are freshwater fish in salt water. Put us in fresh water and we
> function just fine. Put us in salt water and we struggle to survive.
> —Anonymous autistic student

The Sensory Matrix™

Most people are familiar with different types of intelligence—most commonly
intelligence quotient (IQ) and emotional intelligence (EQ). But what about
sensory intelligence (SQ)—our ability to understand how stimulation and
other factors in the built environment affect us? Though we instinctively
know when something is bothering us, we often struggle to articulate these
feelings. Understanding what impacts us enables us to make better choices,
while helping us to articulate those needs to others and advocate for ourselves.

In February 2020, I visited South Africa, where I was introduced to
Annemarie Lombard, a registered occupational therapist and founder of
Sensory Intelligence® Consulting. She had created the Sensory Matrix™, a
test that assesses individuals' sensory styles, categorizing them as sensory-
seeking, sensory neutral, or sensory-avoiders. (Readers interested in learning more about Lombard's Sensory Intelligence® assessments, training, and
coaching can visit sensoryintelligence.com.)

While psychometric tests have long been used by analysts to assess cognitive abilities, personality traits, and behavioral patterns, they can be inaccessible and overly complex and may not reliably measure neurodivergent skills

and abilities. Some experts advocate instead for practical assessments that directly measure work skills rather than relying on abstract standardized tests.

The Sensory Matrix™ measures sensory threshold across whole sensory systems, reflecting the genetic factors that influence how we experience sensory stimulation. This shapes our behavior, habits, and responses, indicating our default comfort zones. According to Lombard, all sensory input is filtered and regulated at a fundamental level in our brains. This process follows a sequence of sensing, feeling, and then acting. While largely unconscious, this sequence has a big impact on our reactions, behaviors, and daily performance.

Lombard's Sensory Matrix™ test was ideal for a pilot we planned for a client interested in designing a workplace for inclusion, and we tested it on 40 individuals from HOK. The 15-minute test was similar to taking a typical personality test but with more intriguing questions. Both the individual and overall group results were surprising. Most of us fell within the sensory-neutral range, with a few elements falling just outside. Some were squarely in the sensory-seeking or avoiding zones for one or more senses. These insights helped us better understand ourselves and our colleagues.

For me, it was eye-opening. While I was primarily sensory-neutral, I leaned toward avoidance of visual stimulation and seeking multisensory experiences. The profile explained that though I enjoyed visual stimulation, excessive chaos or disarray could hinder my concentration. This tendency is relatively common in women.

The report recommended organizing my home and workspace for efficiency and calmness, emphasizing the importance of keeping them clutter-free. The insights from the report reinforced how important it is to consider the entire range of sensory needs when designing inclusive environments. It highlighted that our personal spaces and their organization can have a massive impact on our well-being and productivity—perhaps even in ways we might not recognize right away.

On a Personal Note: Pandemic Revelations

I took Annmarie's Sensory Matrix™ assessment during the early stages of the pandemic lockdown. Four of my five children—mostly teenagers and college students—were living in my house at that time, and we were all working or studying remotely. Our schedules often clashed.

I was early to bed and early to rise, while they stayed up late. Many nights, they would cook feasts at 2 a.m., chatting among themselves. Somehow, using teenage logic, they thought the noise of cooking wouldn't bother me but justified that doing the dishes would, so they left those for the morning. Every morning, I'd wake up to a kitchen full of dirty dishes, which was highly distressing. I couldn't start working until they were done. They suggested leaving the dishes for them to do later, but this was problematic and frustrating for me.

I never fully understood why it bothered me so much besides just being inconsiderate, but the Sensory Matrix™ assessment highlighted that I have a sensitivity to visual clutter and need order and structure. Now it all made sense. Armed with that knowledge, I shared that it wasn't just me being unreasonable. It was a real distractor for me and needed to be addressed.

Many colleagues had similar revelations. Understanding our sensory, cognitive, and behavioral functioning needs more comprehensively helps us get closer to knowing how to put ourselves in environments where we can thrive. Those who shared their assessments with others gained insights into specific behaviors or traits that explained a lot about how to engage with them.

These realizations also highlighted how low our personal sensory intelligence is. We might know that certain things irritate us but lack a full understanding of why and what triggers those reactions. Without this knowledge and experience, it is hard to address or avoid the triggers in built environments that negatively impact us.

Spotlight

How Annemarie Lombard Champions Sensory Intelligence® in the Workplace

Annemarie Lombard, PhD, is the founder and CEO of Sensory Intelligence® Consulting, a thought leader and subject expert on sensory neuroscience with 33 years of global experience. An occupational therapist who has worked extensively with neurodiversity, she

(continued)

(continued)

completed her PhD in 2012, studying the impact of sensory processing within the work environment on workplace productivity. In 2007, she authored the book *Sensory Intelligence: Why It Matters More Than IQ and EQ.*

How did you become an advocate for sensory processing?

> **Annemarie:** As an occupational therapist, I worked with neurodiverse individuals for most of my professional career in South Africa and the United States. After returning to South Africa in 2000, I became involved in professional training, and that's when the light bulb got switched on for me. I was tired of repetitive clinical practice, but loved the sensory modulation theory and understanding how the brain processes the senses. I started exploring sensory processing and how it impacted adults in life, work, and relationships. It was branching into brand new territory and application.
>
> My first personal lightbulb moment was implementing it in my own life. It saved my marriage as I became more understanding and compassionate toward my husband. That started the process of moving away from traditional work to clinic-based work with diagnoses and neurodiversity. I wanted to understand how adults respond to the environment and why certain environments worked for one group but not for another. For example, many people in open-plan workspaces are noise-sensitive, distracted, or don't want to sit too close to others. They find such workplaces stressful, which impacts their capacity to focus, think, and engage.
>
> I started going down that path in 2002 and did market research for about four years, literally just speaking to people. What did sensitivity mean for them? How did it influence their lives and relationships? I learned so much from speaking to people and getting to know their sensory stories. This led me to do my PhD research in call centers.
>
> As a therapist, I went into a commercial call center site and was blown away by literally 500–1,000 people sharing an open-plan office space amidst chaos, having to take phone calls. I thought,

"What are these people on?" It was the perfect place for me to do my PhD because everything gets recorded in this industry and people are put under constant surveillance with data captured at every contact point. I hypothesized that people with more sensitive nervous systems—about 25–30 percent of the population—would be less productive and more absent in call center environments. My hypothesis was supported by the data and results. Having the right technical skills does not guarantee success in call centers; rather, having the best-fit sensory threshold pattern will. This applies to all different workplaces—where the environment is not conducive, people won't thrive.

As I was navigating this growing industry, I observed many workspace "mismatches" and could easily identify how the sensory environment was not conducive to performance. One day, a call center office manager desperately complained about performance issues in their workspace. Upon observation, I found the walls dark gray and it was hot. My immediate response and solution was to repaint the wall—not dark gray, please—and turn down the temperature. The dark walls made it feel like a cave, and warmer temperatures will reduce the arousal level in the brain, switching off focus and attention.

My focus on the environment was purely based on what I saw and how people were getting it wrong. I could immediately identify the disconnect between the sensory stimuli and the human brain. As a result, I started to do Sensory Audits for workspaces to guide design and productivity principles.

Can you tell us more about the Sensory Matrix™ you developed?

In 2005, I decided to develop my own assessment as a result of frustrations with the current tools at the time. I developed the Sensory Matrix™ during and after my PhD work. Since then, we've designed a whole layer of assessments and continue to develop, fine-tune, and analyze data. Fundamentally, we are

(continued)

(continued)

assessing how individuals are wired from a sensory perspective, how they intuitively respond to the environment through all the seven senses, and how it influences their attention, emotion, and behavior. This, in turn, will impact how we live, work, learn, and engage. There is no right or wrong to that—it is just different.

We are all different, and we know that an environment that works brilliantly for one person may not work for another. A one-size-fits-all approach isn't productive and doesn't promote health and well-being.

How does Sensory Intelligence® relate to other forms of intelligence?

This is a very physiological, anatomical way of how the brain processes information, obviously backed by science. The brain first processes, modulates, and regulates the seven senses received through stimuli from the environment. This occurs predominantly in the lower brain structures before it's sent up for our emotional release to coincide with emotion. Then it goes to the executive branch for our intellect, intelligence, strategic thinking, planning, and doing in the upper part of the brain, the cortex.

If we look at the hierarchy within the brain, we see that if the environment isn't conducive, we can't think. This is because the brain first has to sense and modulate information before it gets sent up to the executive centers, the executive cortical brain, for thinking and using.

Sensory Intelligence® refers to the lower part of the brain, where information enters and the initial gut primitive, unconscious, responses occur. It is basically a primitive brain process, occurring in the lower brain structures. This is the initial filtering of information before it reaches the limbic system, which is EQ—emotions. Only then does it go to the cortex and the executive brain for productivity and performance output.

I coined the term Sensory Intelligence® in 2002. It's really about how your body responds to the environment. If you know that, how can you adapt your life, work environment, and relationships to be more conducive rather than being an irritation or annoyance?

Self-awareness is critical. When people go through the assessment and become aware, it is a penny-drop, aha moment.

How many people have taken the Sensory Intelligence® test to date, and what key things have you learned from the assessments?

Collectively, we have done nearly 50,000 sensory-based assessments through our system. We continue to analyze the data, but initial findings showed that 30 percent of people are more sensory seeking, suggesting high thresholds; 30 percent of people are more sensory sensitive and avoiding, suggesting low thresholds; and 40 percent are sensory neutral. This is a fairly equal distribution across the population. The auditory system seems to be the biggest culprit in sensory sensitivities and seems to be the most compromised system across all.

Post-COVID, we've also seen a shift. In general, people seem to be more sensitive to their environments. The sensory sensitive and avoiding group used to be 25 percent before and post-COVID has moved to 30 percent.

What advice would you give designers, architects, and corporate real estate and facilities professionals about creating more neuroinclusive environments?

Having compassion and an understanding that by designing more inclusive workspaces, your business will benefit from it is essential. My biggest frustration is people who talk the talk, but when it comes to doing it, they don't.

(continued)

(continued)

We need to consider diversity and individual differences and create different environments for different kinds of people. This is important because by doing that we are not only going to optimize the people who work for an organization, but it's also going to benefit the company, as their employees will have better focus, better attention, less stress, and less irritation. That will result in a better quality of work.

Space needs to be flexible because people are different and have different needs. Part of me has been grateful that the pandemic showed us that many people can work well from home. There are pros and cons to this, but it showed us that we need to consider options, be mindful of individual differences and needs, and design accordingly.

I'm excited to say that I've seen a much faster embracement of the human element in the workplace design industry, even more so than in HR. Maybe this is just in the spaces where I've been involved, but it's very positive. The workplace design industry is at the forefront of addressing sensory stimulation and an innovative approach, which is fabulous. Keep up the good work!

Client Story

A Place for Everyone at Arup's New Birmingham Office

Arup Office at One Centenary Way

Birmingham, United Kingdom
68,000 sq. ft.
Fit-out: WELL Building Platinum certified
Base building: BREEAM Excellent certified
HOK services: Brief Validation, Space Budgets, Test Fitting, Interior Design

Developer: MEPC
Building architect: Howells

HOK's design for Arup's new Birmingham office showcases neuroin-clusive and sustainable design in a modern workplace. Located across three stories of the new 13-story One Centenary Way building, the workplace accommodates 900 people (Figure 5.1). It is one of the largest offices for Arup, a collective of 20,000 designers, advisors, and experts working across 140 countries.

Arup envisioned "a dynamic, global hub connecting our clients and people." The project reimagines the work environment, focusing on inclusivity, environmental sustainability, well-being, and innova-tion. It sets a new standard for Arup's offices worldwide.

Embracing Neurodiversity

Arup's decision to collaborate with HOK stemmed from a shared vision of creating inclusive work environments. While Arup was

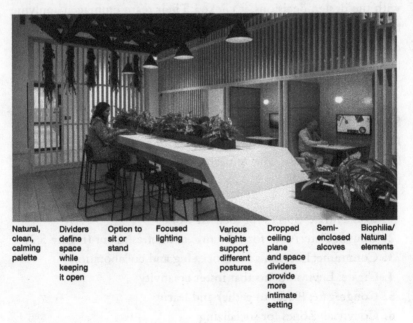

| Natural, clean, calming palette | Dividers define space while keeping it open | Option to sit or stand | Focused lighting | Various heights support different postures | Dropped ceiling plane and space dividers provide more intimate setting | Semi-enclosed alcoves | Biophilia/ Natural elements |

Figure 5.1 Arup Birmingham, UK workplace: Social hub

(continued)

(*continued*)

committed to inclusivity in the built environment, HOK's expertise in neurodiversity-focused design offered a new dimension.

"We wanted a world-renowned expert in the field, a thought leader, and a firm that could guide us," says Alison Kilby, an associate director at Arup who leads its workplace advisory team in the Midlands and acted as the client for this project.

This neuroinclusive approach resonated with Arup's leaders and staff. "As engineers, we likely have a higher-than-average percentage of individuals who are neurodivergent," notes Kilby. "Many people connected with HOK's material. It explained a lot about their own habits, behaviors, and preferences that they perhaps hadn't considered before."

"Engineers are very analytical and driven by facts and data," says Greg Shewan, HOK's project manager. "When we presented a logical approach to aligning Arup's equitable and well-being ambitions with the design decisions, it clicked. Their team embraced applying the science of design to create their new office. They leaned into our research on how environmental elements—thermal, acoustic, and lighting systems—aid in creating a sustainable, neuroinclusive workspace."

Six Modalities of Work
HOK conducted extensive workshops with Arup's staff to understand their daily space use. The resulting design centers around six work modalities:

1. Concentrate: Spaces for focused work
2. Contemplate: Areas for reflection and refreshment (Figure 5.2)
3. Commune: Locations for processing and collaboration
4. Create: Environments that foster creativity
5. Congregate: Places to gather and learn
6. Convivial: Zones for socializing

| Open ceiling creates a more spacious feel | Natural materials/ Biophilia | Option to sit or stand | More private settings mixed into social space | Open access connects floors | Panels for enhanced acoustics | Access to daylight and various lighting levels within space |

Figure 5.2 Arup Birmingham, UK workplace: Contemplate zone

To meet diverse neurotype needs, HOK developed user personas and "Day-in-the-Life" videos. These explored how individuals with different neurological profiles might use the office, including their commute. Each journey highlighted either a hypo- or hypersensitive individual in a different role, demonstrating how the design could serve neurodiverse staff.

Key Neuroinclusive Design Elements
The design incorporates key elements catering to diverse cognitive styles and sensory needs:

1. Thoughtful Space Planning
The layout maximizes comfort and productivity:
- The workspaces optimize natural light and views
- Meeting rooms are carefully placed to avoid blocking light in open areas

(continued)

(*continued*)

- There is a balance between open collaboration spaces and focused work areas
- The design avoids enclosing open areas, maintaining views throughout the day

2. Diverse Space Offerings

HOK's design prioritizes a variety of work settings to support different cognitive styles and tasks:

- Simple, clear circulation around the floor plate
- A range of social, semi-private, and private zones
- Ample daylight access throughout
- Active zones to encourage movement and stimulation
- Dedicated areas for reflection
- Focused workspaces for concentrated tasks
- Quiet contemplation zones for minimal sensory input

"The space does an amazing job of giving people many options and choices," says James Watts, Arup's Birmingham office leader

3. Flexible Seating Strategy

An unassigned seating arrangement empowers employees to choose environments that best suit their daily needs:

- Option to book consistent spots for those who prefer routine
- Freedom to move between different areas and desk types
- Variety of seating options to accommodate different postures and preferences

"The flexible seating is working well for us," says Kilby. "A handful of people sit in the exact same spot daily, using the desk booking system. But most move around, selecting spots based on what they're doing that day, where their colleagues are, or picking their preferred desk or screen type."

4. Acoustic Environment

Recognizing the importance of sound control for neurodivergent individuals, the team implemented innovative acoustic solutions:

- Enhanced absorbent materials throughout, especially in ceilings
- Exposed ceiling design for improved acoustics and aesthetics

- Avoidance of potentially polarizing sound masking techniques "The acoustics in the space are great," says Kilby. "We're in an open environment, but we aren't distracting each other. Even during meetings or Teams calls, which are naturally louder, we have excellent sound control."

5. **Adaptive Lighting**

The office features a sophisticated circadian lighting system that:
- Provides varying light levels to accommodate different sensitivities
- Adapts to time of day and seasonal changes
- Incorporates local desk lamps for personalized lighting control
- Supports staff health and well-being by mimicking natural light patterns
- Offers areas with naturally lower lighting for those preferring more subtle illumination

6. **Biophilic Elements**

Natural elements integrated throughout promote well-being and cognitive function:
- Extensive use of plants and natural materials
- Views of nature where possible
- Natural color palette
- Maximized urban greening throughout the office
- Dedicated "Mindfulness Zones" with abundant plant life, natural light, and city views, located away from busy workspaces

7. **Community Engagement**

Arup's new office catalyzes reconnection with colleagues, consultant, clients, and the community:
- The ground-floor space doubles as a community hub for events
- HOK helped secure ground-level access, giving Arup a street presence with a "shop window" to the city
- The basement at One Centenary Way houses Birmingham's first dedicated cycle hub, promoting sustainable transportation

(continued)

(continued)

"We designed the office to be used for events and social outreach," says Watts. "It has given our team a sense of pride and ownership. We're hosting numerous events, from charity video launches to visits from schoolchildren. This raises the energy level in the office and promotes Arup more broadly."

Blending Office and Home Environments

HOK's design incorporates lifestyle rooms fostering various activities:

- Dedicated spaces for activities ranging from yoga to Legos
- The "Paradise Suite" used for weekly Pilates sessions and social events
- Diverse areas catering to different working styles and preferences

The COVID-19 pandemic influenced the design. "We were on lockdown during the project, so we saw how differently people worked when they were in work environments they had created for themselves," explains Kilby. "On the other side of our Teams' calls, you would have people working hard with their kids playing in the background who were fine with that. Others had to close the door and shut out everything. It became evident that different people need different things."

This insight shifted Arup's thinking about office essentials. "When we surveyed people before we started the project to find out what they wanted, the number one request was for a desk followed by a chair," says Kilby. "But HOK's research and the insights we gained from seeing how people were working from home expanded what we considered essential."

Sustainability Design for Inclusive Well-Being

The design supports Arup's goal to be net-zero carbon by 2030. The project achieved WELL Building Platinum certification, while the base building earned BREEAM Excellent certification. This commitment to sustainable design underscores Arup's dedication to creating a healthy, inclusive environment benefitting all employees, including those who are neurodivergent.

Smart technology is central to this neuroinclusive approach:

- Meeting rooms feature scene-setting lighting and temperature controls, allowing individuals to customize their environment to suit their sensory needs
- CO_2 monitoring ensures optimal air quality, significantly impacting cognitive function and comfort
- Digital totems display occupancy heat maps, empowering staff to choose work areas that suit their preferences

Natural and recycled materials create a visually diverse and tactile environment. The all-electric heating system minimizes noise and air quality issues, enhancing the sensory experience.

Flexible design elements like new slab openings and an atrium promote movement and provide diverse spatial experiences. These features demonstrate how sustainability and neuroinclusion can work together to create an environmentally responsible and adaptable workspace.

Measurable Impacts and Employee Feedback

The neuroinclusive design has had a profound impact on Arup. "It has been positive for many people, and importantly, there's nothing obviously different," says Watts. "People find a desk they like working at and crack on. We've created this broader, more welcoming space without adversely affecting anyone."

Tim Hatton, HOK's senior interior designer, shares an anecdote: "During a recent tour, an Arup engineer sought me out to share that he no longer experiences headaches, fatigue, or anxiety from being in the office. As a designer, that's the ultimate reward—knowing your work has positively impacted occupants."

(*continued*)

(*continued*)

The new workplace has transformed Arup's workplace culture and employee engagement. Watts reports a 10 percent increase in office attendance and a noticeable rise in social activities. "We are seeing the new space become more of a social hub," he says. "People want to spend time here and are socializing more. For example, we have a board game group that has about 40 people. And I've signed off on a soldering iron because a dozen people want to repair model railways."

A Model for Inclusive Workplaces

Arup's office at One Centenary Way demonstrates how neuroinclusive design creates an effective, comfortable, and sustainable workplace for all employees.

"Why wouldn't companies create a more inclusive workplace?" asks Kilby. "We've found it's better on so many levels. These spaces, with more interesting workplace settings, are much more compelling than standard rows. I'd encourage everybody to embrace neuroinclusive spaces."

Watts emphasizes the dynamic nature of the workspace: "In another six months, it may look different again. We need to use the data we're collecting to learn what has and hasn't worked and adapt spaces as needed. We evolve and it keeps going."

6 | Survey Findings

Everybody is a genius. But if you judge a fish by its ability to climb a tree, it will live its whole life believing that it is stupid.
—Often attributed to Albert Einstein, but source unknown

To design spaces that address individual sensory needs, we need to develop a deeper understanding of the factors impacting us. While our research and literature reviews provided a valuable foundation, HOK's team conducted survey, workshops, and pilots to learn directly from the neurodivergent community. Adhering to the principle of "nothing about us without us," involving affected individuals gave us deeper insight into their experiences and gave them a voice in decisions that impact them. This chapter summarizes our survey findings and their implications for how we design space.

HOK's team collaborated with organizational and environmental psychologist and neurodiversity experts to design survey questions exploring how the built environment impacts individuals by neurotypes, age, and gender. The questions covered a variety of elements without leading respondents, attempting to gather objective insights about their reactions to the spaces they use.

Survey One: All Neurodivergent Populations

The first research initiative was conducted to understand the needs of neurodivergents. Along with Genius Within, an organization supporting neurodivergents in finding employment and in their careers, we conducted this research with Tarkett North America, a flooring manufacturer. This study built on years of in-depth research and insights into diversity and inclusion and the impact of workplace environments on performance. Our focus was on identifying key challenges for neurominorities and how businesses can help them thrive.

Key Stats on Participants

- **Respondents:** 202 neurodivergent individuals from the United States, United Kingdom, and Canada.
- **Demographics:** 69 percent female or nonbinary, 82 percent aged 30–60.
- **Neurodiverse Conditions:** 54 percent ADHD, 40 percent autistic, 19 percent dyslexic, 57 percent reported multiple neurodiverse conditions.
- **Sensitivities:** 47 percent had heightened sensitivity to the built environment (hypersensitivity), 22 percent needed more stimulation (hyposensitivity). See QR Code 6.1.

Historically, studies have focused mainly on white male adolescents, underrepresenting Black people, Indigenous people, and people of color (BIPOC); women; and adults of working age.[1,2,3] This imbalance likely stems from society's expectations and biases. For example, girls are often socialized differently than boys, which may affect how neurodivergence is recognized or expressed in different genders. As a result, many neurodivergents who are

QR Code 6.1   Sensory processing neurodiversity and workplace design report

BIPOC, women, or adults of working age may feel compelled to mask their neurodivergent traits or develop coping mechanisms for their sensitivities.

Surveys Two and Three: Mixed Neurotype Population

HOK received a ONEder Grant by One Workplace to assess the sensory needs of an office with a mix of neurotypes. We compared these survey findings to the results from previous research conducted with an all-neurodivergent sample group. Our goal was to identify similarities and differences between the two groups and test our hypothesis: The needs of neurodivergents may not be fundamentally different from those of neurotypicals but rather more intense and specific.

Key Stats on Participants

- **Respondents:** 92 individuals from HOK's San Francisco and Seattle offices, including design, administrative, marketing, accounting, IT, and HR professionals.
- **Demographics:** 19.5 percent identified as neurodivergent, aligning with the United States average of 15–20 percent. 54 percent were female, and 69 percent were between the ages of 30–60.
- **Neurodiverse Conditions:** 13 percent ADHD, 2 percent autistic, 11 percent dyslexic, and 5 percent reported multiple conditions.

The survey findings highlight distinct trends by age, variations of work environments, and work styles.

Work Styles

Understanding how people spend their time in work settings enables us to design spaces tailored to those activities. This involves creating appropriate settings while ensuring people have access to both high- and low-stimulation versions of these settings. Choices allow people to find comfortable levels of social exposure and interaction.

Many people instinctively feel uneasy in a work setting that leaves their back exposed to a room. Yet for some neurodivergent individuals, this feeling can be intolerable. An enclosed office can foster feelings of security and autonomy—or it can further isolate a person who already faces challenges assimilating.

Providing a variety of activity-based workspaces enables everyone to find their ideal work environment. These spaces can include nooks, alcoves, areas of refuge, clusters, neighborhoods, gathering places, and spaces for movement. People who are hypersensitive often prefer settings that are shielded or off to the side because they provide more control and less stimulation. At the same time, some individuals might need more stimulation and thrive in energetic spaces or need to listen to music, physically move, engage, or fidget to process information. If offering workspace choices is not possible, simply asking neurodivergent employees about their preferences can help.

Our research on how respondents spend their time in the workplace shows:

- Deep focused work (concentrated individual tasks): 30–40 percent
- "Alone together" work (individual tasks in shared spaces with occasional interaction): 20 percent
- Meetings and group activities: 18 percent

Solo work dominates, with combined individual work (both deep focus and "alone together") accounting for 50–60 percent of workplace time. People typically underestimate time spent on communal processing work. Employees also feel they spend more time in meetings than they actually do, though they would prefer fewer meetings overall.

Sensory Sensitivities

Our analysis of individual hypersensitivities found that auditory stimulation was the primary factor impacting people, closely followed by visual stimulation. Respondents also noted sensitivities to temperature, smell, patterns, colors, and lighting.

We found many commonalities between the neurodivergent population and the mixed neurotype population regarding hypersensitivities. The mixed neurotype sample showed similar responses but to a lesser degree.

This confirms our hypothesis that sensory stimulation in the built environment affects everyone and there are common triggers for both neurotypicals and neurodivergents, albeit to different degrees.

Hypersensitivity Our research supports the notion that individuals diagnosed with ASD have a heightened sensitivity to sensory stimulation in the built environment and can exhibit different patterns of sensory interventions compared to other neurodivergent individuals (Figure 6.1).

- 77 percent of respondents noted a heightened hypersensitivity to sound.
- 62 percent of respondents reported a heightened hypersensitivity to visual stimulation, finding it distracting. The impact of visual stimulation on neurodivergent individuals is often grossly underestimated. This includes factors such as clutter, patterns, and bold colors.
- About one-third of respondents were sensitive to smell. Scent can be powerful, strongly linked to memory, and capable of triggering vivid childhood recollections.
- One-fourth of respondents reported that their sense of positioning, equilibrium, and balance is impacted by design elements within a space.

Hyposensitivity Visual stimulation was the main factor impacting hyposensitive individuals, with 35 percent reporting a need for added sensory interaction. This was closely followed by 23 percent needing additional auditory stimulation (Figure 6.2).

Our research findings supported our hypothesis that sensory stimulation impacts everyone, both neurotypicals and neurodivergents, to varying degrees (QR Code 6.2). Some people found very quiet environments or empty spaces distracting and disorienting. They noted needing some level of energy, movement, or sound to function effectively in these spaces. Eleven percent of respondents indicated a need for higher tactile experiences. Specifically, ADHDers tended to seek more tactile stimulation (like textured surfaces or materials or interactive screens) while preferring less auditory and visual input.

Sensory Input
To what sensory inputs are you hypersensitive?

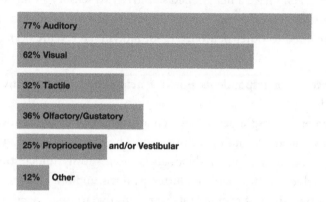

Neurodivergent Population

- 77% Auditory
- 62% Visual
- 32% Tactile
- 36% Olfactory/Gustatory
- 25% Proprioceptive and/or Vestibular
- 12% Other

Mixed Neurotype Population

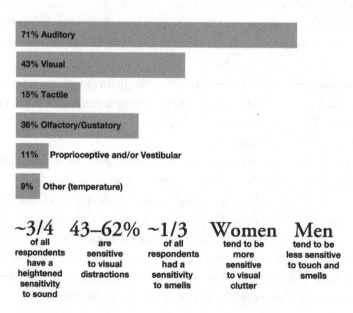

- 71% Auditory
- 43% Visual
- 15% Tactile
- 36% Olfactory/Gustatory
- 11% Proprioceptive and/or Vestibular
- 9% Other (temperature)

~3/4 of all respondents have a heightened sensitivity to sound

43–62% are sensitive to visual distractions

~1/3 of all respondents had a sensitivity to smells

Women tend to be more sensitive to visual clutter

Men tend to be less sensitive to touch and smells

Figure 6.1   Hypersensitivity to sensory stimulation

Sensory Input
To what sensory inputs
are you hyposensitive?

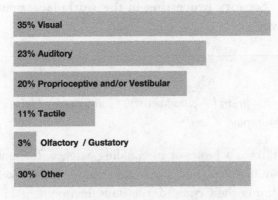

Neurodivergent Population

- 35% Visual
- 23% Auditory
- 20% Proprioceptive and/or Vestibular
- 11% Tactile
- 3% Olfactory / Gustatory
- 30% Other

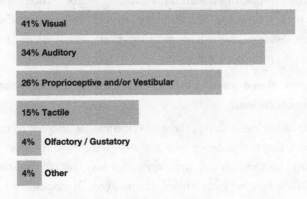

Mixed Neurotype Population

- 41% Visual
- 34% Auditory
- 26% Proprioceptive and/or Vestibular
- 15% Tactile
- 4% Olfactory / Gustatory
- 4% Other

34–41%	25–35%	Women	Men
are sensitive to visual distractions	need more acoustical stimulation or sound	tend to need more visual stimulation than men and are more impacted by visuals than acoustics	tend to be less aware of self-movement and body position

Figure 6.2 Hyposensitivity to sensory stimulation

QR Code 6.2   Sensory processing in the workplace: neurotype workplace survey

Spotlight

Experiential Design and Neurodiversity: Gail Brager's Holistic Approach to Workplace Comfort

Gail Brager, PhD, is a professor in Building Science, Technology & Sustainability in the Department of Architecture at UC Berkeley and associate director of the Center for the Built Environment. For more than 40 years, she has been teaching, mentoring students and colleagues, and conducting research on building performance for energy and occupant well-being. She recently co-authored a book, *Experiential Design Schemas*, aimed at creating rich, variable, multisensory spaces that help humans thrive.

Could you share your path to becoming an advocate for neuroinclusion?

Gail: In my early days, I did and continue to do a lot of research on the thermal side of our sensory systems and how people respond to the thermal environment. I saw that all the standards were based on very controlled experiments in laboratory settings, which were then used to develop models to predict people's comfort. I always thought there was a disconnect between how people might respond in a laboratory setting and how they might respond in real buildings. Like many others in our field, we questioned the universal nature of these standards, based on the assumption that all people in all climates in all building types at any time of the day all felt the same.

In response to these concerns, some of my legacy work includes the development of the adaptive thermal comfort model with my colleague Richard de Dear from the University of Sydney. We showed that people in naturally ventilated and air-conditioned buildings responded differently depending on the context of the outdoor climate. Our hypothesis of why people reacted so differently was a combination of various types of adaptation—physiological, behavioral, and psychological—shifted expectations based on personal control and having a more variable, climate-connected thermal history in the building. All of this started shining a light and focusing on people as individuals, not people as groups, which in turn is related to the needs and preferences of a neurodivergent population.

A second, more recent piece of my legacy work is going beyond thermal comfort and becoming more interested in larger sensory systems and all the attributes of indoor environmental quality, including lighting, acoustic, and olfactory elements.

Can you talk about the work you have been doing recently?

I recently teamed up with Mark DeKay, who shares my interests in the experiences of people and buildings, yet we have complementary backgrounds. I'm an engineer by training and have primarily written scholarly journal publications, and he is an architect who has also written books. Together, we published a book called *Experiential Design Schemas* that translates what we know from building and health sciences into architectural design strategies and speaking more directly to practitioners. It's about bridging the data-driven language of building scientists with the more poetic, sensorial perspective of architects.

The aim is to create environments that help everybody thrive, creating joyful, delightful ways in which buildings are more connected to nature, and subtle variability in the sensory environments. It's about enhancing the positive rather than reducing the

(continued)

(*continued*)

negative, which tends to be the orientation of most research and building standards.

What are some of the biggest challenges that neurodivergent workers are dealing with?

Step one is awareness and education, helping people understand that everybody is on a spectrum of neurodiversity, so it's more than just worrying about the endpoints of people typecast as neurodivergent. We should begin by helping leaders and employees in a workplace understand that all individuals might fall somewhere differently on the spectrum at any given moment. I also think that, too often, decisions are based purely on economic models of efficiency and cost-effectiveness that ignore the health and well-being of people. The reality is that the health and well-being of people have a financial implication, so it is all connected.

What are the obstacles preventing people from thriving in spaces?

In the context of this conversation, the most important factors are lack of agency, choice, and control. We have these fixed spaces designed to be uniform in space and constant in time, with centralized systems where people cannot control their own environments, such as adjusting a thermostat, opening or closing a window, or modifying lighting or acoustic conditions. Many of the existing standards reinforce the idea of designing for the average rather than the individual, and merely reducing the negative, which means another obstacle is just attitude. We need people to look beyond the standards with a fundamentally different mindset.

How can we address these challenges going forward, and what are some things we can do to enhance people's spaces so they can be more successful?

Removing obstacles starts with a mindset, and then design decisions follow. Clients are often economically motivated or perhaps they're used to just doing things the way they've done them before.

I think a good first approach is to identify some low-hanging fruit that naturally integrates with the organization's goals. If it's something that's completely new and different or requires big investments, it's a nonstarter.

Designers need to first find out the organization's goals, speak in a language they will understand, and align their recommendations to those goals.

We have a concept I call experiential programming, where at the earliest stages of design we discuss setting intentional experiential sensory goals and normalize that as part of the programming conversation.

What are some of the successful things that you've seen or experienced that you can share?

One thing to do to create more welcoming environments is to start with a conversation with people that shows your awareness. We need to look at both physical space and workplace culture, so part of it is physical, and part of it is attitude. And we need to normalize the idea that there is a spectrum of needs that we're all on, so anything considered a "special" accommodation benefits everyone. Overall, we need to offer variety, choice, and control to everybody.

Survey Four: Mixed Neurotype Scientific Population

HOK partnered with Advanced Research Clusters (ARC) and Edward Edgerton, an environmental psychologist at the University of the West of Scotland (UWS). ARC's expertise in developing scientific spaces for new-generation exploratory scientists in the United Kingdom made them an ideal partner. Edgerton brought his knowledge of how people experience work and learning environments, and how this relates to building design.

The survey was open to all individuals working in scientific spaces, regardless of neurotype, to obtain a sampling of the current population in these settings. The goal was to better understand how sensory elements in the built environment impact individuals and to develop design considerations for inclusive lab environments. The team conducted a survey and a workshop with a sampling of neurodiverse individuals.

Key Stats on Participants

- **Respondents:** 48 percent identified as neurodivergent, a higher-than-average percentage (Figure 6.3). In contrast, only 30 percent identified as being neurotypical. This unusual distribution may be due to a perception that the survey was perceived as a "neurodiversity survey," potentially attracting more responses from neurodivergent employees. It also could indicate a significant shift in society, with more individuals embracing and acknowledging their whole selves.
- **Neurodiverse Conditions:** 15 percent reported having a comorbidity, and 25.5 percent reported being autistic—10 times the global average.
  - Neurotypical: 29.9 percent
  - Autistic: 25.5 percent
  - Dyslexic: 20.6 percent

Neurodiversity by Age
Mixed Neurotype Scientific Population

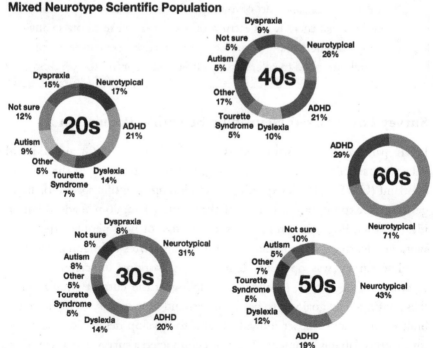

Figure 6.3   Mixed neurotype scientific participants by age group

- ADHD: 18.6 percent
- Dyspraxic: 2.4 percent
- Tourette syndrome: 0.4 percent
- Other: 5 percent
- Not sure: 19 percent
- Prefer not to say: 2.5 percent

Many people have not obtained a formal diagnosis for various reasons. Some may not have access to professional services, while others may not think they meet the prescribed thresholds. Based on previous survey results and the comments from the respondents, we have observed that individuals who identified as "not sure" tended to respond similarly to the neurodivergent population.

Age and Neurotype

Among younger respondents, 71 percent of individuals in their twenties considered themselves neurodivergent, significantly higher than the widely held statistic that 20 percent of the population is neurodivergent (Figure 6.4). This could be due to increased awareness and diagnosis among the younger generation, as well as the tendency that autistic individuals are more likely than the general population and other disabilities groups to gravitate toward STEM jobs.[4]

Neurodiversity by Age
Mixed Neurotype Scientific Population

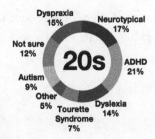
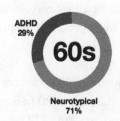

The younger generation reported a much more diverse set of neurotypes.

For the older generations, far less.

Figure 6.4   Mixed neurotype scientific survey: age variances

Among older respondents, those 60 and older reported far less neurodivergence, with only 26 percent identifying as neurodivergent. This disparity could be attributed to underdiagnosis in older generations or different environmental and social factors during their lives.

Neurovariances

The survey reinforced some commonly known attributes of various neurotypes:

- Individuals with comorbidities showed significantly higher sensitivity to visual stimuli compared to those with dyslexia.
- Dyslexics reported significantly higher sensitivity to proprioception stimuli than ADHDers.
- Austistic and dyslexic individuals indicated significantly higher sensitivity to vestibular stimuli than the ADHD group.
- ADHDers tended to seek more tactile stimulation and possibly less auditory or visual input.
- Autistic people demonstrated heightened sensitivity to stimuli in general, aligning with findings from previous studies.

The 15 percent of respondents who reported a comorbidity are more likely to have complex reactions to sensory stimulation in the built environment.

According to a ZenBusiness study,[5] more than half of Gen Z (born between 1997–2012) identify as neurodivergent. Specifically, 22 percent said they definitely were neurodivergent, while another 31 percent expressed having some neurodivergent traits.

The same study revealed that a majority of Gen Zers believe neurodivergents are more likely than others to exhibit traits often associated with entrepreneurship:

- Creativity (90 percent)
- Authenticity (80 percent)
- Hard-working (72 percent)
- Perseverance (72 percent)
- Hustle (64 percent)

Challenges in the Built Environment

When examining the design elements impacting individuals, our research showed that sound, temperature, and light were the most significant challenges in the built environment for both neurotypical and neurodivergent individuals (Figure 6.5). The degree of impact varied between these groups.

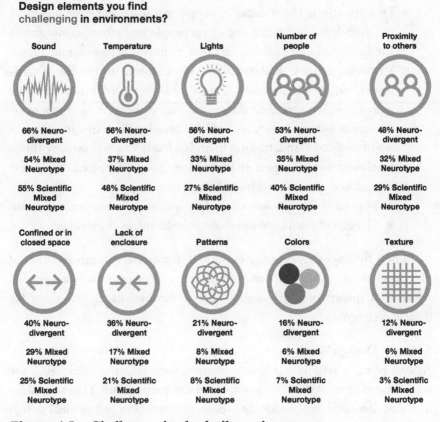

Challenges
Design elements you find
challenging in environments?

Sound	Temperature	Lights	Number of people	Proximity to others
66% Neurodivergent	56% Neurodivergent	56% Neurodivergent	53% Neurodivergent	48% Neurodivergent
54% Mixed Neurotype	37% Mixed Neurotype	33% Mixed Neurotype	35% Mixed Neurotype	32% Mixed Neurotype
55% Scientific Mixed Neurotype	48% Scientific Mixed Neurotype	27% Scientific Mixed Neurotype	40% Scientific Mixed Neurotype	29% Scientific Mixed Neurotype

Confined or in closed space	Lack of enclosure	Patterns	Colors	Texture
40% Neurodivergent	36% Neurodivergent	21% Neurodivergent	16% Neurodivergent	12% Neurodivergent
29% Mixed Neurotype	17% Mixed Neurotype	8% Mixed Neurotype	6% Mixed Neurotype	6% Mixed Neurotype
25% Scientific Mixed Neurotype	21% Scientific Mixed Neurotype	8% Scientific Mixed Neurotype	7% Scientific Mixed Neurotype	3% Scientific Mixed Neurotype

Figure 6.5   Challenges in the built environment

Key Findings

- **Auditory issues:** A majority of respondents in both groups found auditory issues to be the most challenging element in the built environment. Remote work in more isolated environments during the pandemic heightened sensitivity to sound and desensitized many to being in shared spaces. Research on auditory stimulation reinforces these variances and confirms that sound is one of the most impactful sensory elements in the built environment (Figure 6.6).

- **Temperature sensitivities:** Temperature sensitivities edged out lighting sensitivities to round out the top three elements people find challenging. Women tended to perform better when the temperature is slightly elevated, while men preferred cooler temperatures.[6]
- **Densification:** The number of people in a space and close proximity to others had a significant impact on people in the built environment. Pandemic-induced isolation may have exacerbated these sensitivities.
- **Patterns, colors, and textures:** While lower on the list of challenges, patterns, colors, and textures still presented issues for some individuals. We speculate they scored lower because in many environments, especially labs and offices, because these design elements are muted and bland, making them less likely to cause sensory issues.
- **Enclosed versus open spaces:** More people reported discomfort in enclosed spaces compared to open ones.
  - 24 percent of respondents found the lack of enclosure uncomfortable.
  - 31 percent found confined or enclosed spaces distressing.

These findings challenge the common operational recommendation of placing neurodivergent employees in private offices or pods as a universal solution. It underscores the need to create flexible spaces that allow for diverse preferences.

Sensory Design Workshop

As part of the scientific workplace research with Edgerton and ARC, the team hosted a workshop with select survey participants. This workshop included three activities to identify sensory preferences and optimal design strategies.

- **Activity 1:** Participants used cards depicting a range of sensory experiences to express feelings about their current environments. They shared why they selected specific cards and what those cards meant to them.
- **Activity 2:** Participants rated lab and administrative spaces on aspects such as comfort, productivity, and stress levels. The results were discussed to understand preferences and challenges.

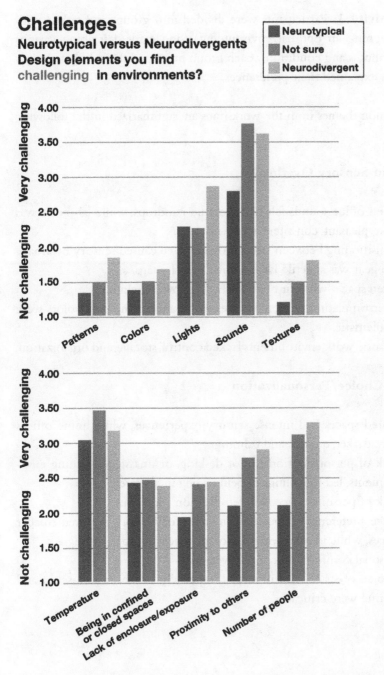

Figure 6.6 Variance in response by neurotype workshop findings

- **Activity 3:** Participants were divided into groups and tasked with designing an optimal environment using cards describing various attributes and conditions. Each group presented their design choices and explained their preferences.

Common themes from the workshops are summarized in the following lists.

Social and Sensory Overload

- Open office sounds felt like sporadic raindrops, while lab noise was more pleasant, consistent white noise.
- Transitioning between lab and office space caused sensory overload.
- Lab gear was a tactile issue, similar to itchy tags.
- Open spaces without boundaries were overwhelming.
- Overstimulating, cluttered spaces with patterns and bold colors were problematic.
- Chaotic work environments lacked control, storage, and organization.

Control/Choice/Personalization

- Shared spaces had intense sensory experiences, while home offices were darker, quieter, and calming.
- Lack of personalization in hot desking, or unassigned seating environments, led to feelings of being a cog in a wheel.
- Lack of personal space and densification were issues.
- Space preferences depended on tasks: focus work required smaller spaces, while ideation or collaboration needed open settings.
- Personal comfort and control were key.
- Choice of space was important, especially in labs where setup and routine were critical.

Reprieve

- No break from noise in lab spaces; bathroom was the only reprieve.
- Dislike for areas where people felt on display.
- Access to quiet rooms and natural elements was important.

Lack of Empathy/Understanding

- Poor wayfinding and navigation were significant workplace challenges.
- Few employers discussed reasons for changes or considered sensory sensitivities when making seating decisions.

Belonging

- Pride in work was a motivating factor.

Neuroinclusive Scientific Neighborhood

To design the neuroinclusive scientific workplace, the team translated survey and workshop findings into a playbook of key design strategies and requirements. These strategies were developed into a set of tangible design concepts used to transform a typical scientific neighborhood into a neuroinclusive "scientific workplace of tomorrow."

Typically, the write-up space within scientific workplaces is open, with regular rows of desks aligned with the lab planning grid. Cellular meeting rooms are usually added with some informal breakout spaces opposite the cores.

The main driver for these uniform lab layouts is maximizing net-to-gross area ratio to drive space efficiency and greatest density of occupants and bench space within a floor plate. This is understandable given the cost premium of lab buildings over more conventional office buildings. However, this uniform layout can have psychological impacts on staff, potentially leading to negative effects on business success and financial outcomes.

The neuroinclusive considerations outlined previously were applied to the typical commercial lab environment as a design brief, resulting in a transformative neuroinclusive scientific neighborhood (see QR Code 6.3).

The most notable difference between the traditional plan and the new neuroinclusive scientific workplace layout is the increased focus on addressing the modalities of work and creating various neurozones (Figure 6.7).

QR Code 6.3   Designing neuroinclusive laboratory environments

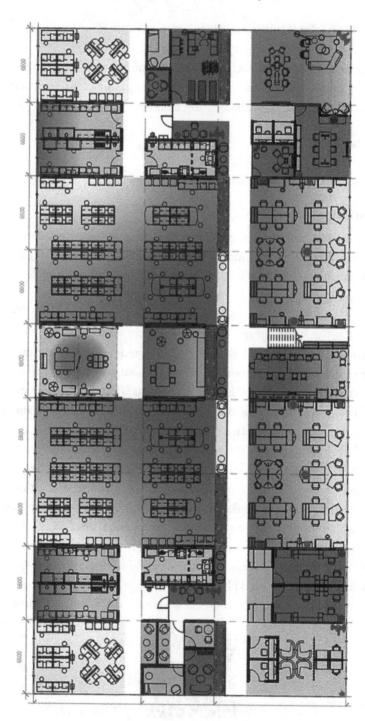

Figure 6.7 Scientific workplace plan

These zones are designed to address the needs of a broader range of individuals, instead of catering to a few. This approach creates a rich and diverse interior landscape, which is at the heart of neuroinclusive design. This richness is not random. The neighborhood has an ordered legibility with clarity about the modalities of work.

Typical Scientific Workplace of Today	Neuroinclusive Scientific Workplace of Tomorrow
1. No access to daylight	1. Access to daylight and views
2. Need for cleanliness often equates to white, sterile, impersonal spaces	2. Elements of hospitality and stylization to humanize the space
3. Limited or no biophilic elements	3. Terrariums for controlled biophilia, color, and natural materiality
4. Noisy equipment	
5. Cluttered spaces	
6. Limited mobility of occupants, as they are often tied to one spot	4. Quiet and buzzy aural environments
7. Lack of variety, choice, control	5. Ordered range of different spaces
8. No space to retreat to	6. Ability to choose type of space

The plan illustrates a wide range of spaces and environments that have been created for our transformative neighborhood and that brings all these ideas together into a rich, vibrant, and diverse scientific workplace that we have collectively imagined.

Spotlight

How Edward Edgerton Applies Environmental Psychology to Neuroinclusive Design

Edward Edgerton, PhD, is an environmental psychologist at the University of the West of Scotland and a leading researcher in environmental psychology. His expertise focuses on the role of the learning environment in the educational process and environmental design within healthcare environments. Recent projects have focused on dementia-friendly design in care homes and identifying

(continued)

(*continued*)

and evaluating the impact of new school buildings. Edward served as a board member for the International Association of People-Environment Studies (IAPS) from 2005–2014 and was president from 2012–2014.

What makes you so passionate about neurodiversity and how the built environment impacts people?

Edward: My background is in psychology, which is essentially about understanding how people think, feel, and behave, but my passion in psychology is about architecture and design. I've always been interested in the design of environments, particularly the idea that when people make mistakes or have problems, it has little to do with the person and actually has a lot to do with the characteristics of the environment.

I took advantage of an opportunity in the United Kingdom to explore the investment in new schools and found two problems: very little evidence supported the positive claims about them, and the new schools often didn't live up to expectations. In the United Kingdom and many Western countries, neurodivergent children are in mainstream schools without recognition of their different needs. Unfortunately, these young people have struggled in these new environments because their needs weren't considered in the design. This is when neurodiversity caught my attention; it was being ignored when there was an opportunity to create more inclusive environments.

Can you tell us about the research you have been involved with recently?

I've been exploring individuals' needs and the gap in what we call person-environment congruence, i.e. whether or not the environment supports our needs. I've come across so many past examples where there is clearly a large gap between a person's needs and their environment. At the same time, many of the adaptations or changes that can be made are relatively simple. It doesn't always have to require the creation of a brand-new environment.

When I talk to architects, there is often a strong desire to do something practical and applied. This is sometimes missing from academia, where there is more of a focus on developing theory and there are often difficulties with conducting applied, real-world research. Hearing about HOK's work and having a specific context, in this case, laboratory design, made it easier than dealing with some vague, large-scale environment. This is a fantastic opportunity to take a multidisciplinary approach to provide evidence that will convince people of what can be done.

What surprised you as you were working through the research?

What surprised me was the prevalence of people who are identifying as neurodiverse, but also how many people are just becoming aware that they may be neurodiverse. That is really interesting.

But the other thing I found interesting was that I don't think neurodivergent individuals are that different from people who are neurotypical. There are parallels between personality traits like extraversion-introversion and neurodiversity. Some people may display their extraversion very differently compared to other extroverts, and I think that's true about neurodiversity.

What do you think accounts for the high number of people identifying as neurodivergent in your research?

In the United Kingdom, particularly in Scotland, there's some value in being identified as neurodivergent in the education systems. Many parents want to obtain a diagnosis for their children in order to access support.

However, this support often isn't available in the workplace, so there are fewer benefits to disclosing neurodivergence there. That's why it's interesting that so many of our study participants reported either being officially or unofficially diagnosed, despite no obvious workplace benefit from this disclosure.

(*continued*)

(continued)

What message would you give to academics, HR professionals, and architects/designers working on inclusivity?

Academics researching inclusion from the operational perspective and HR people working to change recruitment and support practices need to be convinced of the importance of the environment. If space is properly designed and supported by evidence, we can make people much more effective, satisfied, and happier. And we can enhance their well-being. Good environmental design can impact all these things.

For architects and designers, the message is about gathering convincing information or evidence. This involves a more scientific approach. They need to work with other disciplines that have creative, innovative techniques and methodological approaches that can help obtain the information needed to put more rigor into practice.

How can we leverage the current interest in environmental design to create more impactful, evidence-based spaces?

I have worked in this area for 25 years, and the interest in the physical environment is greater now than ever. We need to take advantage of this opportunity.

I have been working within a children's hospital, and the focus has been on reducing the anxiety levels of young people and parents coming in for major operations. The design changes we suggested are relatively simple, yet the benefits are dramatic. There's nothing more powerful than hearing people say, "I can't believe how much better of an experience this was than I anticipated." That is incredibly powerful.

As a hard-nosed scientist, I want to see the statistical evidence, and that's obviously important. But sometimes, what's much more powerful is hearing from someone about the difference something made to their quality of life, well-being, or performance.

Survey Five: ZHAW ADD/ADHD Sensory Challenges Survey

A research initiative by Zurich University of Applied Sciences (ZHAW), led by Clara Weber, PhD, Weber and funded by FRH, Fondation pour la Recherche en faveur des personnes Handicapées, was conducted in partnership with the Birkbeck University of London's Centre for Neurodiversity Research at Work. The study leveraged HOK's neurodiversity questionnaire to identify sensory challenges for workers in Switzerland diagnosed with ADD/ADHD. Their primary objective was to evaluate the effectiveness of adjustments on occupational health.

Their findings aligned with a previous HOK/Tarkett/Genius Within survey of neurodivergent workers with ADD/ADHD.

The research concluded that when workers were satisfied with their workplace adjustments, they were statistically more likely to experience higher levels of well-being, increased workplace satisfaction, and stronger feelings of support from their workplace.

QR Code 6.4   Sensory-Inclusive Office Environments for Workers with ADHD/ADD Poster Report

Gender Variations

Some people are not as affected by sensory experiences as others. In fact, our research showed that men tended to have far fewer hypersensitivities than women and those who identify as nonbinary. (Figure 6.8).

Women were found to:

- Report more sensitivities than men overall
- Be more sensitive to visual stimuli (53 percent reported sensitivity)

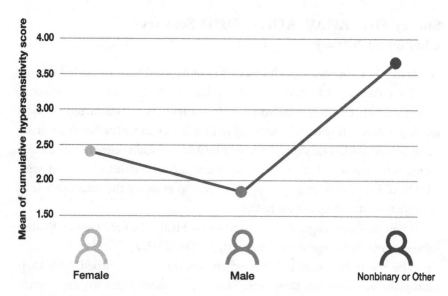

Figure 6.8 Neuroinclusive scientific lab layout

- Be less challenged by open communal spaces
- Have a heightened sensitivity to stimulation (rather than acute responses)
- Be more sensitive to body position in space than men
- Be highly sensitive to auditory stimulation (73 percent reported sensitivity) (Figure 6.9)
- Tend to be more sensitive to visual clutter, yet prefer more visual stimulation, as long as it was ordered and structured

Men were found to:

- Be less sensitive to touch and smell
- Have less awareness of body movement and position
- Be less acutely bothered by stimulation overall
- Tend toward hyposensitivity rather than hypersensitivity
- Be less bothered by auditory stimulation specifically
- Be less bothered by visual stimulation specifically

Auditory Stimulation

Individuals who are hypersensitive or have a heightened sensitivity to auditory stimulation.

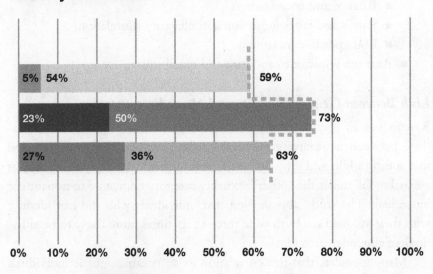

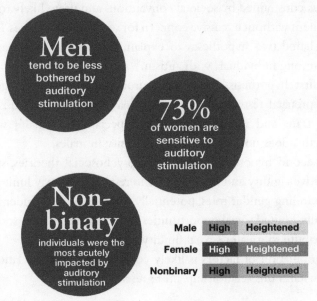

Figure 6.9   Variance in response to auditory stimulation by gender identity

Individuals who identified as nonbinary were found to:

- Be more acutely sensitive to stimulation than both men and women
- Be most acutely impacted by:
  - Balance and coordination
  - Smells and tastes (gustation and olfactory stimulation)
  - Body position awareness
- Be more sensitive to auditory and visual stimuli

Link Between Gender Diversity and Neurodivergence

Research from the University of Cambridge revealed significant correlations between neurodivergence and gender diversity. The study revealed that autistic adults and teens are nearly eight times more likely to identify as asexual or fall under the "other" sexuality category compared to nonautistic individuals. The study also showed that individuals who did not identify with their assigned sex birth were three to six times more likely to be autistic than cisgender individuals.[7]

Many speculate that this correlation exists because autistic individuals may be less constrained by societal conventions and more likely to embrace what fits them without excessive concern for social consequences. Researchers have shared two hypotheses to explain the higher gender and sexual diversity among individuals with autism.[8]

The first hypothesis, based on neurobiologic theories, suggests that increased prenatal testosterone exposure may lead to masculinization and influence traits and sexual preferences, especially in females with ASD. However, this does not explain sexual diversity in males.

The second hypothesis draws from psychosocial theories, suggesting that cognitive rigidity and stereotyped interests in ASD may limit flexibility in understanding gender roles, potentially leading to transgender identities. Additionally, limited social opportunities and less adherence to social norms may contribute to greater sexual fluidity in ASD.

A combination of factors is likely contributing to this relationship. To fully understand this relationship, more research is needed.

Design Strategies and Recommendations

When we asked the survey participants about design strategies and elements that provide comfort, we found many commonalities between neurotypical and neurodivergent respondents. The mixed neurotype group had stronger responses in a few areas—notably plants and access to people-filled spaces. This could reflect the impact of returning to less-populated, lower-energy spaces after the pandemic. The neurodivergent population identified these top 15 elements from a list of more than 30 options:

1. Having the option to select where you will work
2. Spaces that allow you to move and fidget
3. Having a dedicated assigned space
4. Access to daylight
5. Work points in low-traffic areas
6. Dedicated quiet rooms
7. Spaces that have areas to retreat to
8. Spaces with adjustable lighting levels
9. Spaces that incorporate natural elements
10. Adjustable, ergonomic furniture
11. Reduced visual clutter
12. Screens to block and reduce noise and visual distractions
13. Spaces that enable visual connections and clear lines of sight
14. Display walls for information sharing
15. Accessible storage

Interestingly, when we asked the mixed neurotype group, they listed the exact same elements, but in a slightly different order. All these strategies will aid in creating more neuroinclusive spaces that benefit both neurodivergent and neurotypical individuals.

7 | Senses and Degree of Stimulation

> Neurodiversity is not about changing people. It's about changing society's perception of people.
>
> —Dr. Nick Walker, author and activist

Based on the findings from our research, neuroinclusive workplace design relies on these three core principles:

- **Variety** and **options** provide settings with different attributes to accommodate a range of needs and work styles.
- **Choice** means enabling individuals to select from diverse workplace settings.
- **Control** allows individuals to adjust their immediate environment to match their preferences.

These principles should shape specific work settings, lighting levels, acoustics, visual stimulation, color palette, access to daylight, and other aspects of the built environment. Inclusive design gives employees power over their environment.

Accommodating Sensory Needs

Our sensory system includes eight key senses: visual, auditory, tactile, olfactory, gustatory, interoception, proprioception, and vestibular. Each affects us differently in the workplace. Sensory distractions such as sounds, smells, and visual clutter can impede cognitive focus. This reduces engagement and productivity—the last thing we want to do in workplace design. Sensory input can be overwhelming for people with certain neurological conditions. Too much sensory input can cause stress, tiredness, headaches, or nausea. Others need stimulation to focus.

When planning workspaces, we recommend prioritizing accommodations for those with hypersensitivity for two reasons: hypersensitive individuals represent a larger portion of the workforce, and it is easier to add stimulation later than to take it away. To create an optimal environment, we focus on controlled sensory elements such as the following:

- Organic, simple patterns
- Neutral color schemes
- Orderly, uncluttered spaces
- Minimal background noise
- Natural elements
- Ability to incorporate personal boundaries

We also want to avoid excessive stimuli for work environments, including bold colors, bright lights, cluttered or crowded spaces, unfamiliar scents, textures, or significant temperature fluctuations.

It is also important to provide access to active areas. These spaces appeal to individuals with hyposensitive leanings and need more sensory stimuli. When located in transition or social spaces, they also provide stimulation for all. For these areas, design considerations may include the following:

- Textural elements
- More saturated colors
- Visual interest
- Heightened sound levels or music
- Space to move and interact

The following sections address the primary sensory elements affecting us in the built environment and their impact. We also suggest core design strategies for addressing them. You can also find a more detailed list of strategies in Chapter 13, "Design Considerations."

Famous Innovators and Creators: Wolfgang Amadeus Mozart

Wolfgang Amadeus Mozart showed a prodigious talent for music and performed at age six at the imperial court in Vienna. Mozart was known to have perfect pitch and musical memory, but he was also extremely sensitive to loud sounds. He was known for his vulgar language and facial and motor tics and exhibited obsessive-compulsive behavior while constantly fidgeting. A study published in the *Journal of Neurology, Neurosurgery, and Psychiatry* speculated that his "socially unusual behaviors" and musical genius could be attributed to Tourette syndrome, ADHD, or autism.[1]

Visual

Vision is our primary means of perceiving the environment. More than half of the human body's sensory receptors are in the eyes.[2] Some find additional visual stimulation invigorating. Others find excess visual patterns, bold colors, or clutter highly distracting. The Theory of Legibility, the ease of which one can comprehend something, addresses this variation, suggesting that environments should be simple enough for people to intuitively understand which activities and behaviors are most appropriate for that space.[3]

Core Design Strategies: Visual

- Avoid distracting or confusing patterns in spaces where people work for extended periods.
- Balance nonstimulating color schemes with areas of higher stimulation to offer varied sensory experiences.
- Use visual elements—color, patterns, and graphics—strategically to create points of interest and boost energy levels.

- Avoid patterns that create optical illusions, generate visual noise, or cause confusion.
- Limit bold patterns in the peripheral vision of work areas to reduce distractions.
- Leverage subtle changes in patterns, color, or materials in the flooring to aid with wayfinding, navigation, and zone definition. In shared spaces, adjacent floor materials should have a medium contrast to aid those who look down while moving. Transitions should use predictable, gradual color changes.
- Choose low-sheen or matte finish flooring surfaces, as shiny surfaces can appear slippery or wet, potentially confusing those with poor sight or perceptive challenges.
- Incorporate visual aids and cues to facilitate wayfinding and navigation through spaces.
- Provide clear lines of sight to enhance a sense of security and predictability.
- Provide screening options to limit distractions.

Natural light tops the list of desired workspace features. Windows, light wells, and skylights offer views and daylight, enhancing visual comfort, supporting circadian rhythms, and lifting moods.[4] In spaces without outdoor views, people can lose track of time. Providing views enables individuals to orient themselves and stay in sync with natural systems and the time of day. A view of a natural vista or rooftop greenery can be calming or stimulating—or even provide a comforting focal point to those struggling with too much or too little stimulation.

Designers also need to pay close attention to visual accessibility. The World Health Organization reports[5] that at least 2.2 billion people—27 percent of the global population—have vision impairments, with approximately 1 billion cases either preventable or unaddressed.

Spotlight

Travis Hollman's Vision for Neuroinclusive Workplaces

Travis Hollman is a visionary CEO and owner of Hollman, Inc., the world's largest manufacturer of locker solutions. He is also an entrepreneur pioneering innovative solutions to enhance neurodiverse work environments. As someone who failed third grade and navigates the world with dyslexia and ADHD, Travis brings a unique perspective to creating tools that foster inclusivity and optimize productivity for all.

Why is neurodiversity, and designing for it, an important issue for you?

Travis: I was raised in Oregon and was very dyslexic. At a young age, I was struggling in school. At the end of third grade, I remember sitting there with my mom, dad, principal, and teacher—one of the few teachers I remember. In front of all of us, she told me I was the dumbest kid she had ever taught, that I had flunked third grade, and that I had to go to another school. In those days, many neurodiverse conditions were considered to reflect a lack of intelligence.

I struggled through it but had a turning point in high school. I finally had a coach in my sophomore year who asked me to read aloud in class. I told him I was dyslexic and, therefore, he couldn't make me read out loud. After class, he pulled me aside and said he wasn't going to let me use that as an excuse and planned to make me read out loud every day for the rest of the year. And he did. I didn't want to be embarrassed, so I practiced every night.

Back then, you fought through it. I didn't have a choice, so I used raw grit to get me through. It was very difficult, but it worked for me. Other neurodiverse kids may not have been so lucky.

How has your experience shaped your perspective on neurodiversity in the workplace?

Since graduating, I've pretty much worked for myself, which has allowed me to control the type of space I work in. My company designs and manufactures lockers, which means we've worked in a lot of workspaces. When I visit spaces that are rows and rows of desks in open space, I don't know how people do it. That wouldn't work for me.

(continued)

(continued)

Many neurodivergent individuals have above-average intelligence, and many have superpowers. Bill Gates, Elon Musk, Steve Jobs, Henry Ford, Mozart, and Einstein are all brilliant minds who were neurodiverse. If you can get one person with half the brains or creativity of Steve Jobs, it can change your entire company.

What are you currently working on to address neurodiversity in the workplace?

We're working on making products that help create environments where neurodivergent individuals can thrive. We decided to create a personal space where people can work all day. My goal was to make the most versatile space possible where you can control everything—from the lighting to the temperature, the desk height, the tactile surfaces, and a door you can close. The door and window you can either leave clear or press a button and it becomes dark. We want you to be able to control your environment to your preferences, whether you are hypersensitive or hyposensitive, or a little of both.

Often there are too many distractions in shared spaces. If we can give people a great place to work that makes them feel safe, they can be more productive.

What are your thoughts on the future of work for neurodivergent individuals?

AI will increase productivity in the future. The great thing about being neurodiverse is that AI can take over spelling, writing, and all the mundane things that the neurodiverse may not be great at. They tend to excel at creative thinking, communication and interpersonal skills, adaptability and resilience, and complex problem-solving. So, they will be an even greater asset to our future.

My big goal is to get the world to a four-day workweek. The increase in productivity can do this, and research shows that the neurodiverse can do an incredible amount of work in the right environment. We can do this by optimizing the time in the office where we get 40 hours of work done in a 32-hour workweek because you're so efficient.

What message do you have for employers about hiring neurodivergent individuals?

People approach me all the time, aware that both my son and I are dyslexic. They say how sorry they are for us. But my response is, "I'm so sorry for you—it's a superpower. You just have to know how to harness it." People are starting to become aware of the need to hire the neurodiverse. In fact, LinkedIn has added "Dyslexic Thinking" as a trait in their descriptions.

My buddy hires a lot of autistic individuals, and he told me that he has one person who does four times the amount of work that any nonautistic colleagues do. But he has to have a certain pizza from a certain place at 3 p.m. every day on the nose, or else he "goes crazy."

Organizations need to make sure that our managers are in tune with what they need because if you can design for them, you can harness their power. They just need adjustments. By designing something tailored for them, we can create environments that help us all to a better future with a more profitable company and happier employees.

Auditory

HOK's surveys of neurodivergent and mixed neurotype populations have shown that acoustics have the most significant impact on us. Despite the recognized importance, building design codes and requirements pay less attention to acoustics compared to other environmental factors like thermal conditions, indoor air quality, lighting, and electrical systems.

Current acoustic standards are limited, as they are derived from listening tests on healthy 18–25-year-olds.[6] As a result, most sonic experiences do not reflect the vast needs of an aurally diverse population.

Sounds ranging from general conversation levels to transmission between spaces, loud or high-pitched sounds, echoes, and reverberation all impact us. Excessive noise and unwanted sounds can be a major distraction. Autistic individuals often describe hearing electricity, specifically the humming of specific equipment, more acutely than others.

Open environments often raise acoustic concerns. A common myth suggests that offices are too loud and employees want silence. While that can be for some, complete silence and unnaturally quiet spaces are often more distracting than constant ambient sound.[7] Instinctively, silence is a sign of an impending threat or apprehension in our primordial brains. Researchers tested this concept by showing stressed participants an image of a forest. They found that when the image was presented without any sound, it did not reduce stress levels. But when accompanied by natural sounds, the combination of visual and auditory stimuli positively improved the participants' stress level and recovery.[8]

Core Operational and Design Strategies: Acoustics

- Provide varied acoustic levels in distinct zones to support a diversity of activities.
- Design spatial zoning to address sequencing of acoustic zones and transitions between spaces with buffer areas.
- Designate quiet zones for concentrative, heads-down focus work.
- Create spaces with higher energy levels or buzz for social gatherings and individuals who thrive in active, energized spaces.
- Use materials and systems that aid in controlling noise levels and transmission within the space.
- Incorporate water-based natural soundscaping to leverage the therapeutic benefits of nature, using it strategically within the space.
- Offer users personal control of the sonic experience where possible, such as providing noise-canceling headphones.

The Impact of Acoustics in Modern Workspaces

Many modern workspaces lack general background sound, which can allow for distinct conversations to be audible and more distracting than consistent ambient noise. Overhearing one-sided virtual calls or clear conversations across the room, for example, can be far more disrupting than ambient sound. In the workplace, these overheard conversations may reduce people's willingness to openly collaborate due to privacy concerns.[9]

Harsh, sharp, unpredicted sounds tend to be the most jarring. The goal is not to eliminate all sound, but rather to ensure the appropriate levels in these spaces. Effective neighborhood designs can create distinct acoustic zones that enable different work modalities and help employees manage distractions.

Many organizations work within spaces where changes are limited for various reasons, including cost or lease restrictions. When space plans and architectural components cannot be altered, thoughtful material selection becomes one of the best ways designers can control noise. Here is how different materials affect sound in a space:

- Hard, sound-reflecting materials increase noise and reverberation.
- Carpeting and wall panels help reduce reverberation.
- Suspended ceilings, fiberglass, and acoustic ceilings help mitigate noise.
- Acoustic wall panels, cork, and window treatments can absorb sound and reduce reverberation.
- Wood absorbs more noise than other hard surfaces.

Optimal Sound Levels

Not all sound is noise. The sound found in a coffee shop, typically around 70 decibels, is considered optimal for engaged work. Approximately 50 decibels is desirable for a quieter environment.[10] But some researchers believe that quiet environments allow us to focus too much on the task at hand, which actually may inhibit creativity.

The University of Arizona's Institute on Place, Well-being & Performance recently explored the relationship between workplace sound levels and physiological well-being.[11] The study identified 50 decibels as an optimal sound level for well-being in the workplace. The findings suggest that individuals working in quieter home offices may now perceive typical office noise levels as more disruptive, potentially altering their tolerance for sound in work environments. This shift highlights the importance of reassessing optimal noise levels in post-pandemic office settings.

That same research found that while open environments have been linked to more interaction during working hours and lower stress levels at night, they also tend to expose us to more acoustical stimuli. Higher sound levels can decrease physiological well-being, while the reverse is also true. When sounds merge to create a general background hum, we can concentrate better than in spaces that are too quiet or loud. It's about having the right level of sound for the activity at hand.

Benefits of Natural and Water-Based Sounds

Ambient nature sounds can positively impact focus, stimulation, and relaxation. Research has shown that natural sounds, such as gentle rain, wind, or flowing water, can physically change our minds and create a calming environment.[12] Compared to urban or office noise, natural sounds have been shown to expedite recovery and restoration, reduce cognitive fatigue, and increase motivation.[13]

Studies conducted in 2011[14] and 2017 by Annu Haapakangas and colleagues identified that water-based masking sound was preferred over artificial sound masking, such as white noise, pink noise, and instrumental and vocal music. The 2017 study[15] showed that artificial sound masking increased the error rate for individuals within the space more than in a space without it. Yet water-based masking had a significant decrease in error rate and an increase in creativity.

Misophonia is a severe condition affecting many neurodivergents, where ordinary sounds at normal volumes trigger extreme emotional reactions.[16,17] The exact cause of misophonia is unknown, but it may be related to genetic factors, brain responses to certain sounds, or the result of classical conditioning where neutral sounds become associated with negative emotions over time.

Common trigger sounds for those with misophonia are oral (eating, chewing, drinking) or nasal (breathing). They also can include environmental sounds like a ticking clock or clicking computer keyboard. Reactions to these triggers can include anger, irritation, disgust, and anxiety—often accompanied by a need to escape the sound's source. Since these are such common sounds, it can be challenging for those affected to be in the company of others.

Tactile

Our sense of touch is one of the primary ways we interact with space. The surface of a human hand has over 17,000 touch receptors.[18] Some neurotypes seek out more tactile stimulation, while others avoid it. Those who avoid tactile stimulation may resist being touched or hugged and can be irritated by certain textures in textiles or clothing. Many hyposensitive individuals thrive on physical interaction with their environments and seek opportunities to engage with their surroundings.

Vibrations from others, whether through a wall or transmitted from someone at a connected worksurface or seat, can be challenging for many neurodivergents. Tapping of hands or feet, pushing on a shared surface or the back of a chair, can reverberate through surfaces and impact others, often from an unknowing offender.

Core Operational and Design Strategies: Tactile

- Create low-to-no-touch spaces for the hypersensitive with interactive areas for sensory seekers.
- Minimize exposure to shared surfaces.
- Use predictable patterns and symmetry to aid in environmental understanding and navigation.
- Enrich tactile expressions, such as higher textured vertical surfaces or sculptured flooring with low contrast, pattern, and subdued tones to add texture while dampening sound without visual clutter.
- Apply textures strategically: sharp for energy and soft for comfort.
- Create a strong sense of grounding by providing access to spaces with deep-touch tactile elements.

Olfactory

Often undervalued, smell is one of our most potent sensory systems. Our olfactory system connects directly to the limbic brain, which regulates emotions and memory. Smell also impacts our perception of taste, as the two senses work together.[19]

Scents have the power to forge lifelong memory links. Different aromas can evoke various emotions and memories in people. For example, the smell of a fresh apple pie or newly cut grass might conjure up feelings of being relaxed, invigorated or even annoyed, depending on a person's experiences and associations. Many neurodivergents, especially autistic individuals, have hyperosmia, or heightened smell sensitivity.[20]

The Strategic Use of Scent in Business

Realizing the power of aromatherapy, several companies are experimenting with signature smells. Taking a page from the retail playbook and cues from hospitality companies like Marriott International, organizations are using scents to enhance their occupants' experience. Cinnabon and Abercrombie & Fitch are famous for using their signature smells to entice shoppers, so why not employ the same strategy in the workplace?

Three decades ago, Alan R. Hirsch, neurological director of the Smell & Taste Treatment and Research Foundation, authored a study that reported subjects were 84 percent more likely to purchase Nike sneakers in a scented versus unscented room.[21] Commercial real estate giant Hines has introduced a signature scent for many of its buildings internationally.

Using scents in the workplace can be extremely divisive and must be approached with caution. Finding the right balance is key. As noted in the WELL Building Standard, "Excessively strong or distinct odors can disrupt physical and psychological comfort, and even trigger eye, nose, and throat irritation, nausea, and headaches. Limiting these odors is a simple strategy that can greatly contribute to occupant comfort and well-being."[22]

Core Operational and Design Strategies: Olfactory

- Use aromatherapy strategically in select areas or transition spaces.
- Ensure there is good ventilation to reduce negative smells and lower VOC levels within the space.
- Increase the amount of outdoor air introduced into the space.
- Increase filtration and monitor carbon dioxide levels within the space.
- Flush out the spaces to reduce volatile organic compounds (VOCs) with outside air before occupation.
- Locate food service areas or other settings that generate strong smells in enclosed spaces or away from general work areas.

Gustatory

Taste is intertwined with smell. Mindfulness can promote healthier eating, potentially boosting energy levels and overall health. This in turn may contribute to reduced absenteeism in the workplace.[23]

A 2020 study[24] showed that children with autism and ADHD were fussier about their food choices and exhibited greater sensory sensitivity to taste and smell compared to neurotypical children. Autistic children showed a lower preference for vegetables and fruit, which could lead to poor dietary variety, potentially increasing health risks like obesity and cardiovascular disease.

Core Operational and Design Strategies: Gustatory

- Encourage people to eat in designated areas such as cafes instead of their desks to promote mindful eating and healthier habits.
- Provide access to healthy snacks to keep people fueled and energized.
- Offer a variety of healthy choices when food service is provided.
- Reduce access to less healthy food options.

Proprioception, Interoception, and Vestibular

Proprioception is our sense of body positioning and movement. Interoception refers to our internal sensing of bodily signals and thermal comfort. The vestibular sense relates to our equilibrium and balance, which elements within a space can impact.

Core Operational and Design Strategies: Proprioceptive/ Interoceptive/Vestibular

- Design open spaces and circulation paths with clear lines of sight, ample spacing, and limited distractions to aid in wayfinding and orientation.
- Avoid confusing or disorienting patterns. Stripes can be misread as stairs or level changes. Solid blocks can be confused with holes, and diagonal stripes can cause disorientation.
- Allocate areas with generous space and reduced density to accommodate individuals challenged by proximity, density, and balance issues.
- Provide ample, culturally appropriate personal space to enhance spatial comfort.

Thermal Comfort and Workspace Design

Along with acoustics and visual stimulation, thermal comfort consistently ranks among workplace surveys as one of the top environmental irritants. A recent study found that women perform better on specific tasks at higher temperatures, while men prefer cooler settings.[25] However, most environments are set to favor male preferences, based on indoor climate regulations developed in the 1960s using the average male's metabolic rate.[26]

We must acknowledge that in most environments, temperature fluctuates naturally based on factors such as the sun's location, occupancy levels, lighting systems, individual metabolism, and even clothing. To address this, we can:

- Create office layouts that provide individuals with options to choose locations that suit their thermal comfort range.
- Provide more individual control over thermal settings by creating more thermal zones and localized air flow controls.
- Provide adjustable temperature controls, operable windows, or air diffusers. Alternatively, use environmental sensors to identify temperature variations, allowing occupants to choose their desired thermal zone.

Proprioceptive Challenges and Solutions

Autistic individuals often face more challenges with proprioceptive elements.[27] A 2022 study[28] found that proprioception is also often a challenge for ADHDers. Effective solutions can include physical activities that improve balance and proprioception.

Deep pressure and specific tactile elements often have a calming effect by helping with sensory regulation for those challenged with proprioceptive issues as well as emotional and physiological arousal from sensory input.[29] Examples of items that can provide this include the following:

- Oversized beanbags
- Weighted blankets
- Padded walls or booths
- Deep-pile carpet
- Snug seating

Personal Space and Cultural Considerations

Providing ample, culturally appropriate personal space aids in creating spatial comfort. Edward T. Hall's Theories of Proxemics research report[30] defines four primary zones:

- Interpersonal or intimate zone: Up to 18 inches
- Personal or primary territory for interactions among good friends or family members: 1.5–4 feet

- Social or secondary territory for interactions among acquaintances: 4–12 feet
- Public space: 12 feet or more

Personal space comfort zones can vary based on regional or cultural aspects and can change as we mature. Neurodivergents frequently require more generous personal space than neurotypicals, specifically with unfamiliar people.[31] But this preference is not universal among neurodivergents. Some ADHDers and autistic individuals may prefer closer distances and might unintentionally invade others' space[32] This contradiction highlights the importance of providing ample circulation and clearance as essential design elements, especially in unfamiliar environments.

On a Personal Note: A Lesson in Sensory Sensitivity

I recently presented on diversity and inclusion at a university. I was excited to share our research, and the students were eager to learn more as they worked on a project to create an inclusive space. It was a lively group.

I noticed one male student sitting alone in the front, while other cohorts sat together in groups. As I started sharing insights on sensory threshold and the differences between hyper- and hyposensitivity and their impact on individuals, the mood in the group shifted. The smiles, nods, and even giggles I'd been getting quickly faded, and the mood became somber. One of the boys from a gregarious group in the back came forward and sat next to a boy in the front. Something was going on between them, and everyone in the room, including the professor, knew what was happening—except me.

After finishing my presentation, I asked if anyone had questions. The student who had moved up raised his hand. When I called on him, he didn't address me, but turned to his classmate and apologized for not respecting his space.

(*continued*)

(continued)

They led me to two desks in their art studio. One was pristine, clean, and ordered with three pencils lined up perfectly and sharpened to the same height. The desk next to it was a mess. There were papers strewn about, wads of tracing paper, pencil shavings, and ink stains. This student clearly colored outside the lines. He shared that the messy desk was his and that the pristine desk belonged to his colleague. He confessed he had thought it was funny that his classmate was so neat, and every day before class, he had intentionally rearranged the pencils or put shavings or trash onto his fellow student's desk as a joke. But now he realized it wasn't funny and how he was likely negatively affecting his colleague.

This was a vivid example of how each of us has unique ways of dealing with our sensory processing and physical surroundings and that while some find order in chaos, others need structure to function. It was a powerful moment that demonstrated to all the students how our space and its sensory experiences impact us all—and why we need to respect each other's preferences.

Spotlight

Deloitte UK's Alexander Hedlund's Bridges ADHD Experience and Business

Alexander Hedlund is a consultant at Deloitte UK and a passionate advocate for neurodiversity and inclusion in the workplace. Diagnosed with ADHD at a young age, Alexander's personal journey has fueled his commitment to fostering inclusive cultures and driving organizational transformation. He is the head of corporate membership services at Neurodiversity in Business, where he leads initiatives to support and educate corporate members on neuroinclusive practices. Alexander's expertise spans change management, strategy, and DEI implementation.

Tell me about your journey and why you are such a strong advocate for neuroinclusion.

Alexander: I was diagnosed with ADHD at age four in 2000, and they just put me on medications. There was a lack of understanding and poor communication about the full breadth of what ADHD means, so I struggled.

A university therapist introduced me to Dani Donovan's ADHD comics, and it clicked. I understood how much more there is to ADHD—the emotional dysregulation and executive dysfunction. I realized I wasn't dysfunctional. Though diagnosed early, my experience is similar to someone diagnosed later in life.

I brought DEI focus into everything—advocating for equitable curricula at my university and launching a project on student experiences across seven diversity dimensions. The opening line of our report's executive summary stated that the university had consistently violated the U.K.'s Equalities Act 2010. That got their attention.

At Deloitte, I joined the Neurodiversity Network and got involved with Neurodiversity in Business. The rest is history. I continue to work within my own firm, where I've started a local neurodiversity community in my area, leading the way across the firm on innovative neuroinclusion initiatives.

I'm working on a pilot for exciting support mechanisms using neuroinclusion software tools. Our most valuable initiative is a monthly panel series. We recognized that what resonates is taking an intersectional view, focusing on lived experiences to change hearts and minds through storytelling.

Can you tell me about your work with Neurodiversity in Business?

We focus on corporate forums, creating a space for members to expand their network and learn from each other. It's important to

(continued)

(continued)

break down organizational silos. We're also spotlighting the best practices of our corporate members and community partners.

When we talk about neuroinclusion, many organizations tend to focus on onboarding, recruitment, HR, and operations. But there doesn't seem to be as much focus on the environment side.

Are you still seeing that?

It's shifting. We're seeing it come up more in recent sessions, leading to us spinning up a working group on workplace design. We're conducting tours of spaces like Barclays' Glasgow campus and offering more sessions on workplace design.

Interest in addressing the environment is picking up as companies realize the value of transforming spaces, destigmatizing them, and breaking down the structural and systemic barriers. We're starting to see a focus on "fewer barriers, more enablers," which is a natural progression.

We need more definitions around rules and guidelines. If someone's wearing headphones, for example, don't disturb them.

Any other thoughts about how we should be designing more inclusive workspaces?

Take an intersectional approach. Looking at it from only one area risks creating unintentional barriers for other groups. Don't look at neurodiversity in isolation. Consider physical accessibility and gender equity as well. This creates a more holistic approach to inclusion.

8 | Environmental Influences

My core philosophy as an architect and as a person stems from my earliest lessons as a boy: listen very carefully and understand what people want, work hard, and find the best ways to enhance the quality of life around you.

—HOK Cofounder Gyo Obata

As Abraham Maslow's Hierarchy of Needs theory suggests, if a person's physiological and safety needs are not met, their ability to function at a higher level is negatively impacted.[1]

In recent years, we have developed a much deeper understanding of how environmental elements impact us physically and mentally. Psychological and emotional safety help members of an organization connect, collaborate, and create. When there is a sense of trust, individuals feel safe enough to show up to work with their authentic selves. True inclusion means providing an environment where everyone feels safe, supported, and able to be themselves. This process is systemic, not an afterthought.

Neuroaesthetics and the Built Environment

Neuroaesthetics studies how the brain responds to art and beauty. First coined by renowned neuroscientist Semir Zeki in the late 1990s,[2] the term bridges brain science and art. It combines neuropsychological research with aesthetics by investigating the perception, production, and response to artistic elements. Initial research focused on how we perceive and judge works of art. Since then, the field has expanded into the exploration of the built environment as an aesthetic expression that evokes physical and emotional responses.

Anjan Chatterjee, MD, FAAN, founding director of the Penn Center for Neuroaesthetics, developed the Neuro-Architecture Triad to explain how we experience spaces:[3]

- **Coherence:** How organized and legible a space appears
- **Fascination:** How complex and informationally rich the experience of the space is
- **Homeyness:** How much the space engenders a sense of belonging and comfort

Elements in the built environment can trigger reactions through patterns, lighting, and sounds. By controlling these elements, designers can make a space feel more welcoming.

Not all senses are elective. You can close your eyes or avoid touching something, but you cannot close your ears or stop smelling. Environments and their design can cause, amplify, or diminish our reactions to them.

To accommodate different sensitivities, designers can:

- Create different "microenvironments"
- Minimize visual clutter
- Create quiet and tech-free zones
- Incorporate rest areas along circulation areas and stairs

Environmental Factors Affecting Workplace Comfort

Environmental factors play an important role in shaping employees' comfort and cognitive performance, with several elements deserving specific attention.

Air Quality

Our brains need oxygen to function, and the quality of the air we breathe is a factor in our ability to function at a high level. Poor air quality can negatively impact how we think and process information. An increase in fine particulate matter concentration and lower ventilation rates have been associated with reduced response times and accuracy on cognitive tests.[4] Research also indicates that natural ventilation can reduce sick leave by 57 percent.[5]

Consider the following strategies[6]:

- Flush out spaces with outside air to reduce volatile organic compounds (VOCs) before occupancy.
- Increase the amount of outdoor air introduced into the space.
- Put in place improved filtration systems.
- Monitor carbon dioxide levels within the space.

Ergonomics

Personal comfort is also a factor when it comes to optimizing our performance. Poor ergonomics can lead to discomfort, which can negatively affect performance.

It is important to have appropriate environmental conditions to meet the ergonomic needs of users. Proper lighting, temperature, humidity, and acoustics are essential to supporting the individual.

A main theme in modern ergonomics is "the best position is the next position"—in other words, encouraging movement. Ergonomic principles, by nature, are designed to accommodate sitting for extended periods of time, though this is something we often should not be doing in the first place. But sitting limits your movement, and even ergonomically designed chairs can discourage movement by lulling people into a false sense that the problem has been corrected.

Humans were not designed for prolonged sitting. It has only been in recent years, fueled by increased computer use, that people have sat for extended periods of time. This lack of activity means we do not burn off excess calories, which contributes to the rising obesity rate.

Movement and Physical Engagement

Many hyposensitive individuals need to be more physically engaged. Movement is key to their ability to expend excess energy, focus, and digest information. Walking has been shown to enhance divergent creative thinking by 81 percent. Spending even short periods of time in nature can positively impact our mental and physical well-being.[7]

Memory and Familiarity

Our environment can often trigger memory, which is why we might forget our reason for entering a room when we move from one space to another. This phenomenon occurs because doors can act as memory portals.[8] Staying in familiar spaces can enhance memory. Familiar situations may enhance our memory of broader patterns and reduce the number of memories lost,[9] suggesting that having an assigned consistent work zone or neighborhood may help people integrate what they learn.

Principles of Design

The principles of design are the common language and framework design professionals use to address environmental and spatial challenges. They include the following:

- **Scale:** When designing space, we need to ensure that elements within it address both comfort and functionality. For example, the size of furniture should relate to human dimensions.
- **Emphasis:** Designers create focal points to achieve emphasis within a space. Emphasis helps create hierarchy that helps us organize space for easy navigation.
- **Balance:** Balance creates visual equilibrium within an environment, often reconciling opposing forces to achieve visual stability. Balance may be achieved symmetrically, asymmetrically, or radially.
- **Rhythm:** Rhythm is the creation of a flow within a space by leveraging a common element within one's sight line that enables movement and a sense of order within an environment. The use of progression, repetition, or a series of connected design elements can create fluidity or rhythm in an environment.
- **Proportion:** Proportion relates to the size and scale of various elements within a space to ensure it is in sync with other elements and the occupants. Ceiling heights and room proportion are critical to ensure an appropriate feel.

■ **Unity (Harmony and Variety):** Unity creates a sense of cohesiveness within a space when harmony and variety come together. It can be achieved through the repeated use of design elements such as color, pattern, or materiality. Variety brings interest and intrigue by connecting separate but related elements when applied intentionally.

Elements of Design

The elements of design are the tools used to execute on the principles of design, leveraging these concepts:

■ Line   ■ Texture   ■ Space
■ Light   ■ Shape   ■ Pattern
■ Color   ■ Form   ■ Mass

Line

Line refers to the connection of two points in space. They are the foundational element of design and come in a variety of thicknesses and colors. They define spaces, provide direction, and direct the eye through an environment. Designers use lines to add structure to compositions and to highlight or frame elements. Lines can be organic and curved or straight, structured, and formal.

Light

Light is a powerful design tool that enables visual connections. Access to daylight can result in increased happiness, physical well-being, improved mental and emotional health, and increased productivity.[10]

Lighting is key in creating more inclusive spaces, as it is repeatedly identified as a challenge in existing spaces. Research suggests that bright light can intensify our feelings, both positive and negative.[11]

Serotonin and Light Exposure Natural light exposure plays a crucial role in maintaining the optimal balance of serotonin, often referred to as the "happy hormone." Serotonin is associated with mood regulation, while suppressing the production of melatonin, a hormone involved in sleep regulation.[12] Serotonin plays a crucial role in regulating brain development and function.[13] Disruption in serotonin has been linked to various conditions, including depression and anxiety.[14] Thus, proper lighting design can significantly impact mood, sleep, and overall health.

Effects on Mood and Cognition   Lighting can significantly influence mood, cognitive processes, and overall well-being. Circadian lighting helps sync with natural light patterns throughout the day, supporting circadian rhythms, which regulate biophysical functions, and reducing stress levels. Cool color temperatures ("bluish") can create an atmosphere conducive to focus and concentration, while warm color temperatures ("yellowish") are perceived as comfortable, cozy, and inviting, making them suitable for socializing and creative activities. Dimmer lighting tends to be more relaxing and is better for casual social settings compared to brighter lights.[15]

Overhead fluorescent lighting can be harsh and overwhelming to occupants due to distracting flicker and buzzing. Replacing fluorescent fixtures with LED fixtures is a simple way to reduce irritation. Designers also need to consider the quality and color of light waves to create a comfortable and stimulating environment.

Workplace Lighting Standards and Design Guidelines   The benefits of providing occupants access to daylight are so compelling that several European countries have put in place regulations mandating workplace access to daylight.[16] Some studies suggest that the benefits start to kick in with a minimum of three hours of light per day, whether from natural or artificial sources.[17]

Design standards offer guidance on daylight for workplaces. LEED's Daylight credit, for example, requires specified glare-free daylight illuminance levels for 75 percent of regularly occupied spaces. The WELL Building Standard sets a baseline of 95 percent of building inhabitants sitting within 15 feet of the perimeter, with a fallback requirement for appropriate electrical illumination. Other strategies to improve lighting include high-placed windows that allow natural light to penetrate the space while limiting distractions caused by views. Providing occupants the ability to adjust lighting within a space may be one of the most effective ways to positively impact workplace comfort and cognitive well-being as preferences can vary, but lighting levels in spaces rarely do.

Famous Innovators and Creators: Andy Warhol

Andy Warhol was a legendary pop art icon and creative genius. He was a master of color, innovative compositions, and a unique art technique that likely reflected the thinking patterns of his neurodivergence. Though he was a 1960s cultural icon, Warhol exhibited difficulties with social interaction and sensitivity to touch and noise. He was obsessed with repetition, which is apparent in his celebrated works of Marilyn Monroe, Elvis Presley, and the Campbell's soup can.[18]

Color

Color is a powerful design element that can communicate intent, influence mood, and impact behavior and performance. It can also aid individuals with navigating spaces. Certain colors have been associated with increased blood pressure, increased metabolism, and eyestrain. Recent research indicates that chromotherapy—the strategic use of color—has the potential to treat a variety of conditions.[19]

Bold colors or complex color palettes that neurotypical individuals may overlook can adversely impact neurodivergents with heightened visual sensitivity. Color saturation and intensity can also have negative effects. High saturation of color is more stimulating, while lower saturations or muted colors tend to have a calming effect. Colors that are abundant in nature, like browns, greens, and blues, are generally better perceived.[20]

As we age, our color perception changes.[21] People with poor vision may find that contrast between flooring, walls, and ceilings helps in comprehending and navigating space.[22]

Color can have different symbolic meanings and be perceived differently across cultures, making it important to understand cultural references when working in specific regions.[23]

Color theory is an evolving science. Leveraging our professional education, research,[24] and years of experience, including delivering projects around the world, here are some of our observations and insights on color.

Color	Characteristics	Cultural Connotations
White	White is often associated with purity and innocence.	In Western cultures, white symbolizes cleanliness and neutrality. By contrast, in many Eastern cultures, it is associated with death and the supernatural.
Blue	Blue is often perceived as calming, sedative, and stable, due to its association with the vastness of sea and sky. It can aid analytical and rational thinking and is seen as the color of authority. But too much blue without white for contrast can make people feel "blue," sad, or depressed.	Blue is often associated with spirituality and wisdom. Ancient Egyptians connected blue with royalty since it was such a difficult hue to create. In Hinduism, gods like Vishnu, Krishna, and Shiva are depicted with blue skin, symbolic of their cosmic connection. In countries such as Turkey, Greece, Pakistan, and Iran, blue is believed to keep evil away and bring good luck.[25]
Yellow	Yellow, symbolic of the sun, energizes us and promotes creative thinking. Brief exposure to yellow can aid in healing the nervous system and relieving depression. It can also be seen as a warning color, especially when paired with black.	In Mexico, yellow is significant in life and death. In China, yellow has strong historical and cultural associations with royalty. The first emperor was known as the "Yellow Emperor," and subsequently, only they could wear bright yellow. Yellow is also reserved for use by high-ranking individuals in many African nations. It is considered to be a lucky color in many parts of the world.

Color	Characteristics	Cultural Connotations
Red	Red is a warming color and, as a stimulator, increases the heart rate, brain wave activity, and respiration. It is energizing and encourages confidence and courage. Red increases our appetite and circulation and can make us feel aggressive or agitated with prolonged exposure.	Red is universally seen as the color of life and often associated with fire, aggression, and impulse. In Eastern cultures, red is considered a prosperous color that brings good fortune and is often worn by Chinese brides.
Green	Green is calming and can relieve stress while aiding in creating a tranquil environment. Green tends to be the predominant color used in operating room attire because it is the exact opposite of red on the color wheel and provides a contrast that aids in reducing eye fatigue.	Reminiscent of nature, green is universally associated with vitality. In Islamic countries, green is associated with paradise in the Qur'an. In many Eastern and Asian countries, green is symbolic of youth, fertility, and eternal life.
Orange	Orange is associated with warmth and optimism and can be mentally stimulating. It can be used to alleviate fatigue, treat depression, help assimilate new ideas, and remove repression and inhibitions. It can make us feel enthusiastic and increase our energy levels, if not overdone.	Culturally, orange is seen as a socioeconomic neutralizer and applies to a wide range of individuals. In Southeast Asia, orange symbolizes sacredness and spirituality and is worn by monks to communicate their commitment to piety. The Dutch have a strong connection to orange, as it is symbolic of the royal family.

(continued)

(continued)

Color	Characteristics	Cultural Connotations
Pink	Pink can be very soothing. It can have a tranquilizing effect on aggressive behavior and is often used to treat anxiety. It can also be emasculating and reduce aggression.	Pink can be perceived as soft and gentle and has traditionally been associated with femininity. In recent years, pink has been embraced as a liberating color by alt-culture and the LGBTQ+ community.
Purple, Violet, Lavender	These colors are often used to create a peaceful environment and to treat insomnia and compulsive behavior. Purple is often associated with mystery and wealth.	In some countries, like Italy and Brazil, purple is considered symbolic of mourning and bad luck. Similarly, in Thailand, purple is associated with death or mourning. In Europe and the U.S., purple often symbolizes magic, mystery, and religious faith. Historically, purple has been linked to royalty, as the dye was extremely expensive to produce.
Brown	Brown is seen as a neutral color that reminds us of nature and can promote relaxation. It conveys reliability, trustworthiness, and strength.	Brown is associated with resilience, dependability, security, and safety.
Gray	Gray is often perceived as a bland, cold, and draining color on its own. Accents of white can provide some relief. Historically, it has been used to make things seem smaller or less noticeable.	In Western culture, gray is often associated with dignity, practicality, neutrality, and indecision. In China and many Asian cultures, it is perceived as a dignified color.

Color	Characteristics	Cultural Connotations
Black	Black is often perceived as a formal, sleek, and elegant choice in design and fashion.	In many countries, black is often associated with death and doom. In India, black also serves as the color of protection against evil.

Color Variations It is also important to understand the potential variations within a color, as warm and cool variations have different impacts on individuals.

- **Hue:** Hue refers to the pure color, with no black or white added. Vibrant colors tend to be more stimulating, vivid, energetic, and bold. In large quantities, saturated colors can be overwhelming.[26]
- **Tint:** Mixing a pure color with white creates a tint. Lighter colors and tints are seen as more subtle and softer. They also are more pleasing and easier on the eye. Muted colors and pastels are more calming.
- **Tone:** Combining a pure color with gray produces a tint. Grayed or muted colors feel more subdued and subtle. When used in large amounts, muted colors can feel dull and flat.
- **Shade:** Mixing a pure color with black creates a shade. Darker colors and shades tend to be perceived as more serious, authoritative, and sophisticated.
- **Value:** The lightness or darkness of a color. Value can be visualized in a gradient of a hue arranged from the lightest to the darkest.

Color Schemes in Spaces Spaces rarely are made up of a single color, but rather a combination.

Monochromatic color schemes use a single-color tint as the basis for all shades and hues found within a space. They often include an accent color to prevent the space from appearing too flat. For example, blue is a popular, calming color. Yet without a complementary or accent color, it can be overwhelming and depressing.

Complementary color schemes incorporate two colors from opposite sides of the color wheel. When used together, they create variety and harmony in a balanced, visually stimulating palette. Small amounts of color can go a long way in creating interest without being overstimulating.

Analogous color schemes use colors that are next to each other on the color wheel, creating a varied but harmonious palette. Using similar tones and shades in sync with each other can provide cohesion.

Texture

Texture can be used to define, energize, enrich, and punctuate elements. It can help tone down or increase the intensity of stimuli. In addition to adding depth to a two-dimensional surface, texture can add a tactile experience. Upholstered furniture, padded surfaces, plush flooring, and the contrast between smooth and textured surfaces all enrich a space.

For flooring and carpet:

- Low-pile flooring is ideal for heavily trafficked areas that need to be both durable and frictionless.
- Higher-piled or textured carpets should be used strategically in casual, informal spaces to create a more comforting feeling.
- Any hard floors should be used strategically, as they can increase noise in the space and be hard on the feet.

Using a variety of textures and materials can aid in creating a diverse sensory palette. This diversity serves the needs of both hypersensitive and hyposensitive individuals.

Shape

A shape is the external outline of a two-dimensional object that forms a boundary. Shapes can be geometric, organic, or abstract.

People tend to gravitate toward smooth, curved shapes, as they evoke feelings of safety, movement, and playful expression. Sharp angles, on the other hand, can create a sense of danger. Soothing organic shapes and fractal patterns that mimic elements found in nature can elicit positive emotional responses and increase visual interest.[27]

Form

A form encompasses the complete three-dimensional appearance of an object, accounting for depth, width, and height.

Space

Space refers to the area or volume around, within, and between objects. Openness and spaces stimulate areas in the brain associated with movement and expression. The volume of space is important, as higher ceilings can enhance open-minded brainstorming, while lower ceilings aid focused work. Studies have also shown that low ceilings and small windows can increase stress responses.[28]

The area around something, or the area that is not occupied by any elements, is the negative space. This space can be as impactful as the shape itself. Having ample negative space around a work setting can make one feel comfortable, whereas the lack of it can cause discomfort.

Pattern

Patterns found in and inspired by nature tend to be complex, organic, and irregular. While these can be comforting, humans generally seek order in chaos to process information. Hence, we gravitate toward predictable and repetitive patterns to create symmetries and self-referential geometric systems, known as fractal structures. Fractals are complex, repeating geometric shapes and patterns common in nature. Designers use them to give order to space, create interest, and lead the eye in a specific direction. Predictable patterns also help us navigate our world. Recognizing patterns and logical order can result in both acceptance and sensory pleasure.

Large patterns can confuse people with neurological and sensory processing challenges. They often see these patterns as barriers or even level changes. Stripes, solid blocks, perforated materials, and other geometric patterns can be disorienting.[29] Patterns that are visually overwhelming or visually monotonous environments can leave people uninspired with no clear landmarks for orientation or wayfinding.

Patterns also can be used to create optional illusions or emphasis in spaces. Vertical stripes, for example, can make a room feel taller; horizontal stripes can make it appear wider.

Public spaces that use heavy patterned carpets to hide stains can also be disorienting.[30] This is a design strategy casinos use to keep you from easily navigating out of the space.

Mass

Mass is the visual weight of a shape or form, or the volume of space a shape occupies. Designers use mass to give weight to some elements while lightening others. Mass can help ground elements and give them more importance. For example, a bulky lounge chair appears heavier and larger than one of the same dimensions with a pedestal base.

Spotlight

Sean Hoffman's Vision for Neurodiversity at KPMG

Sean Hoffman is the partner-in-charge of risk management for KPMG's Advisory Practice in the United States and the Americas Region. He leads the firm's neurodiversity efforts, which are focused on embracing neurodiverse talent and capturing their untapped potential to benefit the entire workforce. Sean also serves on the board of directors of Melwood, a Washington, DC–based nonprofit focused on employment for people with disabilities.

How did your journey to becoming an advocate for inclusion begin?

Sean: My journey started because of my personal situation. I have a son on the autism spectrum, and I can't tell you how many nights my wife and I agonized trying to figure out what Zachary would do for a job. We wanted to understand what was happening in the marketplace and learn from that, so I was grateful that KPMG fostered an inclusive environment to host sessions around the country to do just that. We've held sessions in Washington, DC; Los Angeles; and Atlanta, where we invited people in the community and clients to discuss their neurodiversity programs so we could all learn from each other.

What you see depends on the lens through which you look at it. I've heard it said that 80 percent of neurodivergent grads are un- or underemployed. Some might look at that as a problem, however, I see it as opportunity. I'm a capitalist at heart. Imagine harnessing the power of this large source of talented unique thinkers. Designing for inclusion isn't just good for the community; it's valuable for business. As a partner in our firm, I want to make sure we're making the difference for our people, clients, and society. That's how this journey started.

How does KPMG create a welcoming environment for neurodivergent individuals?

It starts by how we support neurodivergent talent in three stages of the career lifecycle: getting here, succeeding here and leading here at KPMG. Getting here is focused on attracting and onboarding talent. We have established processes that allow neurodivergent candidates to feel comfortable learning about the firm. As an alternative to the typical interview process, we've developed an immersive process where we bring in candidates for virtual or in-person simulated projects, giving both the firm and the candidates the opportunity to learn about the roles and working styles, ultimately creating a relationship.

Once we've committed to each other and hired an individual, we focus on succeeding here. We've rolled out a lot of learning and development about disability awareness and neurodiversity, not just for neurodivergent talent but for everyone, so that we all understand what neurodiversity is and how we can work together effectively, while ensuring a sense of inclusion and belonging for all.

The last stage is leading here—where we are currently focused on championing neurodiversity in the community. As we gain more

(continued)

(continued)

critical mass of neurodivergent colleagues, I suspect we will be able to share more about best practices for any company looking to support neurodiverse talent.

In the meantime, we've created two subcommunities within our Abilities in Motion Business Resource Group. One of the subcommunities focuses on people like me, caretakers of neurodivergent individuals. We organized a separate group for neurodivergent talent themselves because we recognized that our needs are very different.

Can you elaborate on the support KPMG provides for caregivers of neurodivergent individuals?

We get together monthly. The group has grown about 80 percent over the last year, which tells me we've got a lot of individuals within our firm who are impacted in one way or another by neurodiversity. The group provides advice and shares experiences.

The group's discussions are helping us understand the unique needs of the caregiver group. For example, there are costs associated with different therapies. We're informing our HR department about the needs from an insurance and other standpoints. The sense of community that has formed has provided an outlet for people to come together, be their authentic selves, and share their stories.

Can you tell us about your work with Melwood?

Melwood is a nonprofit based in the Washington, DC, area. Its mission is to find gainful employment for people with disabilities, including neurodivergent talent. In addition to serving on its board of directors, I work with the organization in two other ways: as a teammate where we've successfully delivered projects for clients and as a parent.

My son just graduated from high school, and as part of that, students have to do a senior experience, which is essentially an internship in the community. He was challenged to find one that suited him. Melwood has a program where he became a program assistant, allowing him to fulfill his senior experience requirement. It was an awesome opportunity for him to see what life in the workplace was all about.

What are the biggest opportunities to address neuroinclusion in the workplace?

Simply understanding the breadth of neurodiversity may be one of the largest barriers. For most people, this lack of understanding leads them to downplay the abilities of neurodivergent individuals or not recognize the unique strengths or abilities they bring.

We need to help people understand that these aren't deficiencies. Neurodiversity is simply a difference in how people intake, process, and convey information.

When I put on my "owner of the firm" partner hat, I think about how our clients come to us with complex problems. We provide unique perspectives and solutions. By definition, that's what someone who's neurodivergent does—they bring unique perspectives to complex problems. That's honestly one of the big reasons our firm is so focused on diversity. We value the unique perspectives that a diverse environment or group of people bring to any problem.

What advice do you have for others looking to create more inclusive environments?

My biggest advice is to involve neurodivergent individuals in the process. One thing we subscribe to is the mantra, "Nothing for us without us." It's important that people with the actual experience help to shape the environment we are creating. We want to make sure that what we're building is fit for purpose and meets the needs of our neurodivergent colleagues. In fact, the learning and developmental resources I referenced earlier were created with neurodivergent professionals' and other people with disabilities' input. Neurodivergent professionals also helped test for

(continued)

(*continued*)

accessibility of resources and were part of the communication plan to raise awareness. Additionally, neurodivergent professionals and others with disabilities work with our Accessibility team at KPMG to create resources on how to make environments more inclusive and accessible.

Can you share an example of how neurodivergent thinking can benefit an organization?

I'd love to share a proud dad anecdote. My son recently started doing some weightlifting. When I asked him, "How much weight did you lift today?" He told me "3,000 pounds." I was a bit taken aback, but as we kept talking, I figured out that he was accumulating the total amount of weight he had moved that day. What a unique perspective! He approached a problem in such a different way, and I could think about adapting that in our own business world. For example, a client might approach us with a process problem and need a solution to maximize total throughput and not just maximum one-time capacity.

Client Story

Building Inclusion from the Ground Up in KPMG's New York Office

KPMG U.S. Headquarters at Two Manhattan West
New York, NY
450,000 sq. ft. / 12 floors
HOK services: Workplace Strategy, Interior Design, Sustainability Consulting, Structural Engineering
Certification: Tracking LEED Gold

The pandemic forced many companies to reconsider their offices. KPMG LLP, a firm known for its iterative and innovative approach to workplace design, used it as an opportunity to redefine why its people come into the office. "They wanted to support their hybrid work model—'Flex with Purpose'—the idea that employees should have opportunities for purposeful collaboration as they move between in-person and remote work, supported by flexible spaces." KPMG also wanted to make the space as inclusive as possible for staff and visiting clients.

"Before the pandemic, people went into the office just to work," says KPMG LLP Managing Director of Real Estate Services Vanessa Scaglione. "Now, the office has to be a differentiated experience from what you have at home or in other remote locations."

Led by Scaglione and Executive Director of Architecture & Construction Frank Erickson, KPMG engaged HOK to design its new U.S. headquarters space in New York City. The result is a flexible hub that embodies KPMG's culture and draws employees in with a purposeful design. This new headquarters supports diverse work styles while prioritizing well-being and inclusion.

Incorporating Neurodiversity from the Start

HOK's process began with a "Framing the Possible" session, followed by a deep dive into KPMG's needs through a "Gathering Spaces" workshop to specifically address the requirements for hub spaces and meeting spaces. To work toward holistic solutions from the outset, this process involved stakeholders, design experts, and IT consultants.

KPMG's Business Resource Groups (BRGs) and Sean Hoffman, who leads the firm's neurodiversity design initiatives in addition to serving as partner-in-charge of risk management for its advisory practice in the United States and the Americas Region, were integral to the design process.

After developing the initial design concepts, HOK's team met with KPMG leaders, including inclusion leads, to share their progress and seek additional feedback.

Balancing Consistency with Flexibility

KPMG recognizes that a one-size-fits-all approach to the workplace will not give its diverse workforce the environments they need to

(continued)

(continued)

reach their full potential. "While we've established organization-wide principles and guidelines, we're empowering individual functions, practices, and groups to determine day-to-day experiences that work best for their people, clients, and stakeholders," says Scaglione.

This flexible approach allows KPMG to maintain consistency across offices while accommodating the unique needs of different teams and individuals. Acknowledging that diverse teams require different environmental supports to perform at their best is an essential part of the firm's accessibility and neurodiverse talent strategy.

Key Neuroinclusive Design Elements

1. **Flexible Neighborhood Concept:** KPMG introduced neighborhoods to replace assigned seating. "You don't need a dedicated, specific work seat," says Scaglione. "But you still want to be moored to an area that feels like your home base when you come into the office. This has been a very big change for us."

2. **Egalitarian Open Plan:** The open perimeter has few enclosed individual spaces, creating an equitable employee experience.

3. **Varied Work Settings:** The space offers a range of environments for different tasks and preferences, from quiet focus areas to collaborative zones.

4. **Sensory-Considerate Spaces:** The design team viewed all material selections, finishes, and furniture through a neuroinclusive lens. "We wanted to ensure we were creating environments that reflect the sensory needs of the users," says Beth Ann Christiansen, senior project designer for Interiors at HOK. "We also collaborated with HOK's Experience Design team and KPMG to carefully select the graphics and their locations within the space, wanting to strike the right balance between invigorating visuals without being overwhelming."

5. **Intuitive Wayfinding:** The design incorporates consistent placement of amenities on each floor and visual cues to aid navigation.

6. **Active Design Features:** Pathways circumnavigate each floor's perimeter, and a fire-rated glass staircase links all 12 floors, promoting movement and community.

7. Technology Integration: State-of-the-art systems support hybrid workflows, ensuring seamless collaboration between in-office and remote workers.

See Figure 8.1 for how this came together.

Design Concept: Celebrating New York City

HOK's design draws inspiration from the parallels between New York City and KPMG. Both have rich legacies yet continuously evolve and adapt to stay at the forefront of innovation.

The base palette uses a neutral, timeless aesthetic, with light colors paired with natural materials and refined textures. This forms a backdrop for layers of variety and color, inspired by Manhattan's diverse neighborhoods. The design echoes the city's iconic features. Structural components reflect the regimented grid of New York's streets, while curved architectural features draw from the organic forms of its parks and undulating shoreline. As KPMG's employees move through the

| Natural elements/ Clear definition between planes | Ceiling planes defining space/ Acoustic elements/ Diffused, controlled lighting | Controlled design elements that are non-confusing and keep the focus on the subject at hand | Controlled pops of color | Clear, wide passageways encourage movement | Transparent, non-confining space | Areas to the side that enable controlled interaction | Natural elements/ Clear definition between planes/ Access to daylight |

Figure 8.1 KMPG New York office—gathering space

(*continued*)

(*continued*)

12 floors, they encounter varying colors and patterns, reminiscent of New York's distinct neighborhoods.

This city-inspired approach aligns with HOK's broader approach to creating inclusive spaces. "Designing for inclusion has become second nature for us. It just makes sense and is smart design," says Tara Roscoe, HOK's director of design, Interiors. "Working with innovative clients like KPMG, who understand the importance of this, gave us a great opportunity to lean in and push the boundaries of creating exceptional spaces."

Sustainable and Inclusive by Design

The project is pursuing LEED Gold certification, aligning with KPMG's commitment to sustainability. Addressing sustainability goes beyond meeting certification requirements. For KPMG, human and environmental sustainability are equally important. Providing access to daylight and views for everyone throughout the space reinforces inclusivity and well-being. Responsible sourcing, inclusion of biophilic elements, and access to a variety of settings—including spaces to connect, refresh, focus, and collaborate—are all thoughtfully interwoven into the space.

Overcoming Challenges and Measuring Impact

Implementing these changes was not without challenges. "There's a lot of change management and communication involved," acknowledges Scaglione. "We've incorporated more collaboration spaces and meeting rooms, which meant shrinking individual work spaces. The upside is more variety and choice for our colleagues."

While the new office is still under construction, KPMG is already seeing positive outcomes from its focus on designing for various neurotypes. "As a firm, we believe that in-person collaboration translates to higher engagement, better client work, and more innovative thinking," says Scaglione. "This new environment will foster apprenticeship and mentorship opportunities that are hard to replicate remotely."

HOK Interiors Practice Leader Jennifer Brayer believes designing with neuroinclusion in mind helps teams manage the project more efficiently. "When we can justify the recommendations we're making with facts and research, it expedites decision-making and builds confidence in the design choices," she says. See Figure 8.2.

Lessons for Others

Scaglione offers advice for organizations considering a similar journey:

1. **Actively seek feedback from diverse employee groups.** "They're in the best position to express their preferences and needs for the office," she says. "We were very deliberate in finding a variety of ways to solicit this feedback."
2. **Communicate existing inclusive features.** "For example, some colleagues asked for lighting that changes based on the availability of natural light," says Scaglione. "We already have this, but they weren't aware."

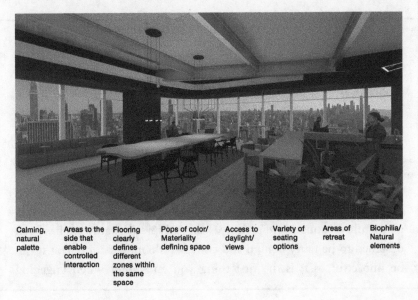

| Calming, natural palette | Areas to the side that enable controlled interaction | Flooring clearly defines different zones within the same space | Pops of color/ Materiality defining space | Access to daylight/ views | Variety of seating options | Areas of retreat | Biophilia/ Natural elements |

Figure 8.2   KMPG New York office—floor common space

(*continued*)

(*continued*)

3. Partner with experts experienced in neuroinclusive design.
"I'd advise that they listen to experts like HOK, because you've done this in other locations for other firms," she says. "Understanding what you have seen that has worked elsewhere and how we can translate that to our offices has been invaluable."

"Creating an inclusive workspace benefits a far broader group than you might initially think," adds Scaglione. "It's like curb cuts. They don't just benefit people in wheelchairs—they help everyone."

Before this project, Scaglione was the champion for the KPMG Business Resource Group Abilities in Motion's Montvale, New Jersey, chapter, which helped to keep her attuned to ensuring the firm had an inclusive workplace. "It has always been top-of-mind for me," she says. "I'm grateful for this opportunity with Manhattan West to build an environment that helps all our colleagues succeed."

On a Personal Note: Addressing What Often Goes Unnoticed

A few years ago, after giving a presentation to students at an Italian university, one of the professors contacted me about potentially collaborating on a neuroinclusive product. The professor worked at pba S.p.A, a manufacturer of high-end door hardware. We partnered with them and design partner RainlightSTUDIO to design a line of hardware embracing inclusive design principles.

Over the next several months, we explored how hardware could play a role creating more inclusive spaces. Typically, hardware has been designed to be fairly benign and convey little information. But it can be impactful, as it is the first thing you encounter when engaging with a space, reaching out to grab the door handle to enter a building. Traditional hardware is hard, sterile, and colorless, often meant to go unnoticed. Case in point: can you visualize the hardware in your office space? We thought we could do better, so we accepted the challenge.

We started by examining the role hardware plays in the built environment and how it affects us from tactile, visual, and thermal perspectives. The materiality, color, touch, and overall feel of the piece are all key components in designing for inclusion. Knowing pba already had an extensive line of successful hardware, we didn't feel like we needed to reinvent the wheel, just make it better. Sometimes the best solutions are the simplest.

Our inspiration came from a usual place—sports. In sports equipment like tennis rackets, hockey sticks, golf clubs, and even sports balls, the feel of the grip is importance for providing a secure hold, warmth, and comfort to the user. Why would door handles be any different?

We introduced color to create visual interest and serve as a signal to occupants. For example, if the door handles in a space are white but one is red, that signals that something is different and cautions users before entering. We leveraged ECONYL®, a 100 percent regenerated nylon from ocean waste, which is warmer to the touch than metal. We also introduced a tactile element, allowing users to choose between a smooth or textured experience. This enables a more secure grip, which is important for children, mature adults, and those with weaker grips due to health conditions. We made it interchangeable so it can be adapted in the field based on user preferences.

pba's TOCCO is the first hardware collection that addresses sensory-sensitivity, sustainability, and interchangeability. It is designed to offer choice and an enhanced sensory experience. Sometimes it's the little things we take for granted, or fail to even notice, that have a big impact.

Spotlight

Erica Anesi Reshapes Architectural Hardware for Neurodiversity

Erica Anesi, PhD, has expertise in engineering, management, and psychology. As the CEO of architectural hardware manufacturer pba S.p.A, she leverages her extensive experience in design and planning. Erica advocates for inclusive space and product design, and her interest in the psychology of architecture drives her to blend technical knowledge with an understanding of human behavior in her designs.

Can you explain how we connected and how our collaboration came to be?

Erica: I was teaching a Strategic Management and Philanthropic Decision course at a university. I needed someone knowledgeable to talk to students about the strategic importance of designing for inclusion and well-being. We thought of you and your work at HOK and asked you to present. Later, we had the opportunity to collaborate on a project. To achieve an outcome that brings value, you have to work with the best experts.

We had two goals: inclusion and sustainability. As a manufacturer, we know our products and have always been committed to creating products that promote accessibility. But designing for inclusion is a level above this. After all, the door handle is your handshake to the room. The first sensation and perception of an environment is transmitted by engaging with the door hardware.

We wanted to collaborate with you to investigate how door hardware, a common accessory, can promote inclusion and address sustainability in the built environment. We also wanted to leverage the research you did with Tarkett on sensory stimulation.

Can you describe the research you commissioned with the University of Venice?

We wanted to understand how the Tocco collection levers and pulls are perceived regarding inclusivity and sustainability. We asked the University of Venice Department of Psychology of Architecture to investigate what the product is communicating.

We discovered that communication occurs on two levels. One is mediated by experience, conventions, and knowledge—cognitive communication or communication through signs. The second level is communication through specific characteristics peculiar to the object, referring to direct and universal communication independent of culture or knowledge.

We had various people assess 10 different models, colors, and designs. We found that:

- Yellow is considered the most inclusive, probably because it's the only color related to nature in the study.
- Round shapes are considered more inclusive, while sharp or edged designs are perceived as less inclusive.
- Metal handles are surprisingly perceived as the most sustainable, which is counter to what is true. This result indicates that our ECONYL® nylon for handles is perceived negatively as plastic despite being 100 percent recycled and 100 percent recyclable.

What are your key takeaways for creating more neuroinclusive environments?

We don't have time to further delay addressing the importance of considering the human condition and diversity as an added value. It's time to act. Responsibility means taking care of things, from small details to bigger ones. Otherwise, there will always be a wrong note in the melody, and I think we're ready to play the melody all together.

9 | Other Elements to Consider

> It is not our differences that divide us. It is our inability to recognize, accept, and celebrate those differences.
>
> —Audre Lorde, intersectional diversity advocate

In addition to the principles and elements of design and the strategies explored in Chapter 8, several key elements are essential for creating neuroinclusive workplaces. These include biophilia, wayfinding, multisensory rooms, safety and well-being, and focus-enhancing strategies. Each plays a vital role in creating welcoming and inclusive spaces.

Biophilia

In today's high-tech environment, our minds and bodies track a wide array of stimuli. But these high-tech spaces can leave us feeling overwhelmed and, at the same time, make us feel like we are missing out on something. One way to balance our high-tech world is to introduce natural elements to the built environment: "high tech = high touch."

As biologist Edward O. Wilson noted, increased urbanization contributes to a growing disconnect from the natural world.[1] Connecting individuals to more natural settings and incorporating biophilic references and elements into the built environment can aid in reinforcing our connection to the natural world. That connection can be made directly, indirectly, or symbolically. For those with sensory processing disorders, green spaces, access to outdoor areas, and sensory gardens can aid in recalibration, allowing individuals to readjust their sensory and social control over their surroundings.[2]

Benefits of Biophilic Design

Biophilic design integrates natural elements and references to nature into the built environment. Creating spaces infused with biophilic elements or references to nature has been found to promote stress recovery, prolonged attention, and increased productivity among employees.[3] Spaces with references to nature can also improve health outcomes and have been shown to reduce stress; improve cognitive function; be calming, refreshing, and relaxing; and enhance mood and creativity among occupants.[4] A recent study found that time spent in natural settings reduced stress hormones by 13–16 percent and blood pressure by about 2 percent.[5]

Incorporating direct connections with nature and multisensory elements is the primary consideration with incorporating biophilic elements into the built environment. But individuals can also benefit from nondirect interpretations and analogies of natural elements. This can include the introduction of organic, symbolic, nonliving, and indirect nodes to elements found in nature—be it color, patterns, imagery, or a pattern of movement that can be very soothing. It can also include biomimicry of natural elements and systems that provide an indirect connection with nature, such as the use of organic shapes or leaf patterns or the inclusion of wood elements that refer to nature and are symbolic of their natural state. Incorporating biomorphic principles into the design of buildings and the spaces within them can leverage the best practices of the natural world while benefiting the individuals who occupy them.

Natural materials are calming, refreshing, and relaxing. Wood gives us a connection to nature, a sense of authenticity, and an organic feel; when sourced responsibly, it is also a renewable and sustainable material.

Studies have shown the exposure to natural elements in healthcare settings can mitigate the stress, depression, anxiety, and fatigue common to patients who visit regularly. This type of exposure to nature can expedite healing and recovery rates while reducing the length of hospital stays.[6,7]

Access to natural light and outdoor views also aids in regulating our circadian rhythms, which promotes better sleep quality and regeneration.

Introducing certain plants and green walls has been scientifically proven to remove air pollutants such as carbon dioxide and VOCs.[8] Plants can also provide a visual shield and sound barrier, enhancing the office's acoustics and providing a better experience in spaces.

Neurodivergent individuals often tend toward rumination, a maladaptive pattern of self-referential thought associated with heightened risk for depression and other mental illnesses.[9,10] However, a Stanford University study showed that spending time in natural surroundings helped reduce rumination.[11] This study reinforces the importance of incorporating natural elements and green spaces into our built environment.

Metaphoric Relationship with Nature

Designers can incorporate symbolic references to nature through the following:

- **Biomorphic forms:** Patterns and textures that occur in nature
- **Simultaneous complexity and order:** Sensory elements that mimic natural patterns
- **Fractal patterns and nonrhythmic sensory stimuli:** Stochastic elements symbolizing organic natural rhythms
- **Nonvisual/local natural materials:** Materials that reflect natural ecosystems

Direct Connection with Nature

These strategies create tangible connections to natural elements:

- **Physical and visual:** A direct connection with or view of natural elements and materials
- **Auditory:** Inclusion of natural sounds such as flowing water or birdsong
- **Olfactory:** Strategic use of scents found in nature such as lavender or sandalwood
- **Water:** Inclusion of water elements

Experiential Connections with Nature

These design approaches create immersive, nature-inspired experiences in space:

- **Natural systems:** A direct connection with natural living systems
- **Dynamic and diffused light:** Introducing fluctuating lighting systems to create shadows and reflect the various lighting levels in nature
- **Thermal airflow variability:** Subtle fluctuations in air movement and temperature
- **Prospect:** The ability to observe your surroundings by having a clear, unimpeded view
- **Refuge:** The ability to withdraw from a space to one that feels more protected and secure
- **Mystery, peril, and excitement:** Spaces that tease and entice the individual to explore the environment
- **Blending the exterior into the interior:** Infusing elements of the outdoors into indoor spaces and blurring the lines between them

Applications of Biophilia in Workplace Design

The natural and varied patterns and rhythms of biophilic design create multisensory environments well-suited to meet the diverse sensory needs and preferences of neurodivergent community. Introducing biomimicry and biophilic design elements into spaces we occupy can have a significant impact on the mental health and well-being of neurodiverse populations.[12] The introduction of airflow that mimics natural air movement supports occupant comfort and well-being.[13]

Work environments with restorative spaces that incorporate natural elements support workers' recovery and well-being.[14] And employees in spaces that incorporate plants show a 15 percent increase in creativity.[15] Studies from the University of Central Arkansas[16] show that the impact of biophilic design can positively impact life expectancy, productivity, mental health, and reduce absenteeism and eye fatigue. All these factors directly benefit not only individuals but also the financial performance of organizations.

Extended use of computers, cell phones, and digital screens can cause visual fatigue. Eye fatigue can also be addressed by taking visual breaks and looking at natural vistas.[17]

Spaces that offer access to natural vistas have been shown to enhance emotional restoration and improve alertness, attention, and the ability to concentrate.[18] Views of nature have also been shown to reduce anxiety, stress, tension, anger, confusion, and overall mood disturbance.[19] Water features, fountains, and water walls can promote relaxation and tranquility[20] as a trickle of water can be both calming and stimulating and can drown out unwanted sounds in a space. See Figure 9.1.

Wayfinding

Many people with neurodistinctions need and thrive on repetition, predictability, and clear boundaries to feel safe and in control.[21] Environments need to make sense, which means effective wayfinding is critical. But overly redundant spaces lack inspiration. Having an intriguing space that is more than meets the eye can make people feel engaged and eager to move through the space but it's important to keep it easy to navigate. Good spatial design creates curiosity and opportunities for exploration, but it should also be intuitive. Visitors, as well as regular occupants, should be able to understand where they are and easily find their way. Neurodivergents often experience a heightened need for legible spatial order in busy spaces, where clear wayfinding becomes essential.

Effective space design strategies include the following:

- Use of signage and visual communication that aids in wayfinding, with strategic use of color, to assist our brains with positioning.
- Creating spaces serve as landmarks, are memorable and use a rhythm of common elements to generate a reassuring sense of order and thus assist the brain's innate positioning systems. Such design should, at the same time, avoid confusing repetition of identical spaces or features.
- Landmarks and focal points (such as a staircase or artwork), viewpoints (such as a mezzanine overlook), and clear lines of sight (including views to the outdoors) can help building users orient themselves.
- Meaningful variations in lighting levels can help as people naturally tend to walk toward brighter spaces or paths.
- The strategic use of materials, colors, and signage.

Metaphoric Relationships with Nature

Biomorphic Forms from Nature   Simultaneous Complexity & Order   Fractal Patterns & Non-Rhythmic Sensory Stimuli   Non-Visual Local/ Natural Materials

Direct Connection Nature

Physical/ Visual   Auditory   Olfactory

Experiental Connection with Nature

Experience Natural Systems   Thermal & Airflow Variability   Dynamic & Diffuse Light   Mystery/ Peril & Excitement

Blurring Exterior/ Interior   Prospect   Refuge

Figure 9.1   Introducing biophilia into the built environment

Multisensory Rooms

Multisensory rooms have become a common design solutions for addressing the needs of neurominorities in public spaces. These controlled environments are intentionally created to provide sensory experiences that support users' needs.

Airports and arenas around the world are increasingly incorporating these spaces, enabling neurodivergent individuals to travel or attend events they might have previously avoided. These spaces are not playrooms or meditation areas, but purposefully designed spaces to meet the unique needs of individuals who may be overwhelmed or under-stimulated in typical spaces. Given their location in the public realm, these rooms must be designed to serve a variety of users of all ages simultaneously—and therein lies the challenge: some visitors may need to be calmed down, while others might need stimulation.

Holistic Approach

While the theory of creating a space that allows someone overwhelmed by sensory stimulation to retreat is well-intentioned, in practice it is often far from ideal. Creating an environment that is welcoming to all goes beyond simply making a space to retreat to, and designing it is far more challenging. As we have shared, to accommodate the vast variety of conditions that exist in the neurodiverse community, we must create options, choices, and variety. The assumption that one room can meet the needs of such a diverse group is unrealistic.

As a firm, HOK advocates a holistic, tiered approach for creating inclusion in public or complex spaces.

- Communicate prior to arrival. Enable individuals to familiarize themselves with the environment before they even arrive on site using an app or the organization's website.
- Streamline the pinch points or stressors within the space.
- Address the entire journey from curbside to destination and identify opportunities for design mitigations.

- Create a variety of experiences in the multisensory zone itself. This may include offering different spaces for various user groups based on age, condition, or function. These can be organized as multiple zones within one space or as separate spaces entirely.
- Leverage technology to guide users, keep them connected, and create varied experiences for different user groups.

Design Considerations

Whether you are designing an airport, a healthcare center, a sports venue, or a workplace, embracing a holistic approach enables us to create better solutions for everyone. When doing so, consider these factors:

- When possible, create a series of rooms or divide the space into smaller areas with varying sensory experiences.
- Allow individuals to see inside a room before committing to enter it via side lights, windows, or subdividing spaces with views from a distance. This affords them a sense of comfort before committing to the experience.
- Provide a level of choice so individuals can determine how they want to engage with the space and other individuals within it.
- Provide adjustable, soft, indirect lighting in spaces that are user-controlled.
- Offer quiet zones with acoustic treatments and spaces with music or natural sounds that can be adjusted.
- Provide a textural palette that promotes a sense of calm.
- Use muted natural colors including blues, greens, and browns—with bolder color accents for interest.
- Incorporate biophilic elements and water features where possible. Consider a skylight or images of the sky, trees, and foliage with slight movement on the ceiling where possible.
- Create areas of active play and opportunities to physically engage via activity walls, interactive screens, or tactile elements.
- Provide fidget furniture, such as rocking stools, to help provide hypersensitive individuals with a way to calm down and refocus.
- Create a variety of seating options, including beanbags or a cocoon feature to allow individuals to nest.

- Create a rest and recovery space where people can lie down with a weighted blanket and dimmable lights.
- Provide soft furniture options and squeezable pillows to aid in releasing muscle tension.
- Ensure that a portion of the space has padded walls and flooring for those with physical reactions, such as head banging or violent outbursts.

Sensory spaces should enable all types of users to find a reassuring sensory level. Ideally, this allows them to experience shared and public spaces in a way that is both manageable and rewarding.

On a Personal Note

A 30-Minute Call That Changed an Airport

In 2023 I got a call from colleagues who were working on the design of a major U.S. airport terminal. During the initial planning, they had set aside a space and labeled it "multisensory room." As the planning progressed, the local airport authority questioned the intent of the space, what it would entail, and whether it was necessary. HOK's team, familiar with our research and recommendations on neuroinclusive design, encouraged them to explore the possibilities. They allocated a 30-minute call for us to share our insights, and I was asked to participate.

My colleagues and I did additional research on precedents in other airports. To our delight, a handful of airports had created multisensory rooms, and many of their officials were eager to share their insights. We reached out to them for feedback on space utilization regarding what they might do differently. One airport team reported that their space was often crowded and misused because it was often occupied by pilots and TSA agents. To us, this did not seem unusual. Few jobs are more stressful than being a pilot or TSA agent. Many of them may even be neurodivergent, and their need for regenerative spaces would affect not only them but all travelers that day. The airport team had not made that

(continued)

(*continued*)

connection, assuming a narrow view of the "typical" neurodivergent user. We inquired whether they had considered creating a specific space for staff and encouraged them to consider it.

Our assessment revealed that most of the multisensory spaces were designed for children and shared a common challenge: trying to make one room suitable for everyone regardless of age or neurotype. Most struggled to balance hyper and hypo settings within a single space. We know there are a variety of neurotypes and cognitive profiles affecting all travelers and airport employees. It's difficult to create a single space that meets everyone's needs. A restless child who just sat through a six-hour flight and has excess energy shouldn't be next to an anxious adult who needs a moment of silence before boarding a flight. We need a tiered approach for these spaces.

We also believe that multisensory rooms alone cannot address the needs of the neurodivergent community. Do you know anyone who finds going to an airport a stress-free experience? We envision a more holistic approach that would address the entire journey through these spaces. These multisensory rooms often are tucked away in the terminal and hard to find. By the time you do find it, you may already be melting down.

Our preferred approach would create a pre-journey engagement enabling individuals to go experience the space online in advance. They could register to be expedited through stressful points, such as check-in, security, and boarding. The goal would be to create a curb-to-gate experience that reduces stress and confusion. This could include opportunities to retreat to or seek refuge; easy-to-follow wayfinding, generous, navigable paths; biophilia, natural materials; art; soothing stimulation; calming palettes; and some control over the experience. As part of this holistic vision, we would incorporate a series of multisensory spaces providing both quiet and more active areas.

I joined the call with the airport authority virtually and presented to a room full of people miles away. We shared background information and explained how they could design for inclusion, along with our thoughts on multisensory spaces. Unable to see the faces of anyone in the meeting, I couldn't read the room. Before I knew it, our

30 minutes had ended and we were off the call. I received a quick "good job" text from a colleague but had no way to gauge how our message was received.

Ten minutes later, my phone rang. It was one of the client's participants from the airport authority. He shared that just prior to the call, the team was wondering whether they needed to join the meeting. He also told me how close they had come to simply changing the space into a smoking room. But they begrudgingly joined the call. He said that within 10 minutes, they were fully committed to creating the multisensory room and embracing a more holistic approach.

That was wonderful, but another revelation was still to come. He confessed that he was embarrassed that they didn't take it seriously initially because he was the father of an autistic child. Even in his role designing airports, he had never envisioned that his son might be able to travel one day, due to anxiety. That 30-minute conversation gave him hope and purpose. He now had a mission—design a space his son would be proud of and that would make it easier for neurodivergents to travel. In the category of best 30-minute calls ever, this ranks high for me. It's the fuel that feeds our dedication to designing purposeful, inclusive, and welcoming spaces.

Safety and Well-Being

The well-being of its employees determines the well-being of an organization. Supporting the physical, mental, and social health of employees in new and creative ways will position your office for long-term resiliency.

The workplace should also serve as a place that helps people decompress and focus rather than heighten feelings of being overwhelmed or isolated. The intentional use of materials, lighting, and environmental graphics can create a calm and inviting atmosphere while avoiding sensory overload.

Mental well-being and inclusion can also be supported by providing access to daylight, fresh air, and views of nature or green space, which ease stress, boost productivity, and help people thrive. Inclusive and accessible design strategies, from clear wayfinding to safety measures, help employees feel secure and supported in their work environment.

We naturally seek places where we feel protected. Many people instinctively pick a spot that allows them to avoid having their back to a corridor and provides a clear view of the entry. This concept of "prospect and refuge" refers to environments where people can observe (prospect) without being seen and have an exit route (refuge).[22] Creating a sense of "prospect and refuge" within spaces can help environments feel secure and meet basic human psychological needs.

Neurodivergents often prefer predictability and clear boundaries to feel safe and in control in shared occupancy spaces. Humans subconsciously want to be able to see into a room before committing to enter. Previewing a space can be accomplished via side lights, glass partitions, windows, or clear views into an area without partitions.

Designing for Psychological Safety

When individuals feel over-stimulated in an environment, they often need a safe space to exit and process negative emotions. Psychological safety in the built environment can mean creating spaces that provide a neutral sensory environment with minimal stimulation that the user can customize to provide the right level of sensory stimulation. "Refuge" provides an escape, be it an exit route or an alcove along a path to step into while others pass.

We use architectural elements to provide clear lines of sight and intuitive wayfinding. Yet removing barriers goes beyond ensuring physical access to spaces. We also need to remove barriers that prevent individuals from succeeding in organizations. The U.S. Surgeon General's *Framework for Workplace Mental Health and Well-Being*[23] outlines five essentials for supporting the mental health and well-being of workers (Figure 9.2). For the neurodivergent community, these essentials can provide physical, social, and emotional security. Along with addressing well-being, they foster a strong sense of belonging and purpose.

As designers, we have learned much about the science of space and design that can be applied to create successful environments. Here are a few examples:

- Mimicking natural environments through subtle changes in air temperature, relative humidity, airflow across the skin, and surface temperatures can enhance comfort and productivity.
- Spaces with numerous enclosed private offices can create a sense of isolation.

- Oversized or vacuous spaces leave people feeling exposed or disconnected.
- When individuals' backs are exposed, they can feel insecure and stressed.[24]

Factors Influencing Workplace Satisfaction

Studies[25] have shown that employee satisfaction with workspace configurations depends on several factors:

- Type of work being performed
- Degree of social interaction surrounding their work point
- Degree of openness, access, and transparency
- Orientation of the work point
- Amount of acoustic and visual interference

The term *view shield* refers to what is in one's line of sight and may be influencing or distracting them.

Figure 9.2 The U.S. Surgeon General's *Framework for Workplace Mental Health and Well-Being*

Blind spots are the spaces around an individual that they cannot see. They may contain elements impacting them, such as people approaching from behind. These factors influence one's sense of safety and security within a space.

Creating Balanced Environments

To create spaces that meet our psychological needs, we should start with the basics. We must ensure that spaces provide optimal ranges for temperature, lighting, air quality, noise, and safety and security.

Lighting research conducted at the University of Toronto has suggested that bright lighting levels can intensify positive and negative feelings, and that dimming the lights can result in more rational decisions.[26] Other studies have found that changing lighting color and intensity over the day to mimic nature's diurnal changes can reduce stress.

After meeting basic environmental conditions, we need to address ergonomic needs and privacy requirements. Only then can we focus on other activities. To go beyond basic needs and achieve meaningful endeavors and well-being, we must create spaces that allow individuals to find the right level of engagement, interaction, and connection. These spaces should also reinforce an organization's values and culture.

Providing a variety of settings where we each can find a location that meets our needs, both functionally and from an orientation standpoint, will be pivotal. This variety helps us feel a sense of control in a world where we often have little.

Focus Flow

It is getting harder to focus, concentrate, and enter a state of "flow" at work. In our research surveys, more than two-thirds of people cite acoustic distractions are their top concern when working in a shared space. During our 2024 workshop with individuals working in scientific settings, several neurodivergent participants compared sporadic sounds in a space to distinct raindrops. In contrast, they described spaces with consistent background noise, like humming equipment or people talking, as a comforting rain shower.

Not all distractions are unwanted. Some neurodivergent thinkers actively seek out buzz spaces full of energy to create their ideal environment for hyperfocus. Others may just need one distraction, such as oral stimulation, or use one to dampen the impact of another.

To help individuals manage distractions, we can design spaces with options and empower people to find solutions that meet their specific requirements. This includes areas for focus, tech-free zones, and even "buzzy spaces" where individuals can get lost in the hum of activity.

Why Flow Is Important

Research by Dr. Gloria Mark, a professor at the University of California, Irvine, and author of *Attention Span: A Groundbreaking Way to Restore Balance, Happiness and Productivity*, shows that the average time individuals focus on a task before becoming distracted has dropped from 2.5 minutes in 2006 to an alarming 47 seconds in 2022.[27]

Neuroscience recognizes flow as a distinct mental state. During focus flow, the Central Executive Network (CEN) is activated, and the Salience Network helps monitor task progress. Flow states are associated with dopamine release, which helps us feel more relaxed and contributes to heightened engagement and reduced fatigue.[28]

When we are free-thinking or letting our minds wander, the Default Mode Network (DMN) kicks in. During focus flow, however, the DMN's activity decreases, allowing for reduced self-reflection and enhanced task engagement.[29]

In addition to workplace noise, technology can be a huge distraction. Studies by Microsoft found that, on average, people check their inboxes 74 times a day.[30] Sixty-eight percent of people do not think they have enough uninterrupted focus time during the workday.[31]

Constant Connectivity

The flow of information coming at us seems never-ending. According to a study by Microsoft, on average people are spending 252 percent more time in virtual meetings than pre-pandemic, and the average workday has been extended with a rise in after-hours work.[32] When we factor in the percentage of time people are multitasking during virtual meetings, it is no wonder we are less focused and burning out faster. A UC Irvine study found that the average worker switched tasks every three minutes.[33] This continuous task switching, which is harder for neurodivergents than neurotypicals,[34] comes at a cost:

- Slower functional speed
- More errors
- Diminished work quality
- Increased fatigue and stress
- Negatively impacted memory
- More distractibility
- Declined cognitive, mental, and physical health

Being on constant scheduled calls also reduces opportunities for the casual interactions and personal connections that ward off loneliness. For neurodivergents, who may already feel isolated, this is an increasing concern. As individuals become more reliant on technology, technostress is taking a toll on their mental health, physical well-being, and social interactions. Many are experiencing an inability to disconnect that is leading to increased levels of anxiety, burnout, and decreased productivity.[35]

It takes about 15 minutes to get into deep meaningful thought. Yet office workers are typically interrupted every seven minutes. Those with active technology alerts are likely to face interruptions every two minutes. After an interruption, it can take 23 minutes to get back into the flow and regain focus.[36] Often referred to as the "ping effect," these distractions make it hard to concentrate.

As the first "digital natives," Generation Z has used technology since they were children. Research suggests this has shaped how they learn, and that they do best in energetic spaces. A study found that "the brains of Gen Zs have become wired to sophisticated, complex visual imagery. As a result, the part of the brain responsible for visual ability is far more developed, making visual forms of learning more effective. Auditory learning (lecture and discussion) is very strongly disliked by this age group."[37]

Improving Focus and Productivity

Research supports breaking tasks into shorter intervals to enhance performance.[38] The Pomodoro Technique[39] uses 25-minute focused work blocks followed by short breaks. Like athletes who train in intervals to optimize their performance, we can achieve better results by alternating between periods of concentrated effort and recovery.

Creating Mindful Work Environments

People are looking for creative ways to enable mindfulness and improve focus. For some, this means more control over when and where they work. For others, it requires companies to provide a greater variety of work zones tailored to different tasks, giving people more options and control over their work environment.

Consider these tips to decrease distraction at work:

- Choose a quiet room or work from home when you require intense concentration.
- Use flex hours to minimize distractions.
- Stay active and move around. Walk and exercise during breaks.
- Use private or semi-enclosed spaces to block out distractions.
- If working in an open space, position yourself in a low-traffic area.
- Decrease clutter on work surfaces.
- Use headsets to tune out background office noise.
- Turn off email and text message alerts and instead check messages for 10 minutes every hour.
- Provide active areas for energy release.

The ability to disconnect, be mindful, and destress is imperative to foster physical and mental health, well-being, creativity, and productivity. We all want and need this. For neurotypicals, it can determine how effectively they work. For neurominorities, it can determine whether they can work at all.

Beyond individual strategies, workplaces need to provide space for focus while promoting connections and a feeling of belonging to the organization. But research by Libby Sander at Bond University suggests that individuals often struggle to maintain energy or inspiration in spaces they routinely frequent because the sameness dulls our minds and senses. She writes that, "At a psychological level, we are biologically disposed to seek out locations where there is some complexity, some interest, and where messages are conveyed in different ways."[40] This suggests space should provide a sense of beauty and delight while offering opportunities for fascination, mystery, and wonder.

While a clean and orderly workspace improves focus for many by reducing visual clutter, others find order in disorder, using a messy desk to spark creativity and pattern-finding.

Spotlight

Benjamin Jensen Brings Neurodiversity Focus to Landscape Design

Benjamin Jensen is a landscape design professional in Washington, DC. His work on neurodiversity in landscape and urban design began when he learned more about his own sensory sensitivities as a master's student in landscape architecture at Cornell University. His research, centered on the autistic experience, explored the wide variety of sensory experiences within the autism spectrum. It examined the needs associated with each sense, as well as extra-sensory needs, and developed a methodology for an iterative process of sensory analysis in design. Benjamin won the ASLA Honor Award in Research for his thesis and continues to expand his expertise by researching the sensory impacts of plants on the landscape experience.

How did you discover you were on the autism spectrum?

Ben: I was pursuing my master's in landscape architecture at Cornell University when I discovered that I'm on the spectrum. Suddenly a lot of things about my life to that point started to make more sense. In learning about my own sensory sensitivities, I realized why so many places make me uncomfortable or anxious, and how much of the built environment is not designed in a way that's friendly to us.

What have you noticed about how landscape architecture takes into account sensory experiences?

In landscape architecture, I often hear people talk about visual and spatial impacts. We have a lot of language surrounding the way things look for the proportions of the space, but rarely is there language around smells and tactile sensations in the natural world.

How does wayfinding impact your experience of spaces?

I want to know when I leave the house what my journey will be. I like it to be predictable. If something is off, or gets changed, it throws me off. And my experience of the building starts before I walk in the front door. It starts when I hit the property line. It starts when I get on the bus.

What are you currently researching?

My current research focuses on the sensory impacts of specific plants. As a landscape architect, my design medium changes seasonally and grows over the years. A tree is more than just a tree. Some generate noise, others absorb it, some are more colorful than others. Each plant has a unique impact on the experience of a space, and my goal is to take advantage of that in curating sensorially accessible spaces.

What are your key takeaways for creating more neuroinclusive environments?

Awareness and design empathy are key. Our baseline of what we design for is what we know. But we all need to practice putting ourselves in someone else's shoes and leveraging design empathy. We have learned to design for physical disabilities. Building that same awareness around neurodiversity is harder. It's not through malice that our spaces are not designed for neuroinclusion; it's a lack of understanding.

10 | Degrees of Inclusive Design

> Neurodiversity may be every bit as crucial for the human race as
> biodiversity is for life in general. Who can say what form of
> wiring will be best at any given time.
> —Harvey Blume, author and neurodiversity advocate

The spaces we occupy have a profound impact on us and our ability to function and thrive. When we design space to be legible, we enable individuals to understand the environment more readily. Employees are more satisfied and productive when offered choices and a variety of workspace types. Inclusive design principles have evolved over the years, and today there are various degrees of inclusion.

Accessible Design

Accessible design is a process in which designers minimize barriers to allow people with disabilities to navigate the built environment. Accessibility codes primarily focus on mobility barriers, not social and sensory elements.

Enacted in 1990, the Americans with Disabilities Act (ADA) prohibits discrimination against people with disabilities in everyday activities.[1] The ADA guarantees that people with disabilities have the same opportunities as everyone else to enjoy employment opportunities, purchase goods and services, and participate in state and local government.[2] In the United Kingdom, the Equality Act 2010 legally protects people from discrimination in the workplace and wider society.[3] These standards cover newly constructed buildings, alterations to existing structures, and the removal of architectural barriers.

Accessible design strives to anticipate, identify, and remove barriers people with disabilities encounter through standards and regulations. These standards lay out the fundamental principles for inclusion and have had a significant impact on making spaces more accessible. However, we need to look beyond these requirements when building environments that might meet the needs of those with different neurotypes.

Universal Design

The Center for Universal Design at North Carolina State University developed and popularized the concept of universal design in 1997. It provides guidance for designing spaces to be accessible, legible, and usable by individuals regardless of their circumstance, age, disability, or other factors.

These seven core principles guide universal design:[4]

- Equitable use
- Flexibility in use
- Simple and intuitive use
- Perceptible information
- Tolerance for error
- Low physical effort
- Size and space for approach and use

Nancy Doyle writes about the importance of universal design in today's workplace: "Neurodiversity is in the transition from hot topic to hot potato, but universal design allows us to include without escalating costs beyond what is reasonable. We need a completely new model to cope with the scale of the change, the opportunity being that an overhaul of working practices leads to a more human-centered workplace for all."[5]

On a Personal Note: The Glass Staircase

One of the most powerful tools in design is empathy. We design spaces for various individuals, many of whom are vastly different from ourselves. Designers need to be able to put themselves in other people's shoes to create spaces that reflect the human condition, reduce physical barriers to accessibility, and make environments more inclusive. Having core principles and guidelines systematically laid out enables us to do so more consistently and with predictable results. But if we fail to consider the vast range of human conditions and neurotypes, we may unintentionally neglect others' needs. As designers who believe the spaces we create can positively impact people within them, we must also acknowledge that poorly designed spaces can have negative effects.

A few years ago, I visited a client who was proud of a new two-story atrium in one of their buildings. The CEO showed me how everyone was mingling in different settings throughout the atrium. The highlight was a sweeping two-story glass staircase that encouraged interaction and visual connections. He was eager for me to experience it. I looked over at the men sitting under the staircase in a casual gathering space, then down at my skirt, and expressed my preference for an alternative. In that moment, the CEO realized why. Horrified, he apologized profusely and took me to the elevator.

This was not intentional and the space was designed by a woman. It is an example of how one's lived experience does not always make you an expert on a situation. It highlights why it is so vital that we define and reinforce best practices for inclusive design.

Inclusive Design

A completely accessible environment might not fully address needs from more complex impairments like brain-based conditions, chronic health issues, or sensory challenges. Accessibility standards focus on physical compliance. Inclusive design encompasses a wider range of human diversity.

It factors in things like socioeconomic status, culture, and varying degrees of abilities—physical, cognitive, or mental. An inclusive design approach tailors solutions for more functional limitations, making environments more usable than just minimal compliance.[6]

As neurodiversity advocate Ludmila N. Praslova writes,[7] "Historically, most organizations have approached inclusion sequentially: gender this year or two, race next, then sexual orientation, and maybe someday disability and age. Or maybe class. Or neurodiversity. But what happens if someone is an older, Black, visibly disabled woman? Sequential inclusion leaves people behind."

Intersectionality, a term coined by Kimberlé Crenshaw,[8] is the concept that overlapping aspects of identity—such as race, culture class, and disability—collectively shape our experiences of both privilege and discrimination. We need a comprehensive approach that considers how multiple factors of identity intersect to define who we are, including the following:

- Race
- Gender
- Sexual orientation
- Ethnicity
- Socioeconomic status
- Age/generation/life stage
- Religion/spiritual beliefs
- Physical abilities
- Mental/cognitive/neural health
- Education

Each of us has intersecting identities that define our true selves. Those who are marginalized are likely to face more challenges.

For a workplace to be inclusive for all, we need to expand design solutions beyond a one-size-fits-all approach. This means creating diverse settings in the built environment that address the needs of users across the spectrum of identities and abilities.

Spotlight

Valerie Fletcher's Vision: Designing for the Edges to Benefit All

Valerie Fletcher has been executive director since 1998 of the Institute for Human Centered Design (IHCD), an international design and education nonprofit whose mission centers on the role of design in social equity. IHCD is a deep content expert in accessibility and inclusive design. Fletcher earned a master's degree in ethics and public policy from Harvard University. She is on the Board of the International Association for Universal Design (IAUD) and a Trustee of the Boston Architectural College. The Helen Hamlyn Centre at the Royal College of Art in London named her Inclusive Design Champion 2022.

What brought you to be an advocate for neuroinclusion?

> **Valerie:** At IHCD, we are keenly attentive to the shifting demographics of ability. We are committed to identifying solutions responsive to people at the edges of the spectrum of ability as a means of delivering design that works better for everyone. The dramatic shift in the relevance of "cognitive" or "brain-based" reasons for disability has been a dominant trend in the United States for years and, in 2023, became the leading reason for disability in America. For the first time, it eclipsed mobility limitations. Neurodiversity is a significant part of that spectrum.

Can you talk about the work that you are doing?

> As deep content experts on accessibility and inclusive design, we have a number of portfolios and serve clients across the nation: higher education; museums; corporate workplace; public agencies at the city, state, and federal levels; public transit; and healthcare. Baseline accessibility is a low floor with no standards or codes responses that address brain-based conditions. Clients want to use design as a tool for equitable experience and to support

(continued)

(continued)

the comfort, confidence, sense of control, and performance of the people they serve.

Our research is participatory, and we directly engage people with lived experiences of physical, sensory, or brain-based reasons for functional limitations: user/experts. Primarily through a variation of contextual inquiry research, we closely document user/experts doing what anyone would do in a given client environment to determine what works, what fails, and what would make a difference. Our clients tend to embrace design changes when they witness what user/experts experience. In the last decade, we have done extensive reviews with neurodiverse user/experts delivering valuable insights for particular environments.

How do you define human-centric design, and why is that such an important concept for us to embrace?

We were founded in 1978 as Adaptive Environments and changed our name on our 30th anniversary to more accurately reflect our work. Though pioneers in the field, we were not ready in 2008 to choose "universal" or "inclusive" design and so chose "human-centered" as the simple name that speaks to design as a social art that significantly impacts people's lives. We work from the World Health Organization's contextual definition of disability. In that model:

Functional limitation is a universal human experience if one lives a typical lifespan. Mental and physical reasons for functional limitation are in parity. The negative, disabling aspects of a functional limitation become disabling at the intersection of the person with the environment—physical, information, communication environments as well as attitude and policy.

Designers are the makers of the human context and we have a powerful opportunity to minimize limitations and enhance experience and performance in the contexts we design. It's critical that we anticipate diversity of ability and design as inherent to good design.

Equitable Design

Equality provides individuals with the same resources and opportunities afforded to others. Equity, by contrast, recognizes that each person has different circumstances and needs. Instead of giving everyone the same thing, it provides the appropriate resources and opportunities needed to reach equal outcomes. True inclusion goes beyond this, requiring every individual's perspective to be understood and integrated into our design process.

HOK's five core equity design principles are as follows:

- Partner with the Community
- Plan for Inclusion
- Provide Equity of Experience
- Promote Health and Well-Being for All
- Champion Environmental Justice

The firm has rolled out the Designing for Equity program globally, identifying Equity Champions in our offices. The program includes a comprehensive framework to systematically address these principles from start to finish, in every stage of a project.

Client Story

*An Inclusive Scientific Workplace for AstraZeneca's
New Kendall Square R&D Hub*

AstraZeneca R&D Site

Cambridge, Massachusetts
570,000 sq. ft.
LEED-CI Platinum certification anticipated
HOK services: interiors, lab programming and planning, sustainable design, experience design, lighting design
Base building architect: Pickard Chilton

What if the next medical science breakthrough hinged not on a molecule but on the minds collaborating to find it? That is part of the

(continued)

(continued)

vision driving the HOK team designing the interiors of AstraZeneca's new Kendall Square tower. Scheduled for completion in 2026, the facility aims to house 1,850 employees and set a new standard for inclusive workplace design in the pharmaceutical industry.

Background and Vision

The COVID-19 pandemic catalyzed AstraZeneca's approach to workplace design, emphasizing the need for diverse standards and individual-focused spaces. AstraZeneca Head of Real Estate and Workplace Design Christine White highlights the strategic importance of this shift: "By aligning our broader diversity goals and corporate responsibility with individual-focused design, we can tap into and nurture an increasingly diverse talent pool."

During the initial Diversity & Inclusion workshop, which was hosted by HOK, the team identified gaps, established priorities, and developed a roadmap for inclusion. They also crystallized a clear project vision: "Lead the industry by example by creating an environment that embodies and demonstrates diversity and inclusion." This vision included the following:

- Creating a feeling of inclusion and belonging by hearing the voices of minority groups
- Designing a welcoming, energizing environment where people feel safe and valued
- Instilling pride in the workplace and amplifying AstraZeneca's Alexion brand
- Empowering all people to thrive and treating everyone as equals
- Paying homage to the area's history and making an impact on the community
- Advancing sustainability efforts

This inclusive vision aligns with AstraZeneca's recognition of its workforce's unique composition. "AstraZeneca is a science-based business, and like many other pharma and STEM companies, there is a widely held belief that nearly 50 percent of our workforces is probably neurodivergent," says Director of Workplace **Design Andy Parry**. See Figure 10.1.

Inclusive Design Process

AstraZeneca and HOK embarked on a unique design journey, integrating inclusivity at every stage.

The team enhanced the typical design process by conducting additional touch bases and meetings with AstraZeneca's workplace design team and facility management team, incorporating inclusivity into every stage of development.

Wayne Nickles, Science + Technology practice leader for HOK, emphasizes the significance of early client engagement: "It started with the fact that AstraZeneca reached out to us very early in the project to ask if we had any tools or methods to use to help push inclusion as a key design driver. Knowing that this was something that

| Flooring defines zones and aids with acoustics | Ample access to daylight and views | Connection between floors | Clear circulation path aids wayfinding | Various ceiling elements help define zones within the space | Lighting creates hospitality vibe | Variety of seating options |

Figure 10.1 AstraZeneca's Kendall Square scientific R&D hub

(*continued*)

(continued)

we as a company have been focused on, it was exciting that a client was just as interested in the idea and willing to make a commitment to it. As we went through the workshops, hearing from people whose lives and abilities are so different from mine greatly expanded my understanding of and appreciation for how spaces can be experienced so differently, with impacts varying from the biggest design moves to the smallest technical details."

"It was an incredibly collaborative and rewarding design process," says Tara Roscoe, HOK's director of design, interiors. "By prioritizing inclusivity at every step, we were able to create spaces that truly welcome and empower all individuals, regardless of their backgrounds or needs."

AstraZeneca Senior Business Transformation Director Suzanne Kennedy describes efforts to engage project stakeholders: "We looked for frequent opportunities for people from our Employee Resource Group to speak up and participate. They influenced the design in many ways. We stripped out a lot of carpets and changed the banquet seating at the mini town hall area because they weren't equitable. We took out the wave access points—the sensors for automatic doors— further than we normally would have done and went well beyond ADA standards to be more accessible."

The commitment to inclusivity extended beyond physical design. Kennedy describes efforts to make engagement assets during the design process more accessible, such as "building audio descriptions for the beautiful renders" and "subtitling the fly-through animations." They also incorporated feedback from neurodiverse colleagues to make assets more accessible, including toning down colors, slowing down movement, and decluttering scenes.

Nickles reflects on the impact of this inclusive approach: "As designers, we are continually expanding the voices we listen to, to learn what we can from them, and to continue to improve our process and designs to be as inclusive as we can going forward." See Figure 10.2.

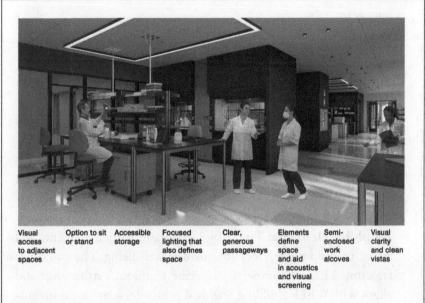

Visual access to adjacent spaces   Option to sit or stand   Accessible storage   Focused lighting that also defines space   Clear, generous passageways   Elements define space and aid in acoustics and visual screening   Semi-enclosed work alcoves   Visual clarity and clean vistas

Figure 10.2   AstraZeneca's Kendall Square scientific lab space

Inclusive Design Features

Based on AstraZeneca's vision and goals, along with the results of the initial D&I workshops and research, HOK designed several innovative features to promote inclusivity and address diverse needs in the new R&D center:

- **Sensory-considerate design:** The open office space features a noise gradient, becoming naturally quieter further from communal areas, such as the pantry and central stairs.
- **Visual calm:** Graphics and digital monitors for branding and messaging were minimized to reduce visual overstimulation.
- **Diverse textures and forms:** The design balances sharp angles with soft curves and offers a varied finish palette across floors,

(continued)

(*continued*)

allowing employees to gravitate to a sensory zone that feels most comfortable.

- **Intuitive navigation:** Clear sight lines to feature stairs provide immediate orientation and a visual anchor on each floor.
- **Flexible work settings:** The layout combines modular lab benches and offices with communal hubs for impromptu gatherings.
- **Deep work areas:** A significant portion of the floor plate is dedicated to quiet, focused workspaces. "We saw the need for more of those spaces and increased the percentage of our floor plate dedicated to that," says Parry.
- **Biophilic elements:** The design integrates natural elements and access to outdoor terraces to enhance well-being. The project is targeting LEED Commercial Interior Platinum certification and aligns with WELL Building Standard principles across areas including air, water, light, sound, and fitness.
- **Community zones:** These replace traditional "neighborhoods," encouraging movement through the workplace.

Impact and Future Outlook

The impact of this inclusive design approach is already resonating across AstraZeneca. Kennedy shares an anecdote: "I was in the coffee queue in our building in Macclesfield, England, where I'm not particularly well known, and people were talking about how the project we are designing in Boston is being done with inclusiveness to address people with different needs. Hearing their excitement about a project three thousand miles away was pretty cool."

HOK Project Manager Erika Reuter underscores the value of the inclusive design process: "The D&I work sessions to review the project were an invaluable process. Allowing everyone to take a step back to hear from a diverse group of end users strengthened the project design. We can rest easy knowing that we've designed something that will be welcoming for all."

Parry highlights a broader cultural shift: "We've seen massive growth in people being able to be their true selves at work, and it's more accepted now. We're much better at creating environments where people no longer have to mask in the workplace." The project is also expected to play a crucial role in talent attraction and retention, adds Parry.

Some organizations fear that neuroinclusive spaces might be costly. For this project, the team found that with the right expertise, inclusive design does not need to be more expensive. The team does, however, recommend allocating additional time for extra meetings, especially when undertaking inclusive efforts for the first time.

The most critical success factor is client commitment. As HOK Director of Interiors Tom Polucci puts it, "Great projects start with great clients. Inclusion starts with committed clients." The team also recommends establishing a working group at the project's inception to champion design review and feedback and conducting an employee survey to capture the workforce's diverse needs.

When it opens in 2026, this project will demonstrate that with the right commitment, expertise, and process, designing for inclusivity can create scientific workplaces where every individual can thrive and contribute their best to the organization. As Parry so aptly says, "Nobody wants to be reasonably adjusted. We all want to be welcomed."

11 | HOK's Approach to Inclusive Design

It's a strange paradox in that there is far more information out there about neurodiversity than 10 years ago, yet that information is not always being transferred into action.
> —Cheryl Winter, neurodiversity consultant

The work we do today is more varied and complex than that of past generations. With this in mind, we need to create work settings and environments that reflect who we are designing for to foster meaningful results for both individuals and organizations. To achieve this, we need to leverage our expertise, experience, and best practices while using a systematic approach. This is where our workplace design expertise and research on neuroinclusion and sensory processing come together to create viable solutions. Our approach extends beyond a simple "do no harm" philosophy. We are committed to creating fit-for-purpose, inclusive spaces.

HOK's tiered approach to optimizing workplace solutions includes these steps:

1. Understand your unique **organizational DNA.**
2. Define **personas**, **work settings,** and **gathering profiles.**

189

3. Address the **six modalities of work** ("the six Cs"): Concentrate, Commune, Create, Congregate, Contemplate, Convivial.

4. Implement **spatial sequencing** and zoning for maximum effectiveness.

5. Consider group and organizational dynamics through the **Power of the 6 to the 48.**

6. Address **DEIA** and sensory needs (see Chapter 10 for details).

7. Develop **planning concepts** based on those factors (see Chapter 13 for details).

8. Apply design **elements and principles** to achieve inclusive spaces (see Chapter 10 for details).

9. Create **journey maps** to define day-in-the-life scenarios.

Organizational DNA

To truly understand an organization, you need to assess its unique organizational DNA. After years of engagements, assessments, and interactions with a variety of companies, we have identified six key strands that make up an organization's DNA:

- Industry
- Regional influences
- Demographics
- Corporate culture
- Organizational structure
- Individual work styles

Understanding where an organization stands in each of those categories helps us define the best solutions. If any of these factors vary, however, the space solution will need to reflect the differences.

We can take a closer look at these factors to understand how each one influences the optimal workplace solution.

Industry

Though industry sectors are varied, they each have distinct characteristics that influence workplace design. For example:

- Teams at professional services firms often work remotely or at client sites.
- Healthcare workers tend to be place-dependent, working in stressful environments for long hours.
- Government agencies are more hierarchical, have an aging demographic, and are often meeting-intensive.
- The financial sector tends to require more individual, concentrative work.

Industries also vary in terms of whether customers are coming into the workplace (legal, healthcare) or employees are going out into the field (sales, consulting). All these factors affect workspace needs, the ability to work remotely, and how to design the space.

Regional Influences

Work environments will vary based on geographic setting: urban, suburban, rural, or virtual. Each setting presents different challenges and advantages that are influenced by factors including traffic, population density, infrastructure, climate, and available workforce. For example:

- Urban centers provide access to communal amenities, so the workforce is less dependent on having on-site services.
- Suburban and rural settings often lack robust public transportation options. Organizations may want to provide on-premise amenities so employees do not have to leave for meals or to run errands.
- Virtual companies can potentially reduce their real estate portfolio but may need to invest more heavily in technology infrastructure.

Demographics

The composition of your workforce significantly influences workplace design. Key demographic factors include age, generational differences, gender, personality types, work schedules, and ethnic diversity.

Different generations have varying work styles and preferences. A company recruiting a lot of recent college graduates will need different spaces compared to one hiring retired military officers. But we also need to consider that life stages often have more impact on people than generational traits. As people mature, their needs, priorities, and behaviors evolve. Millennials are now starting families, and many are gravitating toward the suburbs and communities that are more affordable and have better schools. As Baby Boomers and Gen X become empty nesters and approach retirement, they face their own set of changing needs. Younger workers are often in "sponge mode," while older, seasoned professionals tend to have more managerial and client-facing roles. Different needs require distinct workplace environments.

Corporate Culture

An organization's space should physically embody its culture. For some companies, this might manifest as a formal environment, while others may require an informal, casual, entrepreneurial, empowered, or controlled environment. Understanding and reflecting corporate culture should be a major factor in both the overall design approach and the elements within the space.

Organizational Structure

The organizational structure of a company can take various forms: hierarchical, flat, web-based, hub-and-spoke with decisions radiating from a central point, or completely decentralized. To authentically embody your organizational structure and facilitate the right levels of interaction, the floor plan and space design should align with these frameworks. If you are not aligning these two elements, you may experience operational inefficiencies and operational disconnect.

Individual Work Styles

The work styles of today's knowledge workers range from individually focused to meeting-intensive and highly collaborative. It is becoming increasingly rare for individuals to do the same type of work all day. As a result, we must design spaces that accommodate their predominant work style as well as secondary activities.

Predominant work styles can vary significantly from company to company and department to department. What the accounting team is doing, for example, may be vastly different from what the sales team or researchers are doing. Understanding the unique functional requirements of the different groups within the workforce is key to designing the right space solution that meets their diverse needs.

Defining Personas, Work Settings, and Gathering Profiles

Today's workforce is far more diverse and engaged in a wider variety of tasks than past generations. We can no longer design spaces for the "average" person doing an "average" task. By developing a better understanding of who we are serving, what they are doing, and where they are doing it, we can create more tailored spaces that drive innovation and better outcomes while fostering the physical and cognitive well-being of the workforce.

Personas

HOK's team has developed a guide to aid in creating personas that more accurately reflect the individuals within organizations, allowing us to more holistically meet their specific needs (see Figure 11.1). To do so, we assess the spectrum of work activities and patterns across varying functional groups to find programming commonalities:

- **External mobility:** Time or days spent working in remote locations.
- **Internal mobility:** Level of internal movement and time spent outside of the primary work point
- **Level of interaction:** Degree of interaction with others, solo or group work, and in-person or virtual
- **Privacy/visibility:** Need for acoustical, information, managerial, or visual privacy
- **Work complexity:** Special environments or tools needed to perform one's job, such as a lab

Each persona has implications for space needs, program ratios, and seat-sharing potential. We acknowledge that even within a specific persona, individual needs can vary based on cognitive profile.

Persona Profiles
program 'proforma'

	Residents	Confidants	Flexers	Creators	Networkers	Nomads
Typical Job Roles	Admin Coordinators Analysts	Leadership Legal HR	IT Security Support	Designers Engineers Media Producers	Product Managers Knowledge Workers Marketing	Consultants Sales
Typical / Target % of Staff	10%	5%	5%	30%	45%	5%
Seat Sharing Ratio Work Points / Employees	1:1	1:1	1:12	1:15	1:2	>1:5
Individual Work Point	May be assigned, solo, open	May be assigned enclosed, able to host 2-3 people	Free-choice, team orientation	Free-choice, open, high variety or enclosed, team orientation	Free-choice, open, high variety	Touchdown or alternative workpoint
Collaboration Ratio Work Points / Collaboration Seats	<1:1	<1:1	1:1	1:1	>1:1	>>1:1
Tools & Tech	Basic	Basic	Bespoke (additional equipment)	Enhanced (additional monitors)	Basic	Enhanced (mobile tools)
Specialty Spaces	None	Some dedicated meeting space	Some work rooms, support spaces	Variety of specialty collaboration spaces	Few specialty spaces	Client-facing meeting spaces

Figure 11.1 Persona profiles

Work Settings

To address the needs of the modern, diverse workforce, we must evolve beyond rows of identical cubicles that offer little to no choice or control. HOK's team has developed a process to curate the right work setting for users based on their functional needs. We guide clients through an exercise that addresses the type of work being done and the level of choice, while exploring the primary considerations for determining the right work points that include the following:

- Duration of task
- Degree of privacy required
- Level of interaction with others, whether in-person or virtual
- Degree of flexibility needed

The guide also explores the secondary considerations related to location, technology, and tools and props.

Cultural, legislative, and style issues vary by region, and may require tailored solutions. Companies and their design partners must address regional nuances such as the following:

- Target density
- Personal space zoning and distance spacing
- Infrastructure
- Legislation and regulations
- Demographics and talent preferences

This systematic approach helps the design meet an organization's functional needs while creating environments conducive to collaboration and creative exchange, regardless of the geographic location.

Gathering Profiles

Traditional meeting rooms often fail to serve new ways of working. Shoving a large rectangular table into a room, surrounded by chairs, with a small monitor at one end and glass walls, provides little space for movement or information sharing. This approach does not cut it for today's hybrid gatherings.

Meeting rooms are more than just venues for gathering. They are spaces where teams come together, ideas flourish, and solutions to complex problems are hatched. To create meaningful spaces, designers must understand the true purpose of the gathering, the nature of the exchange, and the experience they are striving to curate. This understanding should inform the design process from the beginning.

To do this, we need a deeper understanding of meeting types and must design gathering spaces to be more fit-for-purpose and tech-enabled. In his 2013 book *Will There Be Donuts,* David Pearl describes seven distinct types of meetings.[1]

1. Discussion
2. Information sharing
3. Selling
4. Innovation
5. Social
6. Problem-solving
7. Decisions

Our team agreed with Pearl's meeting profiles and added two more:

8. Mentoring
9. Coaching

HOK's team uses a discovery process to match work behavior with appropriate settings during the initial programming phase. We guide clients through an exercise that integrates privacy configurations and work postures—whether formal or casual, long duration or short, structured or ad-hoc, or open. This engagement considers factors including level of enclosure, desire for privacy, and confidentiality requirements (QR Code 11.1).

QR Code 11.1   Gathering space matrix

Once you have determined the type of gathering, appropriate room type, number of people to accommodate, and enclosure preference, the next step is to address more specific elements related to how the room will be used. This includes the following:

- **Duration:** Will it be a short engagement or a longer one?
- **Posture:** Does it accommodate a structured meeting or a more ad hoc gathering?
- **Formality:** Is it a formal gathering or more casual?

Understanding these factors will aid in determining the right setup and size of the space. This may involve providing a range of settings, furniture solutions, and tools catering to individual needs and preferences. See Figure 11.2.

Enclosed Huddle

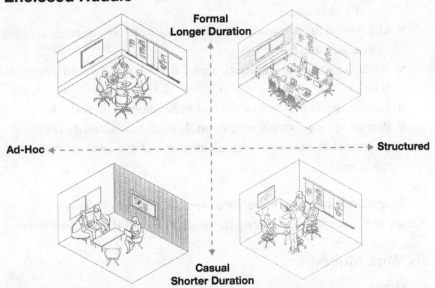

Figure 11.2 Gathering space profile and postures—example

Designers also need to factor in whether the gathering is intended to be:

- Low or high participation
- Structured or reconfigurable
- Virtual or in-person

These factors influence how the room is designed and furnished, and the technology needed to support it.

Where possible, gathering spaces should:

- Enable movement with room for people to stand and move around
- Provide analog tools for visual information sharing and ample space for writing and interaction
- Include a second tier of seating that gives individuals control over their level of engagement and proximity
- Use movable furniture to enhance flexibility and adaptability
- Promote equity and ensure all can engage through thoughtful table shapes and configurations
- Use neutral finishes so videoconferencing cameras accurately capture diverse skin and hair tones
- Be inclusive, ensuring equal access for all physical and cognitive abilities
- Include spaces for both hypo- and hypersensitive individuals
- Provide appropriate acoustic controls so all can be clearly heard
- Represent virtual attendees at full size and eye level for improved integration

To maximize options for everyone, we need to focus on designing spaces that are fit for purpose and address the needs of today's diverse workforce.

Six Work Modes

Per HOK's research into workplace-related issues, many of today's knowledge workers no longer perform the same tasks throughout the day. Workplaces should be dynamic and nimble, offering a balance between spaces for heads-down concentration work and areas for interaction that build bonds, trust, and social capital. HOK has defined six modalities of work, as shown in Figure 11.3.

Modalities of Work / The 6Cs

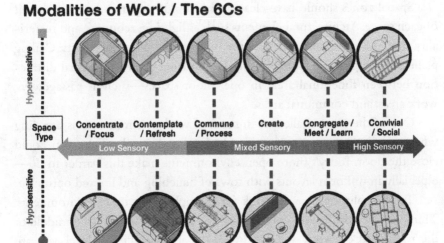

Figure 11.3 Six modalities of work—the six Cs

Beyond assessing the activities within the space, we should strive to give people access to areas that address a range of sensory thresholds, where possible. These spaces should leverage the elements and principles of design to create the right spatial attributes supporting the activity at hand and fostering the appropriate work mode (see Chapter 13).

Spatial Sequencing

Spatial zoning creates distinct areas within a space that address the modalities of work and reflect varying activity and energy levels. Our goal at HOK is to create a sense of flow from one modality to the next throughout the space. This process starts with mapping out activity levels in a logical order based on the desired activity level and sensory thresholds, access, flow, and work settings (QR Code 11.2).

QR Code 11.2 Spatial zoning

Spatial zones should have clear delineation to communicate the intent of each space. Architectural elements such as lighting, acoustics, and materiality should be designed to reflect the functionality of each activity. Ceiling planes, flooring, and materiality should be varied to provide visual distinction between functional areas in open floor spaces—such as passageways, work areas, and communal areas.

One of the main challenges in modern work environments is signaling when you do not want to be disturbed. In traditional offices, you could close the door. Today's more open environments make this harder to do—especially in uniform layouts with rows of benching and limited options.

To find solutions, we can look for examples from other environments. Think about a bar. If you are standing at a high-top table in the middle of the room and everyone walking by you is at the same eye level, you are inviting interaction. But if you choose a side table at seated height and away from the high-traffic area, you reduce the opportunities for engagement. And if you sit in a more secluded and shielded booth in the back, you are telling people you do not want to be bothered. It is all about permission signaling. But you must be in an environment with a variety of settings, in different locations and at varied heights, to successfully enable that. You also need freedom to choose where to work within the space.

Choice, control, and ability for permission signaling aid in creating a high-performing, empowered workplace. Creating spatial zones within an environment gives occupants some control over their level of interaction and stimulation. This creates human-centric and inclusive high-performance spaces (QR Code 11.3).

It is also important to create transitions between spaces to help users recalibrate their senses as they move through different activities and sensory levels. These transitions can be as subtle as a change in materiality or setting. The degree of transition depends on the size of the space and the significance of the change. A transition from a neighborhood zone into a building

QR Code 11.3   Spatial sequencing

atrium space would be intentional and pronounced. This might include a transitional area between the work zone and atrium to help people adjust to changes in spatial volume or lighting. Just as an arrival area, like a foyer in a home, can help individuals transition from the exterior to interior spaces, transition spaces allow people to ease into a situation, assess what is occurring, and get grounded before proceeding.

Power of the 6 to the 48

Social inclusivity is an important factor in creating a sense of belonging and inclusion. But neurodivergents often struggle to fit in. HOK has found that designing spaces that foster meaningful connections, give individuals opportunities to be part of a team, and expand the notion of what is "socially acceptable" are critical steps in reducing the isolation of neurodivergents, creating a sense of belonging, and being truly welcoming.

To create space that supports the psychological safety of individuals and teams, we employ our "Power of the 6 to the 48" approach. Robin Dunbar, a British anthropologist, proposed that people can maintain stable social relationships with about 150 people.[2]

When we provide individuals and teams with a dedicated home base within the workplace, we foster the ability to build community. A recent study observed a 43-person community in a shared office space that included quiet workspaces and opportunities for socializing. Group dynamics change once you reach 43–48 people. You can no longer see everyone's face, know everyone's name, or feel as connected. The occupants most appreciated the access to small rooms, the diversity of settings, and the incorporation of branding elements that reinforced their identity.[3]

Research has shown that individuals tend to form tighter bonds in groups of five people.[4] Leveraging this research, HOK's teams create smaller, tightly connected groupings of four to six people, empowering a "camp" mentality, This approach facilitates community, a sense of belonging, and openness. These camp areas can be grouped in clusters that form a "clan" of up to 24, which feeds into a larger neighborhood, or "tribe," of 36–48.

As social creatures, we thrive on connections and shared experiences. This is why it is so important to design spaces that foster community and create a sense of belonging. Neuroscience shows that when people are physically working together in a group, their brain waves start to sync, promoting innovation. Dr. Hannah Critchlow, a neuroscientist at the

University of Cambridge, describes this phenomenon as "joined-up think-ing" or collective intelligence.[5] When we connect in positive environments, not only do our bodies and brains sync, but we experience a collective effervescence that bonds teams together.

Frank Lloyd Wright reportedly once said that you should never design a dinner table for more than six to eight people; otherwise, you cannot have meaningful conversations. If you have ever sat at a big table, you know that is true. You end up with separate conversations at each end. Thus, smaller group settings of 4–6 people, in neighborhoods that accommodate up to 48 people, are ideal to foster bonding, trust, and social connections.

Journey Mapping

Once we have created a space that strives to be welcoming and inclusive, it is imperative that we aid the occupants in understanding how to use it. To help users understand the dynamics of the new space, we suggest creating journey maps, or day-in-the-life scenarios for different personas (QR Code 11.4).

For example, someone who is hypersensitive and only occasionally comes into the office may use a space very differently from someone who is hyposensitive and in the office every day. Mapping out these various jour-neys can highlight the most advantageous ways to leverage the environ-ment. This also supports effective change management by helping individuals understand and plan how they will use the space.

This process may involve the creation of preset examples or empower-ing individuals to create their own journey through a typical day. When people understand the options and choices at hand and are empowered to use them, we find their satisfaction increases and the space is leveraged to its full potential.

QR Code 11.4 Journey map: a day-in-the-life for a hyposensitive individual

Spotlight

Toby Mildon Champions Sensory-Friendly Workspaces for Neurodiversity

Toby Mildon is a workplace inclusion consultant and the founder of Mildon, with a professional background at the BBC, Deloitte, and Accenture. Through his inclusion agency, he partners with organizations to create bespoke strategies that foster diverse and inclusive workplaces, with a focus on ensuring neurodivergent individuals are included as part of broader diversity and inclusion initiatives.

Toby believes in the transformative power of inclusion to drive innovation, attract top talent, and enhance business performance. He has successfully delivered programs for major organizations like Sony, HarperCollins, Centrica, Mitchells & Butlers, and the National Health Service. Toby is also the author of the Amazon bestsellers *Inclusive Growth* and *Building Inclusivity*.

What was your journey to becoming an advocate for neuro-inclusion?

Toby: I became aware of neurodivergence while working at the BBC and running the disabled staff forum. I learned about the challenges faced by people with non-visible disabilities and worked with neurodivergent individuals, which sparked my interest. I then switched careers from technology and project management to diversity and inclusion to ensure neurodivergent people were included in broader diversity and inclusion strategies.

To what do you attribute the raised awareness for neurodiversity?

The raised awareness can be attributed to increased discussions in the media, as well as companies raising awareness through training and initiatives. However, we should caution against relying on unhelpful stereotypes and emphasize that neurodivergent individuals are found in every industry and role.

(continued)

(continued)

What are the biggest challenges neurodivergent workers face in the workplace, particularly regarding environmental factors?

The most significant challenges for neurodivergent employees often stem from sensory inputs in the work environment. Light, sound, and textures can be particularly overwhelming. For instance, loud open-plan offices without quiet spaces can be highly disruptive. Bright natural sunlight from large windows or disturbing patterns in office decor can also be challenging. Additionally, being positioned in high-traffic areas or near noisy equipment can hinder focus and productivity. These environmental factors can prevent neurodivergent individuals from thriving, making it difficult to perform at their best. It's crucial for employers to recognize these challenges and create more accommodating spaces that consider diverse sensory needs.

What are some of the most successful accommodations employers can make to create a more welcoming environment?

Successful accommodations include creating spaces within the workplace that cater to different needs, like quiet areas or meeting pods, and providing desks with different types of lighting. These accommodations create a variety of modalities to suit the diverse needs of all employees.

How can employers be proactive in designing inclusive workplaces?

Employers can be proactive by actively involving neurodivergent individuals in the design and decision-making processes for workplace policies and environments. This approach aligns with the principle of "nothing about us without us," which emphasizes the need to work directly with those affected by policies or designs. By including neurodivergent employees in these processes, employers ensure that solutions are truly effective and inclusive. This collaborative approach helps create workspaces that are functional for all employees, not just those who are neurodivergent.

12 | Steps Toward Designing for Inclusion

Life would be very boring if we were all the same. Being neurodiverse is a true superpower and employers should celebrate the diversity of their workforce and such talents within their employees. Allowing those who are neurodiverse to play to their strengths whilst supporting them within the working environment is key to enabling them to flourish and reach their potential.
—Dr. Naomi Humber, head of mental well-being,
Bupa Health

Our understanding of disability and the role of inclusive design in supporting neurodiversity continues to evolve. We are on a journey of discovery as research illuminates new aspects of the human condition. Our studies, workshops, and pilot projects deepen our understanding of neuroinclusive design principles. We will continue applying what we know to create environments that welcome and empower everyone, as our knowledge grows.

Redefining Disability

According to the World Health Organization (WHO), social exclusion, which is the inability of people to participate fully in society, is a significant contributing factor when it comes to health inequalities.[1] Physical, cognitive, and social exclusion can occur at a point of interaction between an individual and an environment where there was a misalignment between them.

Individuals have impairments that designers cannot affect. If an environment is well-suited for them, they are less disadvantaged. But if the environment does not meet their specific needs, they are disadvantaged. Since we can only control the environment, we need to focus on creating spaces that are more welcoming and inclusive.

The Social Model of Disability

This notion aligns with the "social model of disability" coined by Mike Oliver, a disabled academic, in 1983.[2] The social model of disability is an alternative to the medical model of disability, which suggests that people are disabled because of impairments or conditions they have.[3] The social model notes that disability is caused when a social structure or environment is not suited to meet individuals' needs. The social model emphasizes how systemic barriers, derogatory attitudes, and social exclusion perpetuate disparities between people with different abilities.

Impairment versus Disability

The social model of disability is based on a distinction between the terms *impairment* and *disability*. An impairment refers to the actual attributes that affect a person, while disability refers to the restrictions caused by society when barriers are in place.[4]

For example, if a person is overwhelmed by sensory stimulation and unable to function in a space, the medical model focuses on making the individual physically able to function. The social model, however, focuses on the built environment as the barrier. A social barrier might include people who understand the need but refuse to make accommodations, such as not providing a sign language interpreter despite knowing there are deaf individuals in society. A physical barrier might be not providing way-finding in a variety of ways, though we know not everyone reads, sees, or speaks the same language.

Creating Inclusive Workplaces

Workplace barriers can be both physical obstacles (such as inaccessible building entries) and operational protocols (such as policies requiring people to work without breaks). The Equal Employment Opportunity Commission (EEOC) lists several possible reasonable accommodations to remove barriers, including making existing facilities accessible.[5] Reasonable accommodations should be designed to address specific individual needs, remove barriers, and make work conditions more inclusive, giving all individuals an equal opportunity to enjoy the benefits and privileges of employment.

A Systematic Approach

As trusted advisors to our clients, we have participated in this process that clients have used to most effectively guide the effort from the beginning to the end. The right professional team addresses each step, whether that involves HR, operational strategies, or design professionals.

We have observed that organizations successful in transitioning and embracing neurodiversity in their workplaces have undertaken comprehensive programs that bring awareness, educate, and sensitize their teams to what their organization is trying to achieve and how to meet those goals. Figure 12.1 outlines a systematic approach to creating an inclusive workplace, from initial consultation and education to design implementation and ongoing evaluation.

Steps for Inclusion

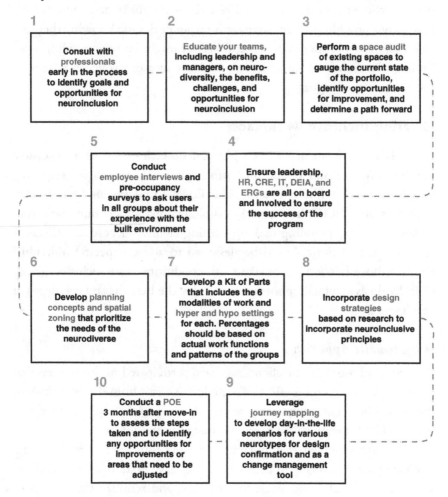

Figure 12.1   Roadmap for inclusion

Spotlight

AJ Paron's Insights on Neuroinclusive Workplace Design

AJ Paron is an executive vice president and design futurist at SANDOW Design Group. A highly accomplished professional with tremendous knowledge and relationships in the design industry, Paron is widely respected as a creative thinker, innovative leader, and engaging speaker and panelist.

How did your journey to becoming an advocate for neuroinclusion begin?

AJ: It started when I was at the University of Minnesota in design school. My professor, Dr. Denise Guerin, one of the few doctors of interior design, required our undergraduate class to do a thesis. I chose to research designing for Parkinson's and Alzheimer's, which were prevalent in my family. That's when I started understanding the effect of space on the mind and how people pick up cues from their environments.

Later, in 1998, my son was diagnosed with severe autism at age two and a half. We noticed he wasn't talking and started regressing, but in the 90s it was hard to get a diagnosis. When we finally did, I felt lost and angry that, as an interior designer, I couldn't directly help him medically or therapeutically.

Then I read *Thinking in Pictures* by Temple Grandin, and it clicked. I knew what I was supposed to be doing. I found some research from the Environmental Design Research Association and an article by healthcare designer Cynthia Leibrock stressing the importance of research. Dr. Guerin gave me some grad students, and we started studying the neural functions of autism, looking at what was happening in the brain and how the built environment could affect symptoms.

What barriers did you encounter, and how did you overcome them?

When we finally got my son into a speech therapy clinic, they were ready to give up after the third session, saying he wasn't making progress. I pointed out they were trying to teach him speech in a gym full of children running around screaming—the worst possible environment. The only private space was a coat closet. When they used it, he started to make progress.

(continued)

(*continued*)

We found that controlling stimulation is crucial, though it doesn't mean eliminating it entirely. It's about managing lighting, sound, and acoustics, and giving individuals choices. For someone with autism, it's like being dropped in a land where you don't speak the language. When you don't know what's happening around you, your polyvagal experiences and sensory systems are on heightened alert, making you more apt to react negatively or be scared.

What should employers consider when trying to create a more welcoming workplace for neurodivergent individuals?

It's important to train other employees about neurodiversity and accommodations. One of the biggest challenges is fear from organizations that hiring neurodivergent individuals might make other employees uncomfortable. But explaining how important it is gives everyone in the organization a sense of purpose.

From a design standpoint, the biggest issue is giving people choice and control. People on the spectrum want to do all the things others do. They just learn from their environment differently. They need different environments where they can be successful or be exposed to more interaction and social situations, which is healthy for them.

What are your thoughts on the recommendation by some organizations that people with special needs should work from home?

That's a huge misconception. Just because someone needs accommodation doesn't mean the best place for them is their home environment. That can be counterproductive to what the individual really needs. Individuals on the spectrum can benefit from being around others. They need to practice social interactions, relationships, and communication skills. Socially isolating individuals on the spectrum is very unhealthy for them.

How do you see the future of neuroinclusive design?

We're just at the tipping point of understanding how to design spaces that take away barriers. What's exciting is that we're on the brink of understanding how to make spaces restorative and start healing people.

There's great work being done by Dr. Stephen Porges, founder of the Polyvagal Theory, about how the body experiences trauma and sensory integration. For example, listening to music can reset your body and put it in a restorative state. The neurodivergent population is the prime candidate for some of these new treatments and therapies.

When we start looking at restorative space, it might be essential for people on the spectrum, but it's also beneficial for others in high-stress environments. Everyone needs some of that restorative element. It's just more of a life-and-death situation for some.

The Role of Workplace Assessment

The challenge today is the known unknowns. If asked whether their organization and spaces are designed to be neuroinclusive, most people could not answer that question because there is no clear definition of what that means. Many companies aspiring to be more inclusive do not know where to start.

A workplace assessment helps employers, HR teams, and corporate real estate and facilities professionals evaluate the current state of neuroinclusivity in their facilities. The assessment can also provide a roadmap for identifying additional planning and design elements that can help create a more inclusive work environment. This can include determining the state of existing conditions, whether they comply with best practices (and to what degree), and recommending modifications or actions needed to make spaces more accessible for a broader range of the population.

Assessment Methodology   HOK has developed an extensive list of Design Considerations (accessible in Chapter 13 via a QR code) that functions as a checklist for designing new spaces and assessing existing ones to identify potential areas to address to improve inclusion. For specific clients, our team has leveraged the tool to assess:

- Current condition for each consideration, ranked on a score from 1 to 5 (1 being poor or most noncompliant, 5 being ideal or most compliant)
- Whether making an accommodation is reasonable (yes or no)
- Whether the accommodation is actionable (yes or no)
- Recommendations for moving forward

Prioritizing Considerations   Once a primary assessment is complete, recommendations can be prioritized based on a ranking system that looks at cost, impact, and complexity of implementation. A recommendation that is high impact, low cost, and easy to implement may be given higher priority than one that is low impact, higher cost, and more complex to implement. The checklist includes an evaluation system to rank the viability of each suggestion based on the following:

- **Actionable:** Degree of difficulty in implementation
- **Effective:** Level of impact for users
- **Affordable:** Cost and financial viability
- **Aligned:** Compatibility with the organization's goals and values

The assessment and ranking helps organizations see where they stand, identify strategies to make their space more inclusive, and prioritize how to do so.

Cost Considerations

Many organizations assume making changes to their workspace to accommodate individuals with disabilities, including neurodivergent employees, will be more expensive. However, this concern is often unfounded. A recent employer survey conducted by the Job Accommodation Network (JAN) found that many accommodations employees request can be implemented for little or no cost. While this survey focused on individual accommodations, many of these solutions can inform broader inclusive design practices. The survey found that 56 percent of the accommodations cost nothing to implement, and an additional 37 percent involved only a one-time expense. Of those that did come with a cost, the median one-time expenditure was $300.[6]

The Society for Human Resource Management data shows the cost of replacing an employee can be three to four times the position's salary.[7] This means the cost of making accommodations can be far less than the cost of recruiting and training new staff.

Through inclusive design practices, we can create environments that proactively address diverse employee needs, often eliminating the need for individual accommodations later. When thoughtfully integrated into the initial design process, these inclusive features typically do not increase overall project costs. Even when specific employee needs extend beyond the built-in elements, the foundation is in place for employers and employees to make additional adjustments through an interactive process.

Client Story

Fidelity's Pioneering Approach to Inclusive Workplace Design

One of the world's leading financial services companies, Fidelity Investments, has launched an initiative to enhance the workplace with neurodiversity in mind. Althea Kearney, director of technology innovation with the Fidelity Investments Real Estate team, is guiding this effort. Kearney, an autistic woman with ADHD, leads a neurodiversity education and awareness workstream while managing her many real estate responsibilities.

The drive for more inclusive workplaces came from within Fidelity. "There was a groundswell of conversations happening at Fidelity within the community of neurodivergent associates," explains Kearney. "At the same time, we had key leaders who were in tune with these signals. Some of our leaders are personally passionate due to their own neurodivergence or because they have neurodivergent family, friends, or associates." These internal discussions, combined with insights about the benefits of customizable workplaces gained during the COVID-19 pandemic, sparked the initiative.

Fidelity's leaders created a Neurodiversity Strategy Working Team made up of leaders from its Diversity & Inclusion office and an associate-led resource group promoting positive and inclusive experiences for all,

(continued)

(continued)

especially those affected by seen or unseen disabilities. That 25-person team then began the important work of raising awareness, educating, and celebrating neurodiversity across the company community.

Neuroinclusive Design Guidelines

The Fidelity team created real estate workplace guidelines that equip Fidelity's architecture and design partners with a single source to help them readapt and reinvent their spaces. To enhance its guidelines for neuroinclusion, Christina Zwart, director of design, partnered with members of Fidelity's neurodivergent community and HOK. This collaboration focused on five key areas:

- Identifying gaps in current design guidelines related to cognitive and sensory well-being
- Developing recommendations for more welcoming and inclusive environments
- Creating planning principles and guidelines for spatial sequencing and space types to support inclusive practices
- Refining guidelines to better address cognitive and sensory well-being
- Developing design considerations to assess existing spaces for inclusive principles

The revised guidelines serve as a checklist for project teams and aid in determining whether modifications can be made to existing spaces to make them more welcoming to a larger population of individuals. These recommendations cover a variety of environmental factors including planning concepts, circulation, amenities, wayfinding, furniture, lighting, acoustics, visual elements, and materiality.

To help prioritize and implement these strategies effectively, Fidelity and HOK developed a four-level assessment system that ranks strategies based on cost, impact, and implementation timeline, ranging from immediate, low-cost changes to more substantial, long-term investments.

Kearney emphasizes the important role of variety and choice in workplace design: "We need to acknowledge that there is no single best work setting to support the near-infinite variety of human experiences and needs. Once we accept this reality, we are able to focus on providing variety and choice."

One example of this approach is the creation of Quiet Spaces. Kearney describes these as "rooms where an associate can drop in for self-regulation, meditation, or focus. These spaces allow control over sensory inputs, including ambient lighting, and offer various seating options—from comfy chairs to yoga mats or more stim-friendly seating with built-in movement."

The benefits of this inclusive approach extend far beyond neurodivergent individuals. "The beauty is that when you support neurodivergent associates, all associates benefit," notes Kearney. This philosophy informs not just physical design but also behavioral shifts and human support systems. There are simple ways to support neurodivergent associates that may not require a formal accommodation, and many of these supports are useful for all associates.

Kearney shares her personal experience: "As an autistic ADHDer (AuDHDer) associate myself, I seek out spaces that support the type of work I'm doing on a particular day. On days where I do not have tasks that require deep focus, I prefer to be in the open office setting because when I'm sitting near others, this is a proxy for body doubling, and that is very useful for the ADHD parts of my particular neurotype."

To ensure these changes resonate with the workforce, Fidelity's Neurodivergent Strategy Team worked with HOK to create day-in-the-life journey maps. These personas illustrate how different individuals might navigate and use the redesigned spaces.

These initiatives are already making a positive impact. "We're hearing feedback from many neurodivergent associates that they're seeing impacts even before a space is officially refreshed," says Kearney.

(continued)

(*continued*)

"But that's due to more than the workspace—it's also due to behavior shifts and the human supports we have introduced."

Lessons Learned

Kearney offers valuable advice for organizations looking to create more inclusive environments:

1. **Create safe spaces for sharing:** "An important step is making sure you're creating a space where associates feel safe sharing their lived experiences."
2. **Focus on impact, not diagnosis:** "Shifting our conversations to the impact of the day-to-day workplace experiences rather than diagnostic status can be helpful."
3. **Listen actively:** "If a neurodivergent individual is willing to tell you their story and put their trust in you, listen."
4. **Prioritize flexibility:** "Embrace the ambiguity of knowing there's no ideal design solution for all. When we do this, we empower people to use spaces in ways that work for them."
5. **Engage key stakeholders:** "If your organization doesn't have a neurodiversity working group that connects neurodivergent associates with key leaders, consider forming one. It's a great way to start."

Fidelity continues to prioritize the holistic associate experience, which includes refining its approach to creating neuroinclusive workplaces and celebrating the entire spectrum of neurodiversity.

13 | Design Considerations

Diversity is being invited to the party; inclusion is being asked to dance.

—Vernā Myers, diversity and inclusion consultant

Legal experts expressed a critical point at the Institute of Government & Public Policy's National Equality, Diversity, and Inclusion in the Workplace Conference in London in 2024. They stressed the importance of shifting our approach to inclusion in the built environment. Instead of focusing on specific issues, they urged that more effort be spent identifying and removing barriers.

To start reducing barriers, we need to take a more comprehensive approach. Light touches will not suffice. Just as adding an accessible restroom to a building does not make it truly barrier-free, neither will adding focus rooms or providing headphones make a space neuroinclusive. We have developed a series of recommendations to aid in addressing potential barriers in shared spaces to strive to be more inclusive and welcoming.

The Premise of Inclusive Design

The premise of inclusive design is that instead of trying to choose or change people to fit their environment, an organization can get the right people for

217

its needs—and simultaneously help them live more fulfilling lives—by changing the environment to welcome all those people who offer unique talents. To incorporate considerations for planning, zoning, and sequencing, teams should integrate inclusivity into the design of a space from the beginning of programming and conceptual design.

For many, the challenge is a lack of understanding of both their current state and how to move forward. Most organizations do not know if their workplace is neuroinclusive. There currently is no definitive way to assess this or guide how to achieve it. We hope our research and findings shared in this book help fill that gap.

Planning Concepts

The open office floor plan has come under increased scrutiny about its effectiveness as a workplace solution. It is important to note that not all open plans are created equally. Many were poorly designed to maximize efficiency, often at the cost of performance. "Open plan" is typically used as a blanket term to describe all environments that feature a uniform layout with low or no partitions or panels separating work points and assigned seats—essentially a one-size-fits-all approach. But open environments do not necessarily equate to open plan.

More than a decade ago, designers pivoted from the "cubeland" model to dynamic ecosystems that enable new ways of working:

- Activity-Based Working (ABW)
- Neighborhood-Based Choice Environments (NCE)
- Maker Environments, Mobile Occupants (MEMO)
- Environment-Based Work (EBW)

These models demonstrate more agile, purpose-driven approaches and empower people with what they want most: options, choice, variety, and control. Instead of constraining employees to a rigid setup, they provide an array of spaces to ignite productivity and innovation. By allowing for choice, individuals can find the right setting because, even if our personal sensory intelligence is poor, we instinctively will navigate to the preferred setting when given the choice.

Few employers ask their people if they have any sensory preferences when assigning them a space. Frankly, I cannot think of a single one that does. By not taking this into account, many individuals are being assigned to a work point that may not be conducive to their sensory needs. For example, if you are hypersensitive but are assigned to sit at the end of a row of work points on a main corridor that also happens to be across from a conference room and your back is exposed to an adjacent open gathering spot, your ability to function would be negatively affected. That assignment is sabotaging your ability to focus.

Given that so many of today's companies are increasing the areas for open collaboration spots, which are loud, and collocating them next to work settings designed for individual, heads-down work, both activities are sabotaging each other. Clinging to an approach that does not allow for some degree of choice and control fails a company's most valuable asset: its people.

Though open environments can have acoustic challenges, the solution is not silence. While many assume employees want quiet, a complete lack of sound can be more distracting than a consistent background hum. The real problem in modern workspaces is often insufficient ambient sound, which makes individual conversations stand out and break concentration. Effective neighborhood design creates various zones that enable different modalities of work and allow employees to manage distractions.

Concept control is a designer's ability to develop a clear concept, avoid overloading or overburdening it with superfluous elements, detail it consistently throughout the space, and execute it well. It is about avoiding overcomplication, so the concept remains clear and the space legible. Keeping things simple and controlled requires discipline and a strong foundational concept.

Activity-Based Working

Though today's knowledge workers no longer do repetitive tasks tied to one spot, many offices still promote sedentary behavior. Enter Activity-Based Working. American architect Robert Luchetti is credited with co-inventing the concept of "activity settings," a precursor to ABW, in 1983.[1] The term *activity-based working* was first coined by Erik Veldhoen, a Dutch consultant and founder of Veldhoen + Company, in his book *The Art of Working* in the early 1990s.[2] The concept was first implemented in 1995 in the Netherlands.[3]

Over the past decades, ABW has emerged as a way to offer task-driven solutions that encourage movement and empower people to choose suitable spaces for what they need to do (Figure 13.1). To design

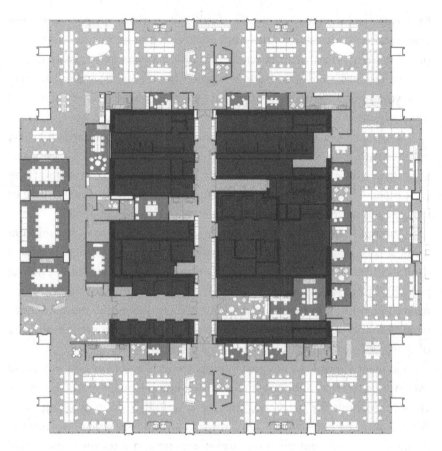

Figure 13.1 ABW planning concept

spaces that encourage movement, we need to promote a healthy and more social work environment. ABW environments typically comprise an ecosystem of spaces. Social hubs with food anchor ABW floors, surrounded by work points with phone booths and team areas. As people move more, they need flexible and task-specific solutions, not one desk per person.

Designing spaces to encourage opportunities for connection and solitude is important. Strategically locating shared amenities such as gathering spaces, social hubs, coffee bars, and printers encourages movement while enabling social connections.

Pinning employees to one spot all day is not just physically limiting—it can dull the mind. Giving employees an assigned space tethers them to that area, limiting their use of other office areas. People crave a change of scenery or a momentary break—a literal "fresh perspective."

A common misconception about free-choice (unassigned) workspaces is that people cannot sit in the same spot every day. While movement is encouraged, consistently choosing the same location is acceptable if it suits an employee or group. When people find spots that meets their functional and sensory needs, they can be more productive—even if they rarely move.

Neighborhood-Based Choice Environments

As companies sought to offer teams a home base—with a sense of belonging and identity—the Neighborhood-Based Choice Environments concept emerged. I first described this term and concept in a 2017 article for *Work-Design Magazine*.[4] This article defined what HOK had been practicing since 2014: the evolution of ABW spaces into smaller neighborhoods that afforded consistency, predictability, and a sense of belonging while still offering choice (Figure 13.2).

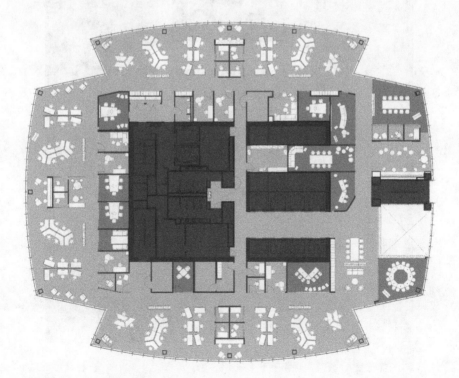

Figure 13.2 NCE planning concept

Our research shows the importance of psychological safety in workspaces. NCEs create a home for teams, balancing the need for a consistent base with the flexibility of diverse work settings. These environments promote team connectivity and belonging, helping to establish a unique team identity and promote a sense of choice and safety.

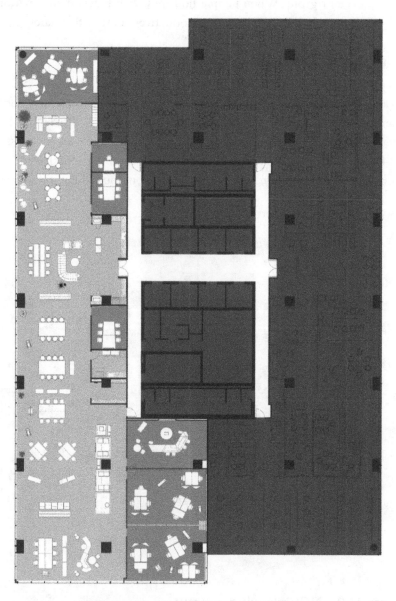

Figure 13.3 MEMO planning concept

Maker Environments, Mobile Occupants

The rise of the maker movement has been a boon to the neurodivergent community, since many are hands-on learners. Creating environments that not only allow but encourage an interactive, hands-on approach can stimulate ideas and channel the creative energy of tactile and visual learners and creators.

Most corporate offices discourage users from rearranging the settings or getting messy in the space. Maker Environments, Mobile Occupants spaces amplify creativity and accelerate innovation by embracing the garage-ification of space, encouraging individuals to experiment within and modify the space as needed. This term and concept were first described in the same 2017 *WorkDesign Magazine* article where we described other planning concepts, including NCE.[5]

MEMO spaces represent the transformation of conventional spaces into dynamic hubs reminiscent of a garage for programmers, creatives, or any employees seeking a scrum or makerspace feel (Figure 13.3). MEMO spaces are especially popular in sectors prioritizing rapid prototyping and the development of new concepts.

Environment-Based Work

Similar to ABW and NCE, Environment-Based Work provides task-driven solutions that offer occupants a variety of settings. The term *EBW* was coined by Andrew Mawson,[6] but the concept of leveraging data from sensors has been discussed since the Edge Building in Amsterdam first started using data to inform choice.[7] EBW spaces leverage technology and the Internet of Things (IoT) to provide data to occupants, enabling them to make informed decisions about where to work (Figure 13.4). These decisions are based on environmental factors such as sound levels, temperature, lighting levels, available settings, and location of colleagues.

EBW represents a more tailored, curated approach to creating human-centric, informed choices. These spaces also provide various sensory zones and support highly flexible, dynamic work.

Six Modalities of Work

Per HOK's research into workplace-related issues, workplaces should be dynamic and nimble, offering a balance of spaces that address the six work modalities: concentrate, contemplate, commune, create, congregate, and convivial.

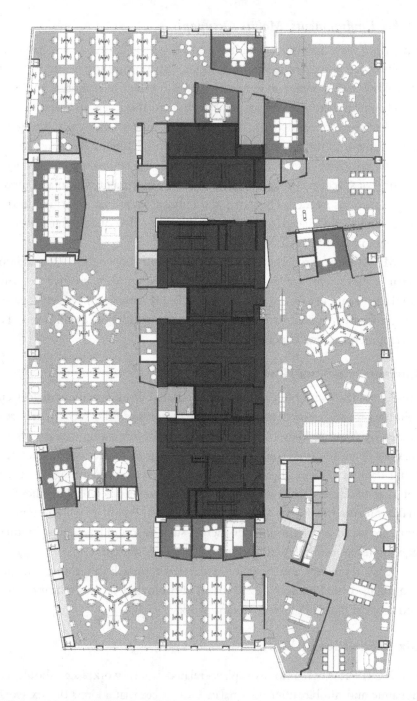

Figure 13.4   EBW planning concept

Concentrate / Focus

It is ideal to create separate spaces to meet the specific needs of hyper- and hyposensitive neurotypes (Figure 13.5). General space considerations include the following:

- Off the beaten path with limited visual distractions
- Circulation paths that discourage lingering
- Ergonomic seating and adjustable work surfaces that provide control over space
- Adjustable, dimmable lighting
- Cool, light colors. Blues, for example, have a calming effect and help with analytical thinking
- Orderly, simple patterns (if any)

Contemplate / Refresh

It is ideal to create separate spaces to meet the specific needs of hyper- and hyposensitive neurotypes (Figure 13.6). General space considerations include the following:

- Off the beaten path with limited visual distractions
- Circulation paths that discourage lingering
- Furniture that promotes sitting or lounging in a comfortable position
- Adjustable, dimmable lighting
- Access to daylight, views, and outdoor space
- Hospitality-inspired elements for comfort
- Non-busy, organic patterns
- Muted, natural colors that occur in nature (such as greens, blues, and browns) for a calming, stress-relieving environment

Communal / Process

Spaces should be designed for inclusive use but zoned with subzones to meet the specific needs of hyper- and hyposensitive neurotypes (Figure 13.7). General space considerations include the following:

- A variety of options and choice of work settings
- Access to daylight and views

Concentrative/Focus

Hyposensitive

● Space that enables movement and hands-on interaction

● Areas for doodling/ drawing

● Active spaces with fidget furniture that enables movement, such as perch seats that rock or sway, and option to stand

● Spaces with tactile elements and texture

● Views to the exterior for visual stimulation

● Semi-enclosed or shielded space

● Personal space boundaries, while not being in confined space

● Ability to self select background noise or music

Figure 13.5   Design considerations for concentrate/focus spaces

Hypersensitive

- Dropped ceiling

- Enclosed or semi-enclosed space

- Snug, personal space boundaries, in sync with human scale

- Strong acoustic controls to limit distractions

- Nature sounds have a calming effect that helps people focus

- Orderly space, clean desk policy

Contemplate/Refresh

Hyposensitive

● Semi-enclosed space

● Ability to be alone / small groups

● Add pops of contrasting color for interest

● Space that enables movement and hands-on interaction

● Tactile elements and texture

● Ability to self-select background noise or music

● Active spaces with fidget furniture that enables kinetic movement

● Ability for aromatherapy

Figure 13.6   Design considerations for contemplate/refresh spaces

Hypersensitive

■ Semi-enclosed or enclosed space to enable some shielding to control distractions

■ Dropped ceiling for intimacy

■ Ability to be alone

■ Frosting or pattern on glass to limit visibility while allowing access to daylight

■ Comfortable seating option

■ Snug, personal space boundaries, in sync with human scale

■ Reduced opportunity for clutter

Communal/Process

Hyposensitive

● Ability to self select background noise or music, headphones

● Access to tactile elements and texture

● Layering of textures and planes

● Strategic visual interest, saturated, contrasting color

● Semi-enclosed or open space

● Allow for pacing, movement

● Options for settings with fidget furniture that enable standing or movement, including perch seats that rock or sway and adjustable height points

Figure 13.7   Design considerations for communal/process spaces

Hypersensitive

◼ More orderly space, clean desk policy, reduced clutter

◼ Access to spaces in a low-traffic area

◼ Enclosed or semi-shielded space

◼ Ability to have some shielding to control distractions

◼ Circulation paths that discourage lingering

◼ Option not to have one's back to an opening or open area

◼ Moderate background noise to create a hum, consider sound masking

◼ Semi-shielding for circulation

◼ Option to have adjustable screening

- Adjustable task lighting
- Ergonomic seating options and work surfaces
- Simple color schemes with limited patterns
- Nature-inspired colors (e.g. greens and blues) for comfort and stimulation

Create

Spaces should be designed for inclusive use but zoned to meet the specific needs of hyper- and hyposensitive neurotypes (Figure 13.8). When possible, provide spaces designed specifically for hypersensitive individuals. General space considerations include the following:

- Areas for impromptu interaction
- Opportunities to reconfigure space or elements within it
- Circulation paths that enable gathering
- Access and collocation with general work zones
- Adjustable lighting: bright or natural light, with views of nature
- Curves and organic forms, minimal geometric patterns
- Limited, simple patterns
- Warm colors (yellow encourages positive thinking and energizes, which stimulates creativity)
- Spaces that encourage movement and physical interaction
- Ample surfaces for information sharing (markerboards, pin-up space, sticky notes)

Congregate

Spaces should be designed for inclusive use but zoned with subzones to meet the specific needs of hyper- and hyposensitive neurotypes (Figure 13.9). General space considerations include the following:

- Bookable spaces for scheduled gatherings and unbookable spaces for impromptu meetings
- Room sizes and proportions allowing all participants to be visible on video with clear views of shared content
- Adjustable, dimmable, zoned lighting
- Ambient lighting over tables

- Surfaces for information sharing, including markerboards and pin-up space
- Limited colors and patterns to keep focus on content
- Neutral tones with color accents for visual relief
- Limit sound transfer between adjacent spaces
- Microphones in larger spaces to ensure all can be heard
- Monitors on side walls for more equal access to the camera and microphone in hybrid meetings
- Ample personal space for distancing and movement

Convivial/Social

Spaces should be designed for inclusive use, with subzones catering to both hyper- and hyposensitive neurotypes (Figure 13.10). General space considerations include the following:

- Reconfigurable spaces and furnishings
- Wide circulation paths that encourage gathering
- Open ceilings and expansive space
- Varied lighting levels, including bright and natural options
- Curved and organic forms
- View of nature, biophilic elements, and outdoor access
- Moderate background sound or music
- Diverse seating options
- Information-sharing surfaces and digital screens
- Warm, stimulating colors

HOK's Design Considerations

Since 2016, HOK has researched neuroinclusive design and developed a comprehensive list of workplace design considerations. These are informed by our experience and collaborations with research partners, including the University of the West of Scotland, the Center for the Built Environment, and others cited in this book.

In 2022, the British Standards Institution issued PAS 6463:2022 *Design for the mind. Neurodiversity and the built environment. Guide.* While the guide addresses a wide variety of spaces, our considerations expand on the design elements specific to creating more inclusive workplaces.

Create

Hyposensitive

● Ability to self select background noise or music

● Open ceiling, expansive space

● Surfaces for doodling/drawing

● Ample space for standing and movement

● Semi-enclosed or open space

● Active spaces with fidget furniture that enables movement

● Saturated, stimulating and energizing pops of color

● Visual interest

● Tactile elements and texture

Figure 13.8 Design considerations for create spaces

Hypersensitive

■ Ambient lighting over the table

■ Moderate background 'hum', consider a sound-masking systema

■ Lower ceiling plane creates the feeling of safety, security, and belonging

■ Semi-enclosed or enclosed spaces

■ Clarity, limited clutter

■ Seating options off to the side

Congregate

Hyposensitive

● Shielded or semi-enclosed space

● Ample space to move or stand

● Fidget furniture that enables kinetic movement, such as perch seats that rock or sway

● Option for adjustable height tables to accommodate standing meetings for active engagement

● Opportunities to physically engage with space, doodle, or write

Figure 13.9   Design considerations for congregate spaces

Hypersensitive

■ Orderly space, limited clutter

■ Size room appropriately for sufficient personal space at the table

■ Semi-enclosed or enclosed space

■ If glass, use frosting or a screen to limit distractionss

■ Additional seating away from main table

Convivial/Social

Hyposensitive

● Active seating area or harvest table

● Visual interest

● Tactile sensory stimulation via elements and texture

● Options to stand and move

● Fidget furniture

● Warmer, invigorating color

Figure 13.10   Design considerations for convivial/social spaces

Hypersensitive

■ Limit visual clutter

■ Differentiate flooring to delineate side seating area, aid with acoustics, and provide comfort

■ Areas of smaller scale off to the side to enhance feeling of safety and comfort

■ Ensure acoustics aren't overwhelming

■ Dropped soffit to create more intimate space

Our considerations also draw on work by Kristi Gaines, Sally Augustin, SensoryIntelligence®, and the WELL Building Standard®. As our understanding evolves, we continue to update these guidelines to incorporate the latest insights on neurodiversity. To access and view the latest iteration of the "HOK Design Considerations," scan QR Code 13.1.

These considerations serve as a foundation for creating inclusive spaces. They also provide practical guidance for managing, renovating, and building facilities. Because the neurodivergent community is diverse, it is important to apply these considerations based on individual needs.

QR Code 13.1   HOK design considerations

Spotlight

Rachel Hodgdon Guides IWBI Toward Research-Backed Neuroinclusive Workplaces

Rachel Hodgdon is the president and CEO of the International WELL Building Institute (IWBI), where she leads a movement to advance human health through healthier buildings, more vibrant communities, and stronger, more equitable organizations. Her motto is "Always be winning for good," which she has put to work at IWBI, developing research-backed tools to help organizations create places where people can thrive. Today, these people-first places extend across more than 5 billion square feet of space in 130 countries—and growing.

Why did IWBI decide to include principles of neuroinclusion in the WELL Building Standard?

Rachel: Over the last decade, IWBI has come to understand the profound impact of WELL spaces and organizations in creating a more level playing field and equitable opportunities for all. When we were working on WELL v2, we wanted to make sure that equity was embedded into the ethos of the standard itself. For each WELL feature, we asked ourselves, "Are we seeing everyone in the creation of this feature, from the facilities manager in the basement to the person working the front desk?"

For every building that gets certified, there are hundreds of other buildings that don't but still experience the impact of the innovation that we've helped to pioneer or codify through the WELL Standard. We translate the evidence into practical, actionable strategies and incentivize their adoption through certifications, ratings, and scores.

In creating the WELL Equity Rating, our Standard Development team elected to include neurodivergent populations as a target beneficiary in addition to people with physical disabilities because there is a massive and growing population within our workplaces that is neurodivergent, as many as one in six. HOK's work on this front has helped educate us on that.

How has your understanding of neurodiversity evolved?

Like many creative professions, design and engineering historically have had higher proportions of neurodivergent individuals who think and process the world differently. Within my own organization, I've noticed that we can be quick to make judgments of individuals whose behaviors—or ways of communicating or working—are atypical. It felt like a blind spot for an organization that really prided itself on being inclusive and open-minded. I started to wonder what the impact would be of leading with curiosity as opposed to judgment.

The journey our team has been on in creating the WELL Equity Rating has driven more awareness and empathy. We've come to realize that quickness to label or judge our colleagues and collaborators isn't serving anyone.

(continued)

(*continued*)

What can organizations do to create more inclusive environments?

An inclusive environment is one that honors people for their strengths, gives them choices about how they work at their best, and approaches differences with a spirit of curiosity. We saw that designers were struggling to locate the research that could inform the creation of more inclusive workplaces. Without evidence-based best practices, there was a lot of educated guessing. We spent two years culling through the research and translating evidence into practice. The result is the WELL Equity Rating, and we hope it serves as a flexible roadmap for creating places that foster a sense of belonging.

What are your thoughts on designing for neuroinclusion in the built environment?

One of our most important learnings to date is that designing neuroinclusive environments begins with arming people with insight into the working conditions that allow them to perform at their best and giving them choices as to where, how, and even when they work. Providing options is one of the most important strategies for supporting neuroinclusive environments.

The impact of improvements made to workspaces will be limited without supportive policies and culture. I believe there are more ways for workplace designers to encourage clients to adopt supportive policies to help them get the most out of the spaces they so intentionally design. While designers don't typically drive policy decisions for their clients, they can be more proactive in informing or motivating policy shifts. The more people experience how powerful interventions that sit at the intersection of policy and place can be, the more they will continue to invest in them.

14

The Three-Legged Stool

Too often the neurodivergent are noted as under-performing. Feedback is often focused on what the individual needs to do in order to improve, instead of looking at environmental factors which could be limiting their ability to be successful.

—Helen Needham, neurodiversity advocate and
Me. Decoded founder

As designers, our expertise is creating physical environments. However, we believe creating truly inclusive environments requires a three-legged stool approach. While we are not HR specialists or medical professionals, we believe organizations should embrace this comprehensive approach, which includes the following:

Leg One: Addressing Operational Strategies
- Focuses on HR practices, onboarding, and organizational policies
- Involves collaboration with HR professionals, neurodiversity advocates, and operational advisors

Leg Two: Designing an Inclusive Built Environment
- Aims to create physical spaces that support diverse needs and work styles
- Involve design professional

243

Leg Three: Addressing Individual Needs
- Allows for personal accommodations within the workplace
- Requires input from various professionals, including occupational therapists, advocates, coaches, and neurodivergents themselves.

When we approach inclusion as a holistic process, our chances for success likely improve. If we address only the operational side and not the environment, it is like putting freshwater fish in saltwater. Conversely, if we address only the environment without addressing operational and organizational aspects, we may still be setting people up for failure. Even if we tackle both operational and environmental factors, the spectrum of needs is so wide and diverse that without allowing for individual adjustments, we are unlikely to get it right.

No single individual or organization has all the answers. As designers, we need to collaborate closely with a wide range of professionals including HR experts, operational advisors, occupational therapists, coaches, and advocates. This collaboration allows us all to leverage our unique skill sets to work together and create holistic solutions.

Leg One: Addressing Operational Strategies

Many neurodivergents face challenges while transitioning into the workforce. These barriers include lack of coordination between organizations, not having the necessary information to navigate the transition process, unfamiliarity with job placement agencies, and the absence of qualified staff to work with young adults during transition.[1]

As design professionals, our expertise lies in how the built environment affects individuals. We are not operational experts or HR professionals, so we defer to experts in those fields who excel at offering advice on operational strategies. For example:

- In the United Kingdom, the Trades Union Congress (TUC) has several good reference guides that address inclusion per neurotype.[2]
- Lyric Rivera, author of *Workplace Neurodiversity Rising 2.0*, addresses workplace surveys, education, and best practices for inclusion.

- Ludmila N. Praslova, PhD, author of *The Canary Code: A Guide to Neurodiversity, Dignity, and Intersectional Belonging at Work*, addresses multiple aspects of workplace inclusion, from the interview process through operational strategies.

During our research, surveys, discussions, and workshops over the past several years, we have learned a lot about the importance of operational strategies as part of an inclusive approach. We will share some of those insights here.

Developing Operational Strategies for Inclusion

Creating an inclusive workplace starts with broadening the group of individuals welcomed into your organization. This requires companies to look at how they recruit, assess, interview, and onboard individuals, and how they prepare their managers and teams to be welcoming. HOK has found that organizations looking to create internal neurodiversity programs often develop an approach that includes the following:

- A targeted recruitment process to identify neurodivergent candidates
- A hiring and assessment process specifically designed to match the user group, often done with the guidance of an agency specializing in neurodiverse employment
- An onboarding program, with coaches if needed, to aid in the immersion
- Buy-in and support from leadership, managers, and workforce
- A targeted educational program for all: neurodivergent employees, managers, and colleagues
- Supportive career services and job coaching

Top Operational Strategies

HOK's survey respondents over the past few years have identified the following actions they would like to see from their employers:

- Awareness training to help staff understand neurodiversity among colleagues

- Flexible work policies that allow employees to work from home
- Flex hours so staff can work during off-hours with minimal distractions
- Ability to have intermittent breaks between tasks
- Having clear action points and assignments
- Ability to book meeting rooms for concentration
- Noise-canceling headphones to reduce auditory distractions

Many offices have unwritten rules and expectations that can be difficult to navigate—especially for neurodivergents, who can be strict rule followers.[3,4] To address this, it is important to provide proper, clear documentation of expectations.

Workplace Accommodations and Flexibility

Neurodivergents are often the first and the most acutely impacted by sensory stimuli. But they are not the only ones affected. When someone requests accommodation, rather than focusing on the cost to address it, consider how many people are being negatively impacted—and what it will cost you if you do not act. The canary is singing. Are you listening?

Katy Hall, an advocate for women in construction and neurodiversity, shared 10 tips on LinkedIn to boost productivity for ADHDers.[5] Her advice advocates for approaches that often challenge conventional wisdom on how to be productive. Delayed starts, encouraging multitasking, and tackling big items later in the day are all things we have heard for years as pitfalls to avoid. Yet Hall shares that these tips have made her far more satisfied and productive in her own work. Regardless of what others think or say, it is important to find what works for you. There is no single right way to work.

Asynchronous communication tools can be effective in enabling individuals to work at their own pace. Shared documents allow people to see each other's contributions without the stress of merging different versions. Virtual collaboration can empower individuals who often feel overwhelmed by dominant personalities, allowing them to be more active in meetings and contribute by raising hands or using chat functions.

Another strategy to accommodate different preferences is designating specific hours for low and high sensory events or activities. For example, Fridays, when most offices are less populated, could be ideal for those with a heightened sensitivity to dense spaces, busy workplaces, or close proximity to others. Conversely, individuals who thrive in buzzy, active spaces might prefer coming in on shared office days, working in social zones, and avoiding low-energy areas.

Recruiting, Hiring, and Onboarding

In the United Kingdom, City & Guilds Foundation is attempting to remove barriers to employment, celebrating best practices on the job, and advocating for inclusion. The City & Guilds Neurodiversity Index 2024[6] shares findings from their latest employment study from the perspective of both employees and employers and offers practical advice for operational inclusion. It also provides a guide to the recruitment and interview process.

Companies are also catering to the needs of neurodivergent applicants by providing accommodative application procedures and increasing accessible features on their websites. Yet even though companies are striving to be more neuroinclusive, a recent study showed that only 23 percent of HR professionals and just 29 percent of senior leaders had received training related to neurodiversity, leaving many ill-equipped to adopt a holistic approach.[7]

HOK and the International Well Building Institute (IWBI) cohosted a workshop on neuroinclusion in New York City. The session brought together more than 40 people in the design community, neurodivergents, HR professionals, neuroinclusion advocates, and environmental and organizational psychologists. One of the most important elements that workshop participants identified to aid with the successful transition of neurodivergents into the workforce is providing a guide. For some, that might be a personal guide or coach, either temporary or permanent. For others, an electronic version of a sherpa can be leveraged to help individuals organize their life and daily tasks.

Leg Two: Designing an Inclusive Built Environment

Neurodivergent employees may require reasonable accommodations to help them work at their full potential. According to a study by Chapman University, one of the challenges for neurodivergents was "finding a work environment that is supportive of a person with a disability."[8] Fifty percent of study participants shared that they received some accommodations from their employer.

There is no obligation for anyone to disclose their condition or disability to an employer. This is a deeply personal choice. In many cases, however, some of the legislative protections most applicable to the day-to-day work environment depend on an individual requesting accommodation.

A Harris Poll by Understood.org found the following[9]:

- 69 percent of respondents knew that the ADA requires employers to provide reasonable accommodations to employees with disabilities.
- 60 percent noted the stigma involved with requesting support.
- 85 percent agreed that accommodations contribute to workplace equality.
- 83 percent noted that accommodations make the workplace better for all.
- 60 percent of neurodivergent respondents did not know what type of accommodations they were entitled to.
- 49 percent did not know how to request a workplace accommodation from their company.
- 59 percent worry that disclosing their needs would adversely affect their career.
- 23 percent of respondents who had asked for an accommodations reported they lost their job or were demoted as a result.

Birkbeck's *Neurodiversity at Work 2023* survey[10] inquired about barriers faced by individuals in disclosing their neurodivergence. Most respondents, 64.7 percent, said they worried about stigma and discrimination from management, while 55 percent had similar concerns about their colleagues. Additionally, 40.5 percent pointed to the lack of supportive and knowledgeable staff as a barrier. Only 11.3 percent reported that they did not experience any barriers.

Leg Three: Enabling Individual Adjustments

Even if you address operational issues and create more inclusive environments, you may not be able to completely meet the vast variety of needs without providing individuals the ability to make personal adjustments. Being neurodivergent in a neurotypical world is not for the faint of heart. It takes courage to own who you are, advocate for yourself, and value your strengths so others will, too.

Top Individual Adjustments

Respondents from HOK's various surveys have identified the following as the top individual adjustments to consider:

- Use visual checklists to track progress.
- If working in an open space, choose a low-traffic area.
- Avoid getting stuck in a daily routine. Schedule breaks and make slight changes to your days.
- Use visual timelines to track dates and break down assignments.
- Break tasks into manageable pieces.
- Perform one task at a time. When possible, do not start a new task until you complete the current one.
- Only attend critical meetings, as defined by your supervisor's interpretation, where you can maintain focus.
- Alter shifts and break times.
- Give advance warning of any changes.
- Have regular meetings with a manager, buddy, or mentor.

Birkbeck's Neurodiversity at Work 2023 survey[11] asked neurodivergents about adjustments they would like to make. Their responses included the following:

- Having a flexible schedule
- Being able to work remotely
- Having a private workspace when required
- Access to dual screens
- Being able to control noise levels

Additional Considerations

Other strategies to consider include the following:

- Starting with easy tasks to gain a sense of accomplishment
- Writing or scheduling reminders
- Turning off phones and other electronic notifications
- Giving yourself extra time to complete tasks

On a Personal Note: A Second Chance

As a designer, I often attend the International Facility Management Association's (IFMA) World Workplace Conference. In fall 2022, I was at IFMA's national conference in Nashville, where I was getting ready to speak on designing for neurodiversity and inclusion with a colleague. A woman approached me and wanted to share the impact of a presentation I'd given a few years earlier on the same topic. She told me that before my previous presentation, she had been on a call with colleagues discussing a "problem" employee. Although he was highly intelligent and had fresh insights, he tended to be disengaged or disruptive in meetings. They had tried to counsel him but had finally come to the difficult decision that he just wasn't fitting in, and they needed to let him go.

Immediately after that call, she attended my presentation on neurodiversity. As I described the attributes of neurodivergent individuals—their amazing skills, the challenges they face, and how they are often perceived as having behavioral issues—her internal alarm bells started to go off. She realized her colleague fit that description and they had not been addressing the situation the right way.

She listened intently to the rest of my presentation and then rushed out to call off the termination. Instead, she circled back with her team, HR, and the employee and had a different conversation about what did and didn't work for him and how they could help him contribute more successfully. The adjustments were fairly simple: excusing him from meetings he didn't need to be in, recording sessions so he could play them back later, allowing him to stand or write on a board during meetings, and creating planned opportunities for his input.

These adjustments made their meetings more successful for everyone, especially him. Today, he has proven to be one of their most successful employees. She said she was delighted to have the opportunity to share this story with me. I was even more delighted to hear it.

When people act differently from what we perceive as the norm, we might just be misunderstanding their needs. But if we approach these situations with curiosity instead of judgment, asking questions instead of acting, we often find simple reasons and solutions.

Spotlight

Breaking Barriers for Neurodivergent Workers with Scott Gibson

Scott Gibson is chief operating officer (COO) at Melwood, an organization that advocates for and empowers people with disabilities by expanding opportunities to work and thrive in the community. As COO, Gibson shapes Melwood's long-term strategic objectives, helping the organization respond to market changes and drive service innovation.

How did you become involved in disability inclusion work?

Scott: Growing up, I had a favorite uncle with a congenital condition that caused him to lose mobility over his life. I saw him go from having a career at Martin Marietta and being a talented musician to struggling to find purpose. At the time, the workplace was not well-equipped to accommodate him.

I started as a family advocate. Since I had a policy background and volunteered for disability organizations, I was recruited to join Melwood. That's when I started to see a disparity in our progress. While we were making great strides on physical accessibility, we languished in the areas of neuroinclusivity and accessibility for what I'll call the "invisible disabilities."

What sparked your interest in neurodiversity specifically?

Dr. Hala Annabi, an associate professor in the Information School at the University of Washington, shared a scholarly report that raised my awareness. The report suggested that if you were

(continued)

(*continued*)

autistic without an intellectual disability, you were three times less likely to be employed than if you were autistic with an intellectual disability. That got me thinking about the underserved middle—folks who aren't disabled enough to receive support services. They're getting through college and are very capable, but they're facing huge barriers to employment. They're falling through the cracks.

Can you tell us about Melwood's history and evolution?

Melwood started in 1963, serving individuals with intellectual and developmental disabilities. Back then, institutional care was still the main path in life for adult children with these disabilities. Most of our founding parents had pediatricians tell them they should put their children in an institutional care setting because their kids were "untrainable and unemployable." We were created by parents who refused to accept that for their kids.

Over 60 years, we've seen so much evolve around our understanding of disability, particularly intellectual or developmental disability. The challenges have changed. It's no longer about just putting somebody in any job. It's about finding a career of their choosing. But the employment process just isn't built for them, and there's enough of a barrier that we need to focus our attention there.

What is the most significant barrier to employment for neurodivergent individuals?

The biggest barrier is lack of education and awareness, which can happen even when you are well aware. Melwood is a pretty aware organization, and we had a training program where a young participant kept wincing every 30 minutes. You could see this clear look of pain when our HVAC was clicking on and creating a whistling sound that wasn't audible to any of us. But she was hypersensitive in her auditory function and was hearing it.

Many employers don't know what the potential triggers are. We'll never be able to address everything, but it's important to create an environment where people feel comfortable raising issues so you can better understand their experience and take steps to mitigate issues.

How can employers create more inclusive environments?

We need to focus more on inviting the conversation of "Are you comfortable?" I've experienced situations where the solution to comfort was as simple as switching which side of the table we were sitting on.

One thing I've been thinking about, based on a comment you made during your Congressional testimony, is how we need to offer a variety of spaces so people can pick what works for them by facilitating a better culture of sharing.

What are your thoughts on the increase in autism diagnoses in recent years?

Much of it stems from legislation in the 1990s when we started better supporting children in public schools. Parents and pediatricians were incentivized to figure out autism and developmental disability diagnoses earlier because more resources were attached to the child once formally diagnosed. So, I think we're diagnosing more people than we were catching in the past, not because more people have it, but because we're more open to diagnosing it and much better at diagnosing it.

Now that one in 40 children are diagnosed as autistic, it is becoming more common and more personal. You're going to meet people you know in your life. That has started to change the conversation.

We still aren't good at diagnosing women. There's a medical bias that made it easier to diagnose in boys. The increase in diagnosis in children is among the leading causes of diagnosis for women

(continued)

(continued)

right now. When previously undiagnosed autistic women are talking to their pediatrician about their child, many are realizing they are facing similar challenges and then having conversations with their own doctor.

How has the concept of neurodiversity affected public perception?

The neurodiversity paradigm has allowed more people to relate to it. While they may not be distinctly neurodivergent, they're recognizing they are impacted by sensory stimuli as well. This could be dangerous if it gets overplayed, but it has increased awareness overall.

Do specific industries or professions attract more neurodivergent individuals?

I don't know if some industries or professions attract more neurodivergents or if they're just more likely to enable neurodivergents to thrive. For example, we hear a lot about neurodivergent people in tech. I don't believe neurodivergent people aspire to tech jobs at greater rates than anyone else. I do, however, believe the tech industry has been better at accommodating many common stressors for neurodivergent individuals and at leveraging the strengths of neurodistinct cognitive function.

15 | Going Forward

We are all different, not less.

— Temple Grandin, American academic

The World Health Organization has deemed neurological disorders among the greatest threats to public health without immediate, coordinated action by planners and health professionals.[1] To address the needs of the growing number of neurodivergents, we need to create inclusive spaces that enable them to fully engage and contribute to society.

To do so, we need to remove the barriers in the built environment and address how sensory elements impact not just neurominorities, but all of us. In collaboration with leading experts, we have identified key trends that will play a pivotal role in shaping the neurodivergent workplace in the future:

- **Growing awareness, increasing diagnoses, and demographic shifts** will elevate the need to address the growing number of people on the spectrum and more comprehensively address their needs within society, the healthcare system, and the built environment.
- **Technological developments** will enhance our ability to identify diverse neurological profiles, improve our understanding of our unique cognitive profiles, and enable us to customize interventions to boost quality of life. These advances will also provide more viable solutions for interaction with both the physical and digital worlds.

- The **changing landscape of work and business dynamics** will transform not only work tasks and processes but also when and where we work and under what conditions we do so.

Many of these themes are intertwined, and we are living in a time of rapid evolution and discovery. While priorities and needs will continue to shift, these trends will all play a role in shaping the future for the neurodivergent community.

Growing Awareness and Increasing Diagnosis

With increased awareness around neurodistinct profiles and a growing number of individuals who identify as such, there is increased pressure to address the needs of neurominorities more comprehensively. Neurodivergent employees have proven to be an asset for many companies when put into the right situation.

As labor shortages challenge business continuity, the untapped talent of the neurodivergent community is an obvious part of the solution. But we need to ensure we set them up for success, and a world designed for neurotypicals presents obstacles we need to remove. This means addressing their operational, environmental, and personal needs.

Nancy Doyle highlights the evolving landscape: "Increased awareness of neurodiversity has led to better diagnoses—prevalence rates have consistently been masked by misdiagnosis of mental health issues and this continues to be so though less than 20 years ago."[2]

Doyle predicts that the increasing neurodiversity diagnoses will trigger a shift in the dynamics of the workplace. With 15–20 percent of the population the identifying as neurodivergent, she says "inclusion will have to move beyond tokenism and into a more radically redesigned workplace that has removed systemic barriers."[3]

A 2024 report by the CDC showed a rise in the number of diagnoses of ADHD among adults in the U.S., reporting that approximately 15.5 million adults had an ADHD diagnosis in 2023. That is the equivalent of approximately 6 percent of U.S. adults.[4]

Demographic Shifts and Environmental Factors

Changing demographics and environmental factors may be impacting the number of people classified as neurodivergent.[5] Research suggests that potential contributing factors for the increase in neurodivergent conditions include improved awareness, broader diagnostic criteria, and possible environmental influences.[6,7] Genetic factors play a big role. For example, it is estimated that between 64–91 percent of autism can be attributed to inherited genetic factors.[8]

Researchers are studying potential links between autism and having either older parents, problematic births, or infections in pregnancy.[9] Parents conceiving children later in life, elevated exposure to pollution from expanding urbanization and environmental conditions, and the proliferation of chronic diseases such as obesity and diabetes are some of the patterns that may be impacting the rise in numbers of diverse neurotypes.

While environmental factors may aggravate underlying genetic factors, they are less likely to be significant contributors. The impact of these factors is still not fully understood, but scientific advances will bring more clarity.

With life expectancy increasing and the retirement ages trending upward across high-income countries, workplaces will continue to have a vital role in our overall quality of life. Combined with rising diagnosis rates, this highlights the need for workplaces to prepare for a more neurodivergent workforce in the years to come.

Spotlight

Tommaso Davi's Insights on Neurodiversity in the Workplace

Tommaso Davi is a neurodivergent entrepreneur, researcher, and advocate dedicated to fostering more neuro-equitable organizations and societies. As the founder of Neuro-Sive, he operates at the intersection of digital technology, education, and transformational change.

What was your journey to becoming an advocate for neuroinclusion?

Tommaso: Much of it started during my research work with a kind of "aha" moment, when I came across the first release of the HOK report that you authored titled "Designing a Neurodiverse Workplace." You discussed challenges experienced by

(continued)

(continued)

neurodivergent individuals in the workplace and offered case studies and insights on best practices for recognizing and overcoming them.

As I read it, I recognized some of what I now identify as my own sensory processing behaviors and preferences impacting my life daily. This led me to question whether I had a neurodivergent brain. For instance, compared to others, I am highly sensitive to certain kinds of lights and buzzing noises.

I am naturally curious. At the time, I was lucky to be able to embark on a journey of self-discovery to better understand the functioning of my own brain. As with many others, for years I had been unaware of being a neurodivergent person.

It was only at age 35 that my diagnostic path helped validate my intuition and make sense of the arc of events that had shaped my journey up to that day. I felt great relief in realizing by the end of the process that my brain is autistic, experiences dyscalculia, and retains high cognitive abilities in its functioning.

Can you talk about the work you are doing now?

I am working on a new startup project, Neuro-Sive. Its work concerns blueprinting and developing solutions to tackle diverse needs and opportunities that are often difficult for organizations to express or identify accurately in their entirety. These needs often start to be noticed as their "tips" emerge and are directly dependent on either cognitive or sensory functioning differences—or both.

Neuro-Sive's work is technology-informed and culture-driven, as well as multidisciplinary in nature. This is because we are dealing with problems connected to the necessity of finding new cultural and organizational meanings under the lens of neurodiversity to act on current opportunities and challenges. We're considering the progressively more neurodiverse workforce on one hand, and on the other, the increasing demand for designing products, services, and environments responding to the emergent neurodiverse needs.

We are in the process of blueprinting one of the first GenAI-powered apps that democratize access to sensory behavioral data. This app, named Project NATA, will enable first-time profiling of personal sensory processing and dependent behaviors, providing customized individual recommendations to help users understand and maintain their sensory well-being.

To what do you attribute the raised awareness for neurodiversity?

Over the past decade, we've seen the convergence of several cultural, social, and technological transformations paired with unprecedented events. There's been a progressive surge in neurodivergence diagnoses and mental health conditions, particularly in the Western hemisphere. The global pandemic has also played a role, during which we developed a more prominent social awareness about mental health and cognitive and sensory diversity.

Today, we are living in a "brain-aware society" overall. In the coming decade, this society will seek to significantly advance its design and planning capabilities for brain-related needs across all societal forms and functions.

This trend is set to continue, and we are only at the beginning of our journey toward creating a neuro-equitable society.

What else do we need to keep in mind when designing a workplace for inclusion?

At Neuro-Sive, we're deeply concerned with finding new meanings for existing cognitive-dependent challenges and opportunities. This approach offers the best chance to create projects and product designs that truly support the multidimensional needs of our brains, which are not static but neuroplastic, changing in response to bio-psycho-social experiences. It's a balancing act between planning for long-term experiences and solving short-term necessities, but when done properly, it can unlock great rewards and opportunities.

Technological Developments

As neuroscience and technology evolve, an array of new tools is reshaping how organizations can support employees with diverse cognitive styles in more inclusive work environments.

Digital Tools and Communications

Mobile devices and tablets already have a huge impact on the ability of neurodivergents to communicate on their terms and in a manner that best suits them. New interfaces and advances in technology are opening avenues for communication, expression, and interaction. Autistic YouTube personality Carly Fleischmann is an example of how tech tools can help. "Once considered a non-verbal, low-functioning autistic person," she now uses a digitally synthesized voice to host her own online talk show.[10]

Up to 30 percent of autistic people may be nonspeaking.[11] Alternative and Augmented Communication (AAC) technology enables many in the non-speaking community to find their "voice" and communicate effectively.

Tools like closed captioning, meeting recordings, eye-tracking readers, and interactive extended reality (XR) are improving opportunities for engagement and challenging misconceptions about intellectual abilities.

Neuroprosthetics

Neuroprosthetics show promise for enabling new interventions to assist or replace visual, auditory, and motor functioning and processing.[12] These breakthroughs will give us a better understanding of our cognitive profiles and how neurodivergents process information, interact with their surroundings, and achieve success in various environments.

AI and Workplace Assistance

AI-powered tools may prove to be invaluable for neurodivergents.[13] AI chatbots can provide personalized assistance for managing daily activities, reducing stress, and staying on task. AI can aid in work tasks like checking spelling, organizing tasks, and providing meeting transcripts. Widespread adoption of AI tools may also help reduce the stigma often associated with assistive tools.

AI–powered building sensors can provide real–time data for automated environmental adjustments including changing the lighting level, reducing glare, adjusting the temperature, and providing the desired sound levels to create a more comfortable and calming work environment.

Changing Landscape

New organizational structures, flattened hierarchies, tech–connected staff, and the emergence of hybrid working give individuals and organizations opportunities to embrace new ways of working. These new work patterns will expand opportunities for neurominorities to participate in more diverse teams and find the right work culture and environment. The ongoing growth of freelance work and the gig economy means employers may need to reconsider strategies for motivating and enhancing the well–being of all employees.

Remote and Hybrid Work

Remote work allows some to contribute who previously were unable to, creating new opportunities for them. But it also has brought new challenges for neurominorities.

The COVID–19 pandemic presented distinct challenges for ADHDers. The loss of routine and structure, isolation, being in confined quarters, concerns about health issues, and for adults, the added pressure of having to monitor their children while juggling their work and daily responsibilities all contributed to heightened challenges. For many, those additional burdens made their challenges more acute and heightened their awareness of their difficulties. This increased awareness may be a factor in the recent rise in ADHD diagnoses.

The pandemic lockdowns had a lasting impact on sensory sensitivities. Many individuals reported increased challenges related to noise and proximity after working in isolation for long periods of time. S. Thomas Carmichael, professor and chair of the neurology department at UCLA's David Geffen School of Medicine, suggests that extended remote work has weakened our ability to focus and filter out distractions. He recommends a solution that those who prefer working from home may not appreciate: spending more time in the office.[14]

Working remotely in an environment tailored for their specific needs allows individuals with sensory sensitivities to be active members of the workforce. Some employers now consider remote work as part of their ecosystem of space solutions. Its appropriateness, however, depends on specific job requirements. Not all positions can be performed effectively from home, and employers must evaluate requests for remote work on a case-by-case basis.

Remote work is not better for everyone. The inability to disconnect can add to stress levels.[15] Distractions found at home, isolation, lack of energy, or loss of direction make remote work unsuitable for some people. Additionally, certain job functions require on-site presence or collaboration.

Nancy Doyle, writing about the impact of COVID-19 remote work, notes, "Interestingly, ADHDers found the lack of structure disorientating and so our typical difficulties with time management and prioritization became disabling. Anxiety and self-consciousness over reading body language and tone was exacerbated by the lack of in person conversation and informal knowledge transfer."[16]

A Skynova survey of more than 1,000 workers with ADHD shows those working remotely found daily tasks 17 percent more challenging and were 54 percent more likely to struggle with impulse control than on-site colleagues.[17]

Exposure therapies, or psychological treatments that help people confront their anxieties and fears, may help some readjust to shared spaces. While various exposure therapies can be effective for conditions often associated with neurodivergence (such as social anxiety disorder[18] and obsessive-compulsive disorder[19]), this approach should be carefully tailored and monitored to avoid heightening stress. What works for one person may not work for another, and while some people might be more effective working remotely, this must be balanced against job functions and business needs.

The ability to visually and physically connect in shared environments can support team dynamics and help determine if there are any budding concerns. In our experience, people also want to feel like they are connected to something bigger than themselves, and that they have a shared sense of purpose and belonging.

There are also concerns about inequity and siloes between on-site and remote workers. Proximity bias, which occurs when people in power tend to treat those physically closer to them more favorably,[20] may lead to inequities between remote and in-office employees. This could potentially entrench deeper racial, gender, and neurotype divides. In 2023, fully remote workers received promotions 31 percent less frequently than their in-office or hybrid counterparts, according to one study.[21] Eight-seven percent of chief executives admitted they favored employees who come into the office for promotions and salary increases.[22]

While remote work might be a good option for some neurodivergent employees, it should not be viewed as the default or only solution. There are significant opportunities to create workplaces that are more inclusive for a greater number of individuals, going beyond patchwork solutions. We must take a more holistic approach to designing and addressing the built environment while considering both employee needs and business requirements.

Work Schedules

If we acknowledge that people communicate and work differently, we need to accept that optimal work times may also vary for individuals. While some people work best in the morning, others are night owls. Some prefer short spurts, while others are marathon workers. For neurodivergents, affordances related to their work schedule can be a critical factor in not only their ability to be successful, but even in their ability to remain employed.

Sixty-one companies in the U.K. participated in a six-month trial of the four-day workweek that included over 3,300 employees. Of those companies, 92 percent continued with the four-day week after the pilot ended, and 18 companies made the change permanent. Belgium became the first European country to legislate a four-day week in 2022.[23] Germany and Portugal are also experimenting with this model.

Many are embracing the 100:80:100 model—"100 per cent of the pay for 80 per cent of the time, in exchange for a commitment to maintaining at least 100 per cent productivity."[24] Several other companies are experimenting with a reduced workweek. Some organizations may be considering providing flexibility in workload, such as working reduced or part-time hours.

More Comprehensive Approach

It is not enough to acknowledge our differences. Nor is it enough to be included but not embraced, or embraced but not enabled. We need to go all in, taking a holistic approach to create a systemic method for operationalizing, designing, and empowering inclusion.

Inclusion requires a long-term commitment. It takes rigor, continuous evaluation, a willingness to remain flexible, and the adoption of best practices for inclusive organizations. Perhaps it is time to reframe the issue and think more about assessing everyone's sensory and cognitive profiles—not just those of neurodivergents—so we can truly know ourselves, understand others, and create situations and environments where all can thrive.

We need to acknowledge that not everyone works in an office. Not everyone works in an office. Many work in the service industry, manufacturing facilities, or other locations. We need to address neuroinclusion in all built environments—transportation hubs, schools, colleges and universities, shopping malls, healthcare centers, sports venues, and urban spaces.

While this book focuses on workspaces, it lays the foundation for addressing inclusion across all types of complex buildings. HOK's market sector leaders in Civic + Justice, Science + Technology, Sports + Recreation + Entertainment, and Healthcare are expanding these principles into their client work, creating a more inclusive world. We are also engaging with university design programs to integrate principles of inclusion into their curriculum.

Afterword
Call to Action

Neurodivergent individuals have the power to change the world.
We just need to give them the opportunity to do so.
—Steve Silberman, neurodiversity advocate

There is a compelling human and business case to be made for ensuring that we approach the design of all workspaces to address mindfulness, health, safety, well-being, and inclusivity. As the stigma associated with neurodiversity diminishes and more people acknowledge the benefits of inclusivity, employers will encounter more existing staff, applicants, and customers who are neurodivergent. The time has come for us to address the needs of neurodivergents in the workplace and design spaces that are inclusive for all.

It is time to take a more comprehensive approach to how we design space so we are truly addressing the sensory needs of the population we are designing for and individuals are not forced to find ways to cope. For neurominorities, masking and coping are all too common and can be both physically and mentally taxing. By incorporating best practices for inclusive design, we can create environments where all can thrive because "when we design for the extreme, we benefit the mean."

On a Personal Note: In Memory of Steve Silberman

> By sharing the stories of their lives, they discovered that many of the challenges they face daily are not "symptoms" of their autism, but hardships imposed by a society that refuses to make basic accommodations for people with cognitive disabilities as it does for people with physical disabilities such as blindness and deafness.
>
> —Steve Silberman, *Neuro Tribes: The Legacy of Autism and the Future of Neurodiversity*

In the summer of 2024, I was invited to participate in a panel discussion about designing for neuroinclusion. One of my fellow panelists was Steve Silberman, renowned author of *Neuro Tribes*. Co-authored with Oliver Sacks in 2016, the book reframed how we talk about neurodiversity and is considered essential reading for those interested in understanding the lived experience of neurodivergents.

The day before the scheduled panel, we gathered one last time to prep for our session and Steve, not one for slides, shared his notes. On the day of our panel, we all joined the call and were ready to go live, but Steve was missing. We learned the tragic news that Steve had suddenly passed away the night before. We were all in shock and immediately decided to postpone so we could absorb this news and regroup.

In the following days, numerous tributes were posted to honor Steve's work and dedication to advocating for the autistic community—all well-deserved. Several weeks later, we did regroup. As a tribute, we began our panel by sharing the words Steve had written in his last days. To ensure we carried the torch forward, we all presented our perspectives on the topic and promised to continue the work Steve had so powerfully influenced. It is my hope that this book serves as another worthy continuation of his legacy.

Notes

Preface

1. U.S. Centers for Disease Control and Prevention, "Disability Impacts All of Us," CDC.gov, accessed October 28, 2024, https://www.cdc.gov/ncbddd/disabilityandhealth/infographic-disability-impacts-all.html.
2. Ibid.
3. Yang-Tan Institute on Employment and Disability at the Cornell University ILR School, *2018 Disability Status Report: United States*, accessed October 28, 2024, https://www.disabilitystatistics.org/StatusReports/2018-PDF/2018-StatusReport_US.pdf.
4. United Nations, "Universal Declaration of Human Rights," (1948), accessed June 27, 2024, https://www.un.org/en/about-us/universal-declaration-of-human-rights.

Chapter 1

1. Centers for Disease Control and Prevention, "Disability Impacts All of Us," U.S. Department of Health and Human Services, accessed September 23, 2024, https://www.cdc.gov/ncbddd/disabilityandhealth/infographic-disability-impacts-all.html.
2. Disabled World, "Invisible Disabilities: List and General Information," last updated May 1, 2023, https://disabled-world.com/disability/types/invisible/.

3. Nancy Doyle, "Neurodiversity at Work: A Biopsychosocial Model and the Impact on Working Adults," *British Medical Bulletin* 135, no. 1 (September 2020): 108–125, https://doi.org/10.1093/bmb/ldaa021.

4. National Institutes of Health, "Scientists Build Largest Maps to Date of Cells in Human Brain," October 31, 2023, https://nih.gov/news-events/nih-research-matters/scientists-build-largest-maps-date-cells-human-brain.

5. Samuel R. Chamberlain et al., "ADHD Symptoms in Non-Treatment Seeking Young Adults: Relationship with Other Forms of Impulsivity," *CNS Spectrums* 22, no. 1 (February 2017): 22–30, https://doi.org/10.1017/S1092852915000875.

6. R. de Graaf et al., "The Prevalence and Effects of Adult Attention-Deficit/Hyperactivity Disorder (ADHD) on the Performance of Workers: Results from the WHO World Mental Health Survey Initiative," *Occupational and Environmental Medicine* 65, no. 12 (December 2008): 835–42, https://doi.org/10.1136/oem.2007.038448.

7. Anselm B. M. Fuermaier et al., "ADHD at the Workplace: ADHD Symptoms, Diagnostic Status, and Work-Related Functioning," *Journal of Neural Transmission* 128, no. 7 (July 2021): 1021–31, https://doi.org/10.1007/s00702-021-02309-z.

8. Amy L. Accardo, Nancy M. H. Pontes, and Manuel C. F. Pontes, "Heightened Anxiety and Depression Among Autistic Adolescents with ADHD: Findings From the National Survey of Children's Health 2016–2019," *Journal of Autism and Developmental Disorders* (November 3, 2022): 1–14, https://doi.org/10.1007/s10803-022-05803-9.

9. Antoinette "Toni" Radcliffe, *A Summary of Evidence Supporting Neurodiversity in the Workplace*, Goodwin College of Professional Studies, Drexel University, September 9, 2023, https://neurodiversityemploymentnetwork.org/wp-content/uploads/2024/01/A-Summary-of-Evidence-Supporting-Neurodiversity-in-the-Workplace.pdf.

10. Johns Hopkins University, "Neurodivergence at a Glance," *The Inclusive Workplace Series*, October 5, 2022, https://imagine.jhu.edu/blog/2022/10/05/neurodivergence-at-a-glance/.

11. The National Autistic Society, *Too Much Information: Employment Report*, accessed September 16, 2024, https://s3.chorus-mk.thirdlight.com/file/1573224908/64036150693/width=-1/height=-1/format=-1/

fit=scale/t=445570/e=never/k=b0347eba/TMI-Employment-Report-24pp-WEB-291020.pdf.

12. Chris Griffiths, "10 Highly Successful People You Didn't Know Were Neurodivergent," *CEO Today* Magazine, June 21, 2024, https://www.ceotodaymagazine.com/2022/06/10-highly-successful-people-you-didnt-know-were-neurodivergent/.

13. Simon Baron-Cohen, "How Autism and Invention Are Connected," *The Wall Street Journal*, December 12, 2020, https://www.wsj.com/articles/how-autism-and-invention-are-connected-11607749260.

14. Harvey Blume, "Neurodiversity: On the Neurological Underpinnings of Geekdom, *The Atlantic*, September 1998, https://www.theatlantic.com/magazine/archive/1998/09/neurodiversity/305909/.

15. Kelly McCain, "Explainer: What Is Neurodivergence? Here's What You Need to Know," World Economic Forum, October 10, 2022, https://www.weforum.org/agenda/2022/10/explainer-neurodivergence-mental-health/.

16. Ibid.

17. Stages Learning, "Five Research-Based Strengths Associated with Autism," *Stages Learning Blog*, accessed September 6, 2024, https://blog.stageslearning.com/blog/five-research-based-strengths-associated-with-autism.

18. Jacqui Taylor-Jackson and Sophie Matthews, "The Influence of Traits Associated with Autism Spectrum Disorder (ASD) on the Detection of Fake News," in HCI International 2020 – Late Breaking Papers: Interaction, Knowledge and Social Media, Lecture Notes in Computer Science, vol. 12427, (Springer, 2020), 464–472, https://link.springer.com/chapter/10.1007/978-3-030-60152-2_35.

19. Simon Baron-Cohen et al., "Talent in Autism: Hyper-Systemizing, Hyper-Attention to Detail and Sensory Hypersensitivity," *Philosophical Transactions of the Royal Society B* 364, no. 1522 (May 27, 2009), https://doi.org/10.1098/rstb.2008.0337.

20. Martine Hoogman et al., "Creativity and ADHD: A Review of Behavioral Studies, the Effect of Psychostimulants and Neural Underpinnings," *Neuroscience and Biobehavioral Reviews* 119 (December 2020): 66–85, https://doi.org/10.1016/j.neubiorev.2020.09.029.

21. Julie Logan, "Dyslexic Entrepreneurs: The Incidence; Their Coping Strategies and Their Business Skills," *Dyslexia* (published online in Wiley

InterScience), https://doi.org/10.1002/dys.388, accessed via https://www.bayes.city.ac.uk/__data/assets/pdf_file/0003/367383/julielogan-dyslexic-entrepreneurs.pdf.

22. Rosie Cope and Anna Remington, "The Strengths and Abilities of Autistic People in the Workplace," *Autism in Adulthood* 4, no. 1 (March 9, 2022), https://doi.org/10.1089/aut.2021.0037.

23. Simon Baron-Cohen, "How Autism and Invention Are Connected," *The Wall Street Journal*, December 12, 2020, https://www.wsj.com/articles/how-autism-and-invention-are-connected-11607749260.

24. U.S. Bureau of Labor Statistics, "Employment in STEM Occupations," accessed October 28, 2024, https://www.bls.gov/emp/tables/stem-employment.htm.

25. Bernard J. Crespi, "Autism As a Disorder of High Intelligence," *Frontiers in Neuroscience* 10 (June 29, 2016), https://doi.org/10.3389/fnins.2016.00300.

26. Eilidh Cage and Zoe Troxell-Whitman, "Understanding the Reasons, Contexts and Costs of Camouflaging for Autistic Adults," *Journal of Autism and Developmental Disorders* 49, no. 5 (2019): 1899-1911, https://doi.org/10.1007/s10803-018-03878-x.

27. Jonathan S. Beck, Rebecca A. Lundwall, and Mikle South, "Looking Good but Feeling Bad: 'Camouflaging' Behaviors and Mental Health in Women with Autistic Traits," *Autism* 24, no. 4 (2020), https://doi.org/10.1177/1362361320912147.

28. Praslova, "Autism Doesn't Hold People Back at Work. Discrimination Does."

29. Maria Panagiotidi, Paul G. Overton, and Tom Stafford, "The Relationship Between ADHD Traits and Sensory Sensitivity in the General Population," *Comprehensive Psychiatry* 80 (January 2018): 179–185, https://doi.org/10.1016/j.comppsych.2017.10.008.

30. Mehzabeen Mannan and Sami G. Al-Ghamdi, "Indoor Air Quality in Buildings: A Comprehensive Review on the Factors Influencing Air Pollution in Residential and Commercial Structure," *International Journal of Environmental Research and Public Health* 18, no. 6 (March 2021): 3276, https://doi.org/10.3390/ijerph18063276.

31. "Indicators: Employee Engagement," Gallup, Inc., accessed July 1, 2024, https://www.gallup.com/394373/indicator-employee-engagement.aspx.

32. Sylvia Ann Hewlett, Melinda Marshall, and Laura Sherbin, "How Diversity Can Drive Innovation," *Harvard Business Review*, December 2013, https://hbr.org/2013/12/how-diversity-can-drive-innovation.

33. Karen Brown, "To Retain Employees, Focus on Inclusion — Not Just Diversity," *Harvard Business Review*, December 4, 2018, https://hbr.org/2018/12/to-retain-employees-focus-on-inclusion-not-just-diversity.

34. Well Living Lab, "International Healthy Building Accord," Well Certified, accessed June 30, 2024, https://resources.wellcertified.com/articles/international-healthy-building-accord-sign/.

Chapter 2

1. Catherine Caruso, "A New Field of Neuroscience Aims to Map Connections in the Brain," *Harvard Medical School*, January 19, 2023, https://hms.harvard.edu/news/new-field-neuroscience-aims-map-connections-brain.

2. Piper Hutson and James Hutson, "Neurodiversity and Inclusivity in the Workplace: Biopsychosocial Interventions for Promoting Competitive Advantage," *Journal of Organizational Psychology* 23, no. 2 (2023), https://digitalcommons.lindenwood.edu/faculty-research-papers/493.

3. Centers for Disease Control and Prevention, "Disability Impacts All of Us," Disability and Health Promotion, accessed August 12, 2024, https://www.cdc.gov/ncbddd/disabilityandhealth/infographic-disability-impacts-all.html.

4. Monique Botha, Robert Chapman, and Nick Walker, "The Neurodiversity Concept Was Developed Collectively: An Overdue Correction on the Origins of Neurodiversity Theory," *Autism* 28, no. 6 (2024), https://doi.org/10.1177/13623613241237871.

5. Nancy Doyle and Almuth McDowall, "Diamond in the Rough? An 'Empty Review' of Research into 'Neurodiversity' and a Road Map for Developing the Inclusion Agenda," *Equality, Diversity and Inclusion* 41, no. 3 (2021), https://emerald.com/insight/content/doi/10.1108/EDI-06-2020-0172/full/html.

6. Nancy Doyle, "Neurodiversity at Work: A Biopsychosocial Model and the Impact on Working Adults," *British Medical Bulletin* 135, no. 1 (September 2020): 108–125, https://doi.org/10.1093/bmb/ldaa021.

7. World Health Organization, "Neurological Disorders: Public Health Challenges," Geneva: World Health Organization, 2006, accessed July 15, 2024, https://who.int/publications/i/item/9789241563369.

8. Kerry Magro, "Autism is One Word Attempting to Describe Millions of Different Stories," *Autism Speaks*, accessed July 10, 2024, https://autismspeaks.org/blog/autism-one-word-attempting-describe-millions-different-stories.

9. Diversability, "Invisible Disabilities 101: What You Need to Know," published January 30, 2021, https://mydiversability.com/blog/invisible-disabilities.

10. Lauren Rylaarsdam and Alicia Guevara-Guevara, "Genetic Causes and Modifiers of Autism Spectrum Disorder," *Frontiers in Cellular Neuroscience* 13 (2019): 385, accessed July 15, 2024, https://doi.org/10.3389/fncel.2019.00385.

11. Oliver Grimm, Thomas M. Kranz, and Andreas Reif, "Genetics of ADHD: What Should the Clinician Know?" *Current Psychiatry Reports* 22, no. 4 (February 27, 2020): 18, https://doi.org/10.1007/s11920-020-1141-x.

12. Sundar Gnanael et al., "Attention Deficit Hyperactivity Disorder and Comorbidity: A Review of Literature," *World Journal of Clinical Cases* 7, no. 17 (September 6, 2019): 2420–2426, https://doi.org/10.12998/wjcc.v7.i17.2420.

13. Steven D. Targum and Lenard A. Adler, "Our Current Understanding of Adult ADHD," *Innovations in Clinical Neuroscience* 11, no. 11–12 (November–December 2014): 30-35, https://www.ncbi.nlm.nih.gov/pmc/articles/PMC4301030/.

14. National Institute of Mental Health, "Attention-Deficit/Hyperactivity Disorder (ADHD)," *National Institute of Mental Health*, accessed September 23, 2024, https://nimh.nih.gov/health/statistics/attention-deficit-hyperactivity-disorder-adhd.

15. Centers for Disease Control and Prevention, "Data and Statistics on ADHD," last modified May 16, 2024, https://www.cdc.gov/adhd/data/index.html.

16. Tricia Kinman, "Gender Differences in ADHD Symptoms," *Healthline*, last modified March 22, 2016, https://www.healthline.com/health/adhd/adhd-symptoms-in-girls-and-boys.

17. Ibid.

18. Mayo Clinic, "Adult Attention-Deficit/Hyperactivity Disorder (ADHD)," *Mayo Clinic*, accessed September 23, 2024, https://www.mayoclinic.org/diseases-conditions/adult-adhd/symptoms-causes/syc-20350878.

19. Martine Hoogman et al., "Subcortical Brain Volume Differences in Participants with Attention Deficit Hyperactivity Disorder in Children and Adults: A Cross-Sectional Mega-Analysis," *Lancet Psychiatry* 4, no. 4 (2017): 310-319, https://doi.org/10.1016/S2215-0366(17)30049-4.

20. Ana Aceves, "Key Brain Regions Found to Be Smaller in People With ADHD," NOVA Next, February 17, 2017, https://www.pbs.org/wgbh/nova/article/largest-adhd-study-finds-link-to-brain-size/.

21. Maria Panagiotidi, Paul G. Overton, and Tom Stafford, "The Relationship Between ADHD Traits and Sensory Sensitivity in the General Population," *Comprehensive Psychiatry* 80 (January 2018): 179–185, https://doi.org/10.1016/j.comppsych.2017.10.008.

22. Brandon K. Ashinoff and Ahmad Abu-Akel, "Hyperfocus: The Forgotten Frontier of Attention," *Psychological Research* 85, no. 1 (2021): 1–19, https://doi.org/10.1007/s00426-019-01245-8.

23. Caterina Gawrilow and Sara Goudarzi, "Are People with ADHD More Creative?" *Scientific American*, June 11, 2019, https://www.scientificamerican.com/article/are-people-with-adhd-more-creative/.

24. Warren Magnus et al., "Attention Deficit Hyperactivity Disorder," *StatPearls*, last modified August 8, 2023, https://www.ncbi.nlm.nih.gov/books/NBK441838/.

25. Keath Low, "Are ADD and ADHD the Same Condition? How the Name and Diagnosis Have Changed Over the Years," *Verywell Mind*, updated May 31, 2023, https://www.verywellmind.com/is-add-the-same-thing-as-adhd-20467.

26. Russell Barkley, "How ADHD Shortens Life Expectancy: What Parents and Doctors Need to Know to Take Action," *ADDitude*, August 28, 2023, https://www.additudemag.com/webinar/life-expectancy-russell-barkley/.

27. Centers for Disease Control and Prevention, "Key Findings: Estimated Number of Adults Living with Autism Spectrum Disorder in the United States, 2017," *Centers for Disease Control and Prevention*, last modified May 16, 2023, https://www.cdc.gov/autism/publications/adults-living-with-autism-spectrum-disorder.html.

28. Kyler Shumway and Daniel Wendler, *Neurodiversity and the Myth of Normal* (The Great Courses, 2024), audiobook, 4 pages, Audible Audio.

29. Patrick F. Lee, Roger E. Thomas, and Patricia A. Lee, "Approach to Autism Spectrum Disorder," *Canadian Family Physician* 61, no. 5 (May 2015): 421–424, https://www.ncbi.nlm.nih.gov/pmc/articles/PMC4430056/.

30. Alex P. A. Donovan and M. Albert Basson, "The Neuroanatomy of Autism – A Developmental Perspective," *Journal of Anatomy* 230, no. 1 (January 2017): 4–15, https://doi.org/10.1111/joa.12542.

31. Shumway and Wendler, *Neurodiversity and the Myth of Normal.*

32. Tiffany D. Rogers et al., "Is Autism a Disease of the Cerebellum? An Integration of Clinical and Pre-Clinical Research," *Frontiers in Systems Neuroscience* 7 (May 2013), https://doi.org/10.3389/fnsys.2013.00015.

33. Centers for Disease Control and Prevention, "Signs and Symptoms of Autism Spectrum Disorder," *CDC*, last reviewed May 16, 2024, https://www.cdc.gov/autism/signs-symptoms/index.html.

34. National Autistic Society, "Obsessions and Repetitive Behaviour – A Guide for All Audiences," *National Autistic Society*, accessed September 23, 2024, https://www.autism.org.uk/advice-and-guidance/topics/behaviour/obsessions/all-audiences.

35. Amanda Chan, "Autistic Brain Excels at Recognizing Patterns," *Live Science*, May 30, 2013, https://www.livescience.com/35586-autism-brain-activity-regions-perception.html.

36. Michael Alexander Pelzl et al., "Reduced Impact of Nonverbal Cues During Integration of Verbal and Nonverbal Emotional Information in Adults with High-Functioning Autism," *Frontiers in Psychiatry* 13 (2022): 1069028, https://doi.org/10.3389/fpsyt.2022.1069028.

37. Xie, Fan, et al., "Functional Echolalia in Autism Speech: Verbal Formulae and Repeated Prior Utterances as Communicative and Cognitive Strategies," *Frontiers in Psychology* 14 (February 23, 2023): 1010615, https://doi.org/10.3389/fpsyg.2023.1010615.

38. Apoorva Rajiv Madipakkam et al., "Unconscious Avoidance of Eye Contact in Autism Spectrum Disorder," *Scientific Reports* 7 (2017): 13378, https://doi.org/10.1038/s41598-017-13945-5.

39. Wang, Chenyu, et al., "Impaired Cerebellar Plasticity Hypersensitizes Sensory Reflexes in SCN2A-Associated ASD," *Neuron* 112, no. 9 (May 1, 2024): 1444-1455.e5, https://doi.org/10.1016/j.neuron.2024.04.0055.

40. Om Patil and Meghali Kaple, "Sensory Processing Differences in Individuals With Autism Spectrum Disorder: A Narrative Review of Underlying Mechanisms and Sensory-Based Interventions," *Cureus* 15, no. 10 (October 2023): e48020, https://doi.org/10.7759/cureus.48020.

41. Hannah Rappaport et al., "'I Live in Extremes': A Qualitative Investigation of Autistic Adults' Experiences of Inertial Rest and Motion," *Autism* 28, no. 5 (May 2024): 1305–1315, https://doi.org/10.1177/13623613231198916.

42. Amanda Chan, "Autistic Brain Excels at Recognizing Patterns," *Live Science*, May 30, 2013, https://www.livescience.com/35586-autism-brain-activity-regions-perception.html.

43. Henry O'Connell and Michael Fitzgerald, "Did Alan Turing Have Asperger's Syndrome?" *Irish Journal of Psychological Medicine* 20, no. 1 (March 2003): 28-31, https://doi.org/10.1017/S0790966700007503.

44. Richard K. Wagner et al., "The Prevalence of Dyslexia: A New Approach to Its Estimation," *Journal of Learning Disabilities* 53, no. 5 (September-October 2020): 354–365, https://doi.org/10.1177/0022219420920377.

45. Zoï Kapoula et al., "Education Influences Creativity in Dyslexic and Non-Dyslexic Children and Teenagers," *PLOS ONE* 11, no. 3 (2016): e0150421, https://doi.org/10.1371/journal.pone.0150421.

46. Victoria Masterson, "People with Dyslexia Have 'Enhanced Abilities', According to a New Study," *World Economic Forum*, July 27, 2022, https://www.weforum.org/agenda/2022/07/dyslexia-enhanced-abilities-studies/.

47. Azadeh Kushki et al., "Changes in Kinetics and Kinematics of Handwriting During a Prolonged Writing Task in Children with and without Dysgraphia," *Research in Developmental Disabilities* 32, no. 3 (May–June 2011): 1058–1064, https://doi.org/10.1016/j.ridd.2011.01.026.

48. "Eunice Kennedy Shriver National Institute of Child Health and Human Development, "Learning Disabilities," *National Institutes of Health*, https://nichd.nih.gov/health/topics/factsheets/learningdisabilities."

49. Ibid.

50. Stefan Haberstroh and Gerd Schulte-Körne, "The Diagnosis and Treatment of Dyscalculia," *Deutsches Ärzteblatt International* 116, no. 7 (February 2019): 107–114, https://doi.org/10.3238/arztebl.2019.0107.

51. "National Institute of Neurological Disorders and Stroke, "Developmental Dyspraxia," *National Institutes of Health*, https://ninds.nih.gov/health-information/disorders/developmental-dyspraxia."

52. "Dyspraxia," *UNESCO Mahatma Gandhi Institute of Education for Peace and Sustainable Development*, accessed July 15, 2024, https://mgiep.unesco.org/dyspraxia.

53. Andreas Hartmann et al., "Tourette Syndrome Research Highlights from 2022," *F1000Research* 12 (2023): 826, https://doi.org/10.12688/f1000research.135702.2.

54. National Institute of Neurological Disorders and Stroke, "Tourette Syndrome," *NIH*, accessed September 23, 2024, https://ninds.nih.gov/health-information/disorders/tourette-syndrome.

55. National Institute of Mental Health, "Obsessive-Compulsive Disorder," NIMH.gov, accessed October 29, 2024, https://www.nimh.nih.gov/health/topics/obsessive-compulsive-disorder-ocd.

56. Michael J. Banissy, Clare Jonas, and Roi Cohen Kadosh, "Synesthesia: An Introduction," *Frontiers in Psychology* 5 (2014): 1414, https://doi.org/10.3389/fpsyg.2014.01414.

57. Psychology Today Staff, "Synesthesia," *Psychology Today*, accessed October 29, 2024, https://www.psychologytoday.com/us/basics/synesthesia.

58. S. Gnanavel, P. Sharma, P. Kaushal, and S. Hussain, "Attention Deficit Hyperactivity Disorder and Comorbidity: A Review of Literature," *World Journal of Clinical Cases* 7, no. 17 (September 6, 2019): 2420-2426, https://doi.org/10.12998/wjcc.v7.i17.2420.

59. "Understanding ADHD: What You Need to Know," *MedlinePlus*, NIH MedlinePlus Magazine, accessed July 15, 2024, https://magazine.medlineplus.gov/article/understanding-adhd-what-you-need-to-know.

60. Melissa L. Danielson et al., "ADHD Prevalence Among U.S. Children and Adolescents in 2022: Diagnosis, Severity, Co-Occurring Disorders, and Treatment," *Journal of Clinical Child & Adolescent Psychology* 53, no. 3 (May 22, 2024): 343-360, https://doi.org/10.1080/15374416.2024.2335625.

61. Camille Hours, Christophe Recasens, and Jean-Marc Baleyte, "ASD and ADHD Comorbidity: What Are We Talking About?" *Frontiers in Psychiatry* 13 (2022): 837424, https://doi.org/10.3389/fpsyt.2022 .837424.

62. Haewon Kim et al., "Impact of Comorbid Oppositional Defiant Disorder on the Clinical and Neuropsychological Characteristics of Korean Children With Attention-Deficit/Hyperactivity Disorder," *Psychiatry Investigation* 20, no. 10 (2023), 962–971, accessed September 23, 2024, https://doi.org/10.30773/pi.2023.0091.

63. Kerstin Konrad et al., "Sex Differences in Psychiatric Comorbidity and Clinical Presentation in Youths With Conduct Disorder," *Journal of Child Psychology and Psychiatry* 63, no. 2, accessed September 23, 2024, https://doi.org/10.1111/jcpp.13428.

64. Elisa D'Agati, Paolo Curatolo, and Luigi Mazzone, "Comorbidity between ADHD and Anxiety Disorders across the Lifespan," *International Journal of Psychiatry in Clinical Practice* 23, no. 4 (2019): 238–244, https://doi.org/10.1080/13651501.2019.1628277.

65. Martin A. Katzman et al., "Adult ADHD and Comorbid Disorders: Clinical Implications of a Dimensional Approach," *BMC Psychiatry* 17, no. 302 (2017), https://doi.org/10.1186/s12888-017-1463-3.

66. Andrea Sandstrom et al., "Prevalence of Attention-Deficit/Hyperactivity Disorder in People with Mood Disorders: A Systematic Review and Meta-Analysis," *Acta Psychiatrica Scandinavica* 143, no. 5 (2021): 380–391, https://doi.org/10.1111/acps.13283.

67. Olumide O. Oluwabusi, Susan Parke, and Paul J. Ambrosini, "Tourette Syndrome Associated with Attention Deficit Hyperactivity Disorder: The Impact of Tics and Psychopharmacological Treatment Options," *World Journal of Clinical Pediatrics* 5, no. 1 (2016): 128–135, https://doi .org/10.5409/wjcp.v5.i1.128.

68. Bahadar S. Srichawla et al., "Attention Deficit Hyperactivity Disorder and Substance Use Disorder: A Narrative Review," *Cureus* 14, no. 4 (2022): e24068, https://doi.org/10.7759/cureus.24068.

69. Bengü Yücens, Ayşegül Kart, and Selim Tümkaya, "Obsessive Beliefs and Clinical Features in Patients with Comorbid Obsessive-Compulsive Disorder and Attention-Deficit/Hyperactivity Disorder," *Psychiatry and Clinical Psychopharmacology* 31, no. 4 (2021): 408–416, https://doi .org/10.5152/pcp.2021.21200.

70. Ye Rim Kim et al., "Clinical Characteristics of Comorbid Tic Disorders in Autism Spectrum Disorder: Exploratory Analysis," *Child and Adolescent Psychiatry and Mental Health* 17 (2023): 71, https://doi.org/10.1186/s13034-023-00625-8.

71. NHS Dorset, "Neurodiversity and Mental Health," *NHS Dorset*, accessed July 15, 2024, https://nhsdorset.nhs.uk/neurodiversity/explore/mentalhealth/.

72. ChildNEXUS, "Navigating the Challenges of Social Media for Neurodivergent Youth," *ChildNEXUS* (blog), November 4, 2023, https://childnexus.com/blog/article/navigating-the-challenges-of-social-media-for-neurodivergent-youth-65464eb50ea4f.

73. Reinert, M., D. Fritze, and T. Nguyen, "The State of Mental Health in America 2023," *Mental Health America*, October 2022, Alexandria, VA., https://mhanational.org/sites/default/files/2023-State-of-Mental-Health-in-America-Report.pdf.

74. The Lancet Global Health, "Mental Health Matters," *The Lancet Global Health* 8, no. 11 (2020): e1352, accessed September 24, 2024, https://doi.org/10.1016/S2214-109X(20)30432-0.

75. Ginger Christ. "Burnt Out: Stress on the Job [Infographic]," *EHS Today*, May 7, 2016, https://www.ehstoday.com/health/article/21917550/burnt-out-stress-on-the-job-infographic.

76. Reinert, M., et al., "The State of Mental Health in America 2023," 2022.

77. Hazel Muir, "Einstein and Newton Showed Signs of Autism," *New Scientist*, April 30, 2003, https://www.newscientist.com/article/dn3676-einstein-and-newton-showed-signs-of-autism/.

78. "Autism Rates Increase," *Newcastle University Press Office*, March 29, 2021, https://www.ncl.ac.uk/press/articles/archive/2021/03/autismratesincrease/.

79. Gary Wenk, "Why Does Autism Affect More Boys Than Girls?" *Psychology Today*, October 30, 2020, https://www.psychologytoday.com/us/blog/your-brain-on-food/202010/why-does-autism-affect-more-boys-than-girls.

80. Meng-Chuan Lai, Simon Baron-Cohen, and Joseph D. Buxbaum, "Understanding Autism in the Light of Sex/Gender," *Molecular Autism* 6, no. 24 (May 13, 2015), https://doi.org/10.1186/s13229-015-0021-4.

81. Charlotte Skoglund et al., "Time after Time: Failure to Identify and Support Females with ADHD – A Swedish Population Register Study,"

Journal of Child Psychology and Psychiatry 65, no. 6 (2024): 832–844, https://doi.org/10.1111/jcpp.13920.

82. Darby E. Altoe and Emma A. Climie, "Miss. Diagnosis: A Systematic Review of ADHD in Adult Women," *Journal of Attention Disorders* 27, no. 7 (May 2023): 645–657, https://doi.org/10.1177/10870547231161533.

Chapter 3

1. Amy E. Hurley-Hanson and Cristina M. Giannantonio, eds., *Journal of Business and Management*, vol. 22, no. 1, Chapman University, 2016, Special Issue: Autism in the Workplace, accessed October 29, 2024, https://www.chapman.edu/business/_files/journals-and-essays/jbm-editions/jbm-vol-22-no-1-autism-in-the-workplace.pdf.

2. Amy Jane Griffiths et al., "Developing Employment Environments Where Individuals with ASD Thrive: Using Machine Learning to Explore Employer Policies and Practices," *Brain Sciences* 10, no. 9 (September 2020): 632, https://doi.org/10.3390/brainsci10090632.

3. ManpowerGroup, *2024 Global Talent Shortage*, accessed October 29, 2024, https://go.manpowergroup.com/hubfs/Talent%20Shortage/Talent%20Shortage%202024/MPG_TS_2024_GLOBAL_Infographic.pdf.

4. Rob Wile, "Employment Among People with Disabilities Hits Post-Pandemic High," NBC News, July 7, 2023, https://www.nbcnews.com/business/economy/jobs-for-people-with-disabilities-hit-new-post-pandemic-high-rcna93084.

5. Wile, "Employment Among People with Disabilities."

6. Almuth McDowall, Nancy Doyle, and Meg Kiseleva, *Neurodiversity at Work: Demand, Supply and a Gap Analysis* (London: Birkbeck, University of London, 2023), https://eprints.bbk.ac.uk/id/eprint/50834/.

7. Alan Price, "Neurodiversity and the Workplace," *Forbes*, February 15, 2022, https://www.forbes.com/sites/forbeshumanresourcescouncil/2022/02/15/neurodiversity-and-the-workplace/?sh=6dc59ba32a22.

8. Juliet Bourke and Bernadette Dillon, "The Diversity and Inclusion Revolution: Eight Powerful Truths," *Deloitte Review*, Issue 22, January 2018, https://www2.deloitte.com/content/dam/insights/us/articles/4209_Diversity-and-inclusion-revolution/DI_Diversity-and-inclusion-revolution.pdf.

9. Nancy Doyle, "Schools Crisis: Today's Children Are Tomorrow's Employees," *Forbes*, July 24, 2024, https://www.forbes.com/sites/drnancydoyle/2024/07/24/schools-crisis-todays-children-are-tomorrows-employees/.

10. Richard Branson, "Opening the Door to Bigger Thinking on Neurodiversity," *Virgin*, April 4, 2021, https://www.virgin.com/branson-family/richard-branson-blog/opening-the-door-to-bigger-thinking-on-neurodiversity.

11. Samuel Osborne, "Dyslexia Should Be Recognised as a Sign of Potential, Says Richard Branson," *The Independent*, April 30, 2017, https://www.independent.co.uk/news/people/dyslexia-richard-branson-potential-intelligence-genius-advantage-virgin-a7710676.html.

12. Maureen Dunne, *The Neurodiversity Edge* (Hoboken, NJ: Wiley, 2024).

13. Jared Lindzon, "Why Companies Who Hire People with Disabilities Outperformed Their Peers," *Fast Company*, March 13, 2019, https://www.fastcompany.com/90311742/why-companies-who-hire-people-with-disabilities-outperformed-their-peers.

14. Louis Carter, "4 Neurodiverse Friendly Companies Loved by Their Employees: SAP, HP, Dell, and Home Depot," Most Loved Workplace, accessed September 24, 2024, https://mostlovedworkplace.com/four-neurodiverse-friendly-companies-loved-by-their-employees/.

15. Allaya Cooks-Campbell, "Unlock Creativity by Making Space for Neurodiversity in the Workplace," BetterUp, June 24, 2022, https://www.betterup.com/blog/neurodiversity-in-the-workplace.

16. Robert D. Austin and Gary P. Pisano, "Neurodiversity as a Competitive Advantage," *Harvard Business Review*, May-June 2017, https://hbr.org/2017/05/neurodiversity-as-a-competitive-advantage.

17. Darren Hedley, Mathilda Wilmot, Jennifer Spoor, and Cheryl Dissanayake, "Benefits of Employing People With Autism: The Dandelion Employment Program," Melbourne, Australia: La Trobe University, School of Psychology and Public Health, Olga Tennison Autism, 2017, https://ecommons.cornell.edu/items/9b0b28a8-e74d-4d66-9286-40f3f8450503.

18. Michael Bernick, "Effective Autism (Neurodiversity) Employment: A Legal Perspective," *Forbes*, January 15, 2019, https://www.forbes.com/

sites/michaelbernick/2019/01/15/effective-autism-neurodiversity-employment-a-legal-perspective/.

19. Microsoft, "Inclusive Hiring for People with Disabilities," Microsoft Global Diversity and Inclusion, accessed August 13, 2024, https://microsoft.com/en-us/diversity/inside-microsoft/cross-disability/hiring.

20. Nancy Doyle, "IBM Explain What Works in Neurodiversity at Work," *Forbes*, August 23, 2022, https://www.forbes.com/sites/drnancydoyle/2022/08/23/ibm-explain-what-works-in-neurodiversity-at-work/.

21. Leah Carroll, "How EY is Focusing on Neurodiverse Talent – and Why It Benefits Everyone," BBC, March 21, 2024, https://www.bbc.com/worklife/article/20240320-ey-karyn-twaronite-neurodiversity-bbc-executive-interview.

22. Life At The BBC, "Project Cape Neurodiverse Immersive 360VR Experience," YouTube video, 5:07, September 13, 2016, https://www.youtube.com/watch?v=ZLyGuVTH8sA.

23. Job Accommodation Network, "Costs and Benefits of Accommodation," *AskJAN.org*, last updated April 5, 2024, accessed September 4, 2024, https://askjan.org/topics/costs.cfm.

24. Katie Navarra, "The Real Costs of Recruitment," SHRM, April 11, 2022, https://shrm.org/topics-tools/news/talent-acquisition/real-costs-recruitment.

25. United Nations, Resolution Adopted by the General Assembly on 27 July 2015: Addis Ababa Action Agenda of the Third International Conference on Financing for Development (Addis Ababa Action Agenda), A/RES/69/313, July 27, 2015, https://www.un.org/en/development/desa/population/migration/generalassembly/docs/globalcompact/A_RES_69_313.pdf.

26. Fortesa Latifi, "Spoon Theory: What It Is and How I Use It to Manage Chronic Illness," *The Washington Post*, January 14, 2023, https://www.washingtonpost.com/wellness/2023/01/14/spoon-theory-chronic-illness-spoonie/.

27. Nicole Gilroy, "Neurodivergent Children Are Twice as Likely to Experience Chronic Disabling Fatigue in Adolescence," University of Sussex, July 24, 2024, https://www.sussex.ac.uk/broadcast/read/65116.

Chapter 4

1. Shiv Gautam et al., "Concept of Mental Health and Mental Well-Being, Its Determinants and Coping Strategies," *Indian Journal of Psychiatry* 66, Suppl. 2 (January 2024): S231-S244, https://doi.org/10.4103/indian jpsychiatry.indianjpsychiatry_707_23.

2. National Academies of Sciences, Engineering, and Medicine, "Cognitive Tests and Performance Validity Tests," in *Psychological Testing in the Service of Disability Determination* (Washington, DC: National Academies Press, 2015), accessed September 25, 2024, https://www.ncbi .nlm.nih.gov/books/NBK305230/.

3. Aayush Dhakal and Bradford D. Bobrin, "Cognitive Deficits," *StatPearls* [Internet], updated February 14, 2023, National Library of Medicine, accessed September 25, 2024, https://www.ncbi.nlm.nih.gov/books/ NBK559052/.

4. Robyne Hanley-Dafoe, "Harnessing the Power of Social Awareness," *Psychology Today*, April 26, 2024, https://www.psychologytoday.com/ us/blog/everyday-resilience/202404/harnessing-the-power-of-social-awareness.

5. Debra Umberson and Jennifer Karas Montez, "Social Relationships and Health: A Flashpoint for Health Policy," *Journal of Health and Social Behavior* 51, Suppl. (2010): S54-S66, https://doi.org/10.1177/ 0022146510383501.

6. NeuroLaunch editorial team, "Architecture's Impact on Human Behavior: Shaping Our Lives Through Design," NeuroLaunch, September 22, 2024, https://neurolaunch.com/how-architecture-affects-human-behavior/.

7. Jenny L. L. Csecs et al., "Joint Hypermobility Links Neurodivergence to Dysautonomia and Pain," *Frontiers in Psychiatry* 12 (February 2, 2022): 786916, https://doi.org/10.3389/fpsyt.2021.786916.

8. Nancy Doyle, "Neurodiversity at Work: A Biopsychosocial Model and the Impact on Working Adults," *British Medical Bulletin* 135, no. 1 (September 2020): 108–125, https://doi.org/10.1093/bmb/ldaa021.

9. Exceptional Individuals, "We Are Exceptional Individuals," Exceptional Individuals, accessed September 25, 2024, https://exceptionalin dividuals.com.

10. Maureen Dunne, The Neurodiversity Edge (Hoboken, NJ: Wiley, 2024).

11. The de Bono Group, "Lateral Reading," accessed August 15, 2024, https://www.debonogroup.com/services/core-programs/lateral-thinking/lateral-reading/.

12. Marije Stolte et al., "Characterizing Creative Thinking and Creative Achievements in Relation to Symptoms of Attention-Deficit/Hyperactivity Disorder and Autism Spectrum Disorder," *Frontiers in Psychiatry* (July 1, 2022), https://doi.org/10.3389/fpsyt.2022.909202.

13. Chris Griffiths, "10 Highly Successful People You Didn't Know Were Neurodivergent," *CEO Today*, June 2024. https://ceotodaymagazine.com/2024/06/10-highly-successful-people-you-didnt-know-were-neurodivergent/.

14. STAR Institute, "Your 8 Senses," STAR Institute for Sensory Processing, accessed September 25, 2024, https://sensoryhealth.org/basic/your-8-senses.

15. Paloma Yáñez Serrano et al., "Understanding Individual Heat Exposure Through Interdisciplinary Research on Thermoception," *Humanities and Social Sciences Communications* 11 (2024): article 572, https://doi.org/10.1057/s41599-024-03091-5.

16. Scott A. Armstrong and Michael J. Herr, "Physiology, Nociception," *StatPearls* [Internet], updated May 1, 2023, National Library of Medicine, https://www.ncbi.nlm.nih.gov/books/NBK551562/.

17. George Markowsky, "Physiology," *Encyclopaedia Britannica*, last modified July 2, 2024, https://www.britannica.com/science/information-theory/Physiology.

18. P. R. A. Heckman, A. Blokland, J. Ramaekers, and J. Prickaerts, "PDE and Cognitive Crocessing: Beyond the Memory Domain," *Neurobiology of Learning and Memory* 119 (March 2015): 108-122, https://doi.org/10.1016/j.nlm.2014.10.011.

19. National Institute of Mental Health, "Mental Illness," National Institute of Mental Health, accessed September 25, 2024, https://www.nimh.nih.gov/health/statistics/mental-illness.

20. Rebecca Burch, Paul Rizzoli, and Elizabeth Loder, "The Prevalence and Impact of Migraine and Severe Headache in the United States: Updated Age, Sex, and Socioeconomic-Specific Estimates from Government Health Surveys," *Headache* 61, no. 1 (January 2021): 60–68, https://doi.org/10.1111/head.14024.

21. Rosemarie Kobau, Cecily Luncheon, and Kurt Greenlund, "Active Epilepsy Prevalence Among U.S. Adults Is 1.1% and Differs by Educational Level—National Health Interview Survey, United States, 2021," *Epilepsy & Behavior* 142 (May 2023): 109180, https://doi .org/10.1016/j.yebeh.2023.109180.

22. Silvana Mareva and The CALM Team, "Mapping Neurodevelopmental Diversity in Executive Function," *Cortex* 172 (March 2024): 204–221, https://doi.org/10.1016/j.cortex.2023.11.021.

23. Antonio de Lucas Ancillo, Sorin Gavrila Gavrila, and María Teresa del Val Núñez, "Workplace Change Within the COVID-19 Context: The New (Next) Normal," *Technological Forecasting and Social Change* 194 (September 2023): 122673, https://doi.org/10.1016/j.techfore .2023.122673.

24. Annemarie Lombard, "Sensory Stories # 78: Research and Sensory Style Data," YouTube video, 10:51, posted by "Sensory Intelligence Consulting," March 31, 2023, accessed August 29, 2024, https://www .youtube.com/watch?v=vMtvySzRWeo.

25. S. E. Chidiac, M. A. Reda, and G. E. Marjaba, "Accessibility of the Built Environment for People with Sensory Disabilities—Review Quality and Representation of Evidence," *Buildings* 14, no. 3 (2024): 707, https://doi.org/10.3390/buildings14030707.

26. Lucy Jane Miller et al., "Identification of Sensory Processing and Integration Symptom Clusters: A Preliminary Study," *Occupational Therapy International* 2017 (November 2017): 2876080, https://doi.org/10 .1155/2017/2876080.

27. Elaine Aron, *The Highly Sensitive Person*, accessed September 25, 2024, https://hsperson.com.

28. Sarah A. Schoen et al., "Physiological and Behavioral Differences in Sensory Processing: A Comparison of Children with Autism Spectrum Disorder and Sensory Modulation Disorder," *Frontiers in Integrative Neuroscience* 3 (2009): article 29, https://doi.org/10.3389/neuro.07.029 .2009.

29. Ashley Soderlund, "Is Your Child a Dandelion, an Orchid, or a Tulip? Understanding Your Child's Biological Sensitivity," *Nurture and Thrive* (blog), accessed October 29, 2024, https://nurtureandthriveblog.com/ is-your-child-a-dandelion-or-an-orchid/.

30. Kayla Sheridan et al., "Uncertainty and Autism: How Changing with the Times is Harder for Some," in *Research and Teaching in a Pandemic*

World, ed. Basil Cahusac de Caux et al. (Singapore: Springer, 2023), 195–212, https://doi.org/10.1007/978-981-19-7757-2_13.

31. Fabian Herold et al., "Thinking While Moving or Moving While Thinking – Concepts of Motor-Cognitive Training for Cognitive Performance Enhancement," *Frontiers in Aging Neuroscience* 10 (August 2018): 228, https://doi.org/10.3389/fnagi.2018.00228.

32. Larry E. Humes, "Age-Related Changes in Cognitive and Sensory Processing: Focus on Middle-Aged Adults," *American Journal of Audiology* 24, no. 2 (June 2015): 94–97, https://doi.org/10.1044/2015_AJA-14-0063.

33. Danielle Miller, Jon Rees, and Amy Pearson, "'Masking Is Life': Experiences of Masking in Autistic and Nonautistic Adults," *Autism in Adulthood* 3, no. 4 (December 2021): 330–338, https://doi.org/10.1089/aut.2020.0083.

34. Steven K. Kapp et al., "'People Should Be Allowed to Do What They Like': Autistic Adults' Views and Experiences of Stimming," *Autism* 23, no. 7 (October 2019): 1782–1792, https://doi.org/10.1177/1362361319829628.

35. National Autistic Society, "Stimming," *National Autistic Society*, accessed September 25, 2024, https://www.autism.org.uk/advice-and-guidance/topics/behaviour/stimming.

36. Tyler C. McFayden, Sheila M. Kennison, and J. Michael Bowers, "Echolalia from a Transdiagnostic Perspective," *Autism & Developmental Language Impairments* 7 (January–December 2022): 23969415221140464, https://doi.org/10.1177/23969415221140464.

37. Amanda Reill, "A Simple Way to Make Better Decisions," *Harvard Business Review*, December 5, 2023, https://hbr.org/2023/12/a-simple-way-to-make-better-decisions.

38. Annabelle Merchie and Marie Gomot, "Habituation, Adaptation and Prediction Processes in Neurodevelopmental Disorders: A Comprehensive Review," *Brain Sciences* 13, no. 7 (July 2023): 1110, https://doi.org/10.3390/brainsci13071110.

39. Patil and Kaple, "Sensory Processing Differences," e48020.

40. Apoorva Rajiv Madipakkam et al., "Unconscious Avoidance of Eye Contact in Autism Spectrum Disorder," *Scientific Reports* 7 (October 2017): 13378, https://doi.org/10.1038/s41598-017-13945-5.

41. National Autistic Society, "Sensory Differences – A Guide for All Audiences," National Autistic Society, accessed September 25, 2024, https://www.autism.org.uk/advice-and-guidance/topics/sensory-differences/sensory-differences/all-audiences.

42. Dinah Murray, Mike Lesser, and Wendy Lawson, "Attention, Monotropism and the Diagnostic Criteria for Autism," *Autism* 9, no. 2 (May 2005): 139–156, https://doi.org/10.1177/1362361305051398.

43. Dwight J. Peterson and Marian E. Berryhill, "The Gestalt Principle of Similarity Benefits Visual Working Memory," *Psychonomic Bulletin & Review* 20, no. 6 (December 2013): 1282–1289, https://doi.org/10.3758/s13423-013-0460-x.

44. Ann Sussman and Katie Chen, "What Neuroscience Says About Modern Architecture Approach," ArchDaily, September 18, 2020, https://www.archdaily.com/947890/what-neuroscience-says-about-modern-architecture-approach.

45. Lindsay M. Oberman and Alvaro Pascual-Leone, "Hyperplasticity in Autism Spectrum Disorder Confers Protection from Alzheimer's Disease," *Medical Hypotheses* 83, no. 3 (September 2014): 337–42, https://doi.org/10.1016/j.mehy.2014.06.008.

46. Michelle A. Patriquin et al., "Autonomic Response in Autism Spectrum Disorder: Relationship to Social and Cognitive Functioning," *Biological Psychology* 145 (July 2019): 185–97, https://doi.org/10.1016/j.biopsycho.2019.05.004.

47. Shelly J. Lane et al., "Neural Foundations of Ayres Sensory Integration®," *Brain Sciences* 9, no. 7 (2019): 153, https://doi.org/10.3390/brainsci9070153.

Chapter 6

1. Kelly Mo et al., "Sex/Gender Differences in the Human Autistic Brain: A Systematic Review of 20 Years of Neuroimaging Research," *NeuroImage: Clinical* 32 (2021): 102811, https://doi.org/10.1016/j.nicl.2021.102811.

2. David Mason et al., "Older Age Autism Research: A Rapidly Growing Field, but Still a Long Way to Go," *Autism in Adulthood* 4, no. 2 (June 2022): 164–172, https://doi.org/10.1089/aut.2021.0041.

3. Desiree R. Jones et al., "An Expert Discussion on Structural Racism in Autism Research and Practice," *Autism in Adulthood* 2, no. 4 (December 2020): 273–281, https://doi.org/10.1089/aut.2020.29015.drj.

4. Xin Wei et al., "Science, Technology, Engineering, and Mathematics (STEM) Participation Among College Students with an Autism Spectrum Disorder," *Journal of Autism and Developmental Disorders* 43, no. 7 (July 2013): 1539–1546, https://doi.org/10.1007/s10803-012-1700-z.

5. Business Wire, "New ZenBusiness Research Finds Class of 2023 Sees Neurodiversity as an Asset in Leadership, is Primed to be the Most Entrepreneurial," *Business Wire*, June 14, 2023, https://www.businesswire.com/news/home/20230614082058/en/New-ZenBusiness-Research-Finds-Class-of-2023-Sees-Neurodiversity-as-an-Asset-in-Leadership-is-Primed-to-be-the-Most-Entrepreneurial.

6. Tom Y. Chang and Agne Kajackaite, "Battle for the Thermostat: Gender and the Effect of Temperature on Cognitive Performance," *PLOS ONE*, May 22, 2019, https://doi.org/10.1371/journal.pone.0216362.

7. Elizabeth Weir et al., "The Sexual Health, Orientation, and Activity of Autistic Adolescents and Adults," *Autism Research* (September 18, 2021), https://doi.org/10.1002/aur.2604.

8. Laura A. Pecora et al., "Sexuality and Gender Issues in Individuals with Autism Spectrum Disorder," *Child and Adolescent Psychiatric Clinics of North America* 29, no. 3 (July 2020): 543–556, https://doi.org/10.1016/j.chc.2020.02.007.

Chapter 7

1. Aidin Ashoori and Joseph Jankovic, "Mozart's Movements and Behaviour: A Case of Tourette's Syndrome?" *Journal of Neurology, Neurosurgery, and Psychiatry* 78, no. 11 (2007): 1171–1175, accessed July 10, 2024, https://www.ncbi.nlm.nih.gov/pmc/articles/PMC2117611/, doi:10.1136/jnnp.2007.114520.

2. Ibraheem Rehman and Bita Hazhirkarzar, "Anatomy, Head and Neck, Eye," in *StatPearls* (Treasure Island, FL: StatPearls Publishing, 2023), https://www.ncbi.nlm.nih.gov/books/NBK482428/.

3. Thea Snow, "The (il)logic of Legibility: Why Governments Should Stop Simplifying Complex Systems," *Medium*, February 10, 2021,

https://medium.com/centre-for-public-impact/the-il-logic-of-legibility-why-governments-should-stop-simplifying-complex-systems-f8822752d753.

4. Mohamed Boubekri et al., "Impact of Windows and Daylight Exposure on Overall Health and Sleep Quality of Office Workers: A Case-Control Pilot Study," *Journal of Clinical Sleep Medicine* 10, no. 6 (June 15, 2014): 603–611, https://doi.org/10.5664/jcsm.3780.

5. World Health Organization. *World Report on Vision.* Geneva: World Health Organization, 2019, accessed August 23, 2024, https://cdn.who.int/media/docs/default-source/blindness-and-visual-impairment/9789241516570-eng.pdf?sfvrsn=dd15adbb_3.

6. International Organization for Standardization (ISO), *ISO 226:2003 - Acoustics — Normal Equal-Loudness-Level Contours.* Withdrawn Edition 2, August 2003, accessed September 6, 2024. https://www.iso.org/standard/34222.html.

7. Örn Kolbeinsson et al., "No Sound Is More Distracting Than the One You're Trying Not to Hear: Delayed Costs of Mental Control of Task-Irrelevant Neutral and Emotional Sounds," *BMC Psychology* 10 (2022): 33, https://doi.org/10.1186/s40359-022-00751-6.

8. M. Annerstedt et al., "Inducing Physiological Stress Recovery with Sounds of Nature in a Virtual Reality Forest: Results from a Pilot Study," *Physiology & Behavior* 118 (June 13, 2013): 240–250, https://doi.org/10.1016/j.physbeh.2013.05.023.

9. John E. Marsh et al., "Why Are Background Telephone Conversations Distracting?" *Journal of Experimental Psychology: Applied* 24, no. 2 (June 2018): 222–235, https://doi.org/10.1037/xap0000170.

10. Adi Gaskell, "What Is the Ideal Noise Level for the Office?" *Forbes*, March 21, 2023, https://www.forbes.com/sites/adigaskell/2023/03/21/what-is-the-ideal-noise-level-for-the-office.

11. Karthik Srinivasan et al., "Discovery of Associative Patterns Between Workplace Sound Level and Physiological Well-being Using Wearable Devices and Empirical Bayes Modeling," *npj Digital Medicine* 6, no. 5 (2023), https://doi.org/10.1038/s41746-022-00727-1.

12. Cassandra D. Gould van Praag et al., "Mind-Wandering and Alterations to Default Mode Network Connectivity When Listening to Naturalistic Versus Artificial Sounds," *Scientific Reports* 7 (2017): Article 45273, https://doi.org/10.1038/srep45273.

13. Paul B. Baltes and Jacqui Smith, "New Frontiers in the Future of Aging: From Successful Aging of the Young Old to the Dilemmas of the Fourth Age," Public Health Reviews 32, no. 2 (2010): 476–483, https://www.ncbi.nlm.nih.gov/pmc/articles/PMC2872309/.

14. Annu Haapakangas et al., "Effects of Five Speech Masking Sounds on Performance and Acoustic Satisfaction: Implications for Open-Plan Offices," Acta Acustica United with Acustica 97, no. 4 (July 2011): 641–655, https://doi.org/10.3813/AAA.918444.

15. Valtteri Hongisto et al., "Perception of Water-Based Masking Sounds—Long-Term Experiment in an Open-Plan Office," Frontiers in Psychology 8 (2017): 1777, https://doi.org/10.3389/fpsyg.2017.01177.

16. Antonia Ferrer-Torres and Lydia Giménez-Llort, "Misophonia: A Systematic Review of Current and Future Trends in This Emerging Clinical Field," *International Journal of Environmental Research and Public Health* 19, no. 11 (June 2022): 6790, https://doi.org/10.3390/ijerph19116790.

17. Louisa J. Rinaldi et al., "Autistic Traits, Emotion Regulation, and Sensory Sensitivities in Children and Adults with Misophonia," *Journal of Autism and Developmental Disorders* 53, no. 3 (2023): 1162–1174, https://doi.org/10.1007/s10803-022-05623-x.

18. Giulia Corniani and Hannes P. Saal, "Tactile Innervation Densities Across the Whole Body," *Journal of Neurophysiology* 124, no. 4 (October 19, 2020), https://doi.org/10.1152/jn.00313.2020.

19. Benjamin Branigan and Prasanna Tadi, "Physiology, Olfactory," in *StatPearls*, last modified May 1, 2023, https://www.ncbi.nlm.nih.gov/books/NBK542239/.

20. Chris Ashwin et al., "Enhanced Olfactory Sensitivity in Autism Spectrum Conditions," *Molecular Autism* 5 (2014): 53, https://doi.org/10.1186/2040-2392-5-53.

21. Ray A. Smith, "The Boss's New Secret Weapon: Pumping Perfume Into the Office," *The Wall Street Journal*, February 21, 2024, https://www.wsj.com/articles/workers-return-office-mood-fragrance-1751be44.

22. International WELL Building Institute, "77. Olfactory Comfort," International WELL Building Institute, accessed August 24, 2024, https://standard.wellcertified.com/v3/comfort/olfactory-comfort.

23. Janet M. Warren, Nicola Smith, and Margaret Ashwell, "A Structured Literature Review on the Role of Mindfulness, Mindful Eating

and Intuitive Eating in Changing Eating Behaviours: Effectiveness and Associated Potential Mechanisms," *Nutrition Research Reviews* 30, no. 2 (December 2017): 272–283, https://doi.org/10.1017/S0954422417000154.

24. Bobbie Smith et al., "The Relationship Between Sensory Sensitivity, Food Fussiness and Food Preferences in Children with Neurodevelopmental Disorders," *Appetite* 150 (July 2020): 104643, https://doi.org/10.1016/j.appet.2020.104643.

25. Tom Y. Chang and Agne Kajackaite, "Battle for the Thermostat: Gender and the Effect of Temperature on Cognitive Performance," *PLOS ONE*, May 22, 2019, https://doi.org/10.1371/journal.pone.0216362.

26. Pam Belluck, "Chilly at Work? Office Formula Was Devised for Men," *The New York Times*, August 3, 2015, https://www.nytimes.com/2015/08/04/science/chilly-at-work-a-decades-old-formula-may-be-to-blame.html.

27. Emma Gowen et al., "From 'One Big Clumsy Mess' to 'a Fundamental Part of My Character': Autistic Adults' Experiences of Motor Coordination," *PLOS ONE* 18, no. 6 (2023): e0286753, https://doi.org/10.1371/journal.pone.0286753.

28. Heather S. McCracken et al., "Sensorimotor Integration and Motor Learning During a Novel Force-Matching Task in Young Adults with Attention-Deficit/Hyperactivity Disorder," *Frontiers in Human Neuroscience* 16 (2022): 1078925, https://doi.org/10.3389/fnhum.2022.1078925.

29. Masahiro Hirai et al., "Greater Reliance on Proprioceptive Information During a Reaching Task with Perspective Manipulation Among Children with Autism Spectrum Disorders," *Scientific Reports* 11 (2021): 15974, https://doi.org/10.1038/s41598-021-95349-0.

30. Roger Kreuz and Richard Roberts, "Proxemics 101: Understanding Personal Space Across Cultures," MIT Press Reader, accessed August 24, 2024, https://thereader.mitpress.mit.edu/understanding-personal-space-proxemics/.

31. Kathryn A. McNaughton and Elizabeth Redcay, "Interpersonal Synchrony in Autism," Current Psychiatry Reports 22, no. 3 (2020): 12, https://doi.org/10.1007/s11920-020-1135-8.

32. Chris R. H. Brown and Sophie Forster, "Lapses in the Person Radar: ADHD Symptoms Predict Difficulty in Interpersonal Distancing," *Journal of Attention Disorders* 27, no. 4 (2023), https://doi.org/10.1177/10870547221149200.

Chapter 8

1. Wichita State University, "Maslow's Hierarchy of Needs," Wichita.edu, accessed September 30, 2024, https://wichita.edu/services/mrc/OIR/Pedagogy/Theories/maslow.php.

2. Susan Magsamen, "Your Brain on Art: The Case for Neuroaesthetics," *Cerebrum* (July 1, 2019), 2019: cer-07-19, PMCID: PMC7075503, PMID: 32206171, https://www.ncbi.nlm.nih.gov/pmc/articles/PMC7075503/.

3. Anjan Chatterjee, "The Neuro-Architecture Triad: A Cheat Code for Designers," *Psychology Today* (January 24, 2024), https://www.psychologytoday.com/au/blog/brain-behavior-and-beauty/202401/the-neuro-architecture-triad-a-cheat-code-for-designers.

4. Jose Guillermo Cedeño Laurent et al., "Associations between Acute Exposures to PM2.5 and Carbon Dioxide Indoors and Cognitive Function in Office Workers: A Multicountry Longitudinal Prospective Observational Study," *Environmental Research Letters* 16, no. 9 (2021), https://doi.org/10.1088/1748-9326/ac1bd8.

5. Donald K. Milton, P. Mark Glencross, and Michael D. Walters, "Risk of Sick Leave Associated with Outdoor Air Supply Rate, Humidification, and Occupant Complaints," *Indoor Air* 10, no. 4 (2000): 212–221, https://doi.org/10.1034/j.1600-0668.2000.010004212.x.

6. International WELL Building Institute, "WELL v2," WELL Certified, accessed September 30, 2024, https://v2.wellcertified.com/en/wellv2/overview/.

7. Marily Oppezzo and Daniel L. Schwartz, "Give Your Ideas Some Legs: The Positive Effect of Walking on Creative Thinking," *Journal of Experimental Psychology: Learning, Memory, and Cognition* 40, no. 4 (2014): 1142–1152, https://doi.org/10.1037/a0036577.

8. Gabriel A. Radvansky, Sabine A. Krawietz, and Andrea K. Tamplin, "Walking through Doorways Causes Forgetting: Further Explorations," *Quarterly Journal of Experimental Psychology* 64, no. 8 (2011): 1632–1645, https://doi.org/10.1080/17470218.2011.571267.

9. Hyojeong Kim et al., "Predictability Changes What We Remember in Familiar Temporal Contexts," *Journal of Cognitive Neuroscience* 32, no. 1 (2020): 124–140, https://doi.org/10.1162/jocn_a_01473.

10. Mohamed Boubekri et al., "Impact of Windows and Daylight Exposure on Overall Health and Sleep Quality of Office Workers: A Case-Control Pilot Study," *Journal of Clinical Sleep Medicine* 10, no. 6 (2014): 603–611, https://doi.org/10.5664/jcsm.3780.

11. Alison J. Xu and Aparna A. Labroo, "Incandescent Affect: Turning on the Hot Emotional System with Bright Light," *Journal of Consumer Psychology* 24, no. 2 (2014): 207–216, https://doi.org/10.1016/j.jcps.2013.12.007.

12. Joshua J. Gooley et al., "Exposure to Room Light Before Bedtime Suppresses Melatonin Onset and Shortens Melatonin Duration in Humans," *Journal of Clinical Endocrinology & Metabolism* 96, no. 3 (March 1, 2011): E463–E472, https://doi.org/10.1210/jc.2010-2098.

13. Susanne Brummelte et al., "Developmental Changes in Serotonin Signaling: Implications for Early Brain Function, Behavior and Adaptation," *Neuroscience* 342 (2017): 212–231, https://doi.org/10.1016/j.neuroscience.2016.02.037.

14. Omar A. Bamalan, Marlyn J. Moore, and Yasir Al Khalili, "Physiology, Serotonin," *StatPearls*, last updated July 30, 2023, https://www.ncbi.nlm.nih.gov/books/NBK545168/.

15. Sally Augustin, "How Lighting Choices Can Affect Your Mood," *Psychology Today*, June 29, 2021, https://www.psychologytoday.com/us/blog/people-places-and-things/202106/how-lighting-choices-can-affect-your-mood.

16. Jozef Hraška and Jakub Ćurpek, "The Practical Implications of the EN 17037 Minimum Target Daylight Factor for Building Design and Urban Daylight in Several European Countries," *Heliyon* 10, no. 1 (January 15, 2024): e23297, https://doi.org/10.1016/j.heliyon.2023.e23297.

17. Mustafa K. Alimoglu and Levent Donmez, "Daylight Exposure and the Other Predictors of Burnout Among Nurses in a University Hospital," *International Journal of Nursing Studies* 42, no. 5 (July 2005): 549–555, https://doi.org/10.1016/j.ijnurstu.2004.09.001.

18. Vanessa Thorpe, "Was Autism the Secret of Warhol's Art?" *The Guardian*, March 13, 1999, https://www.theguardian.com/uk/1999/mar/14/vanessathorpe.theobserver.

19. Samina T. Yousuf Azeemi et al., "The Mechanistic Basis of Chromotherapy: Current Knowledge and Future Perspectives," *Complementary Therapies in Medicine* 46 (October 2019): 217–222, https://doi.org/10.1016/j.ctim.2019.08.025.

20. Ashwini S. Nair et al., "A Case Study on the Effect of Light and Colors in the Built Environment on Autistic Children's Behavior," *Frontiers in Psychiatry* 13 (2022): 1042641, https://doi.org/10.3389/fpsyt.2022.1042641.

21. Chloe Taylor et al., "Color Preferences in Infants and Adults Are Different," *Psychonomic Bulletin & Review* 20 (2013): 916–922, https://doi.org/10.3758/s13423-013-0411-6.

22. Clare Gilbert and Karin van Dijk, "When Someone Has Low Vision," *Community Eye Health Journal* 25, no. 77 (2012): 4–11, https://www.ncbi.nlm.nih.gov/pmc/articles/PMC3404439/.

23. Domicela Jonauskaite, Ahmad Abu-Akel, and Christine Mohr, "Universal Patterns in Color-Emotion Associations Are Further Shaped by Linguistic and Geographic Proximity," *Psychological Science* 31, no. 10 (2020), https://doi.org/10.1177/0956797620948810.

24. Stephen R. Kellert, Judith H. Heerwagen, and Martin L. Mador, eds., *Biophilic Design: The Theory, Science, and Practice of Bringing Buildings to Life* (Hoboken, NJ: John Wiley & Sons, 2008).

25. Ibid.

26. Ibid.

27. Ibid.

28. Avishag Shemesh et al., "The Emotional Influence of Different Geometries in Virtual Spaces: A Neurocognitive Examination," *Journal of Environmental Psychology* 81 (June 2022): 101802, https://doi.org/10.1016/j.jenvp.2022.101802.

29. Ashwini S. Nair et al., "A Case Study on the Effect of Light and Colors in the Built Environment on Autistic Children's Behavior," *Frontiers in Psychiatry* 13 (2022): 1042641, https://doi.org/10.3389/fpsyt.2022.1042641.

30. An T. D. Le et al., "Discomfort from Urban Scenes: Metabolic Consequences," *Landscape and Urban Planning* 160 (2017): 61–68, https://visualstress.info/2016-238.pdf.

Chapter 9

1. Edward O. Wilson, *Biophilia* (Cambridge, MA: Harvard University Press, 1986).
2. James Hutson and Piper Hutson, "Neuroinclusive Workplaces and Biophilic Design: Strategies for Promoting Occupational Health and Sustainability in Smart Cities," *GHES* 1, no. 1 (2023): 0549, https://doi.org/10.36922/ghes.0549.
3. Ibid.
4. Stephen R. Kellert, Judith H. Heerwagen, and Martin L. Mador, eds., *Biophilic Design: The Theory, Science, and Practice of Bringing Buildings to Life* (Hoboken, NJ: John Wiley & Sons, 2008).
5. Bum Jin Park et al., "The Physiological Effects of Shinrin-yoku (Taking in the Forest Atmosphere or Forest Bathing): Evidence from Field Experiments in 24 Forests Across Japan," *Environmental Health and Preventive Medicine* 15, no. 1 (2010): 18–26, https://environhealthprevmed.biomedcentral.com/articles/10.1007/s12199-009-0086-9.
6. Seong-Hyun Park and Richard H. Mattson, "Ornamental Indoor Plants in Hospital Rooms Enhanced Health Outcomes of Patients Recovering from Surgery," *Journal of Alternative and Complementary Medicine* 15, no. 9 (2009): 975–80, https://doi.org/10.1089/acm.2009.0075.
7. Roger S. Ulrich, "View through a Window May Influence Recovery from Surgery," *Science* 224, no. 4647 (1984): 420–1, https://doi.org/10.1126/science.6143402.
8. Raghavendra Kumar et al., "A Systematic Review on Mitigation of Common Indoor Air Pollutants Using Plant-Based Methods: A Phytoremediation Approach," *Air Quality, Atmosphere & Health*, March 11, 2023, https://doi.org/10.1007/s11869-023-01326-z.
9. Zachary J. Williams, Erin E. McKenney, and Katherine O. Gotham, "Investigating the Structure of Trait Rumination in Autistic Adults: A Network Analysis," *Autism* 25, no. 7 (October 2021): 2048–2063, https://doi.org/10.1177/13623613211012855.

10. Ali Kandeger, Serifre O. Ünal, and Muhammed T. Ergün, "Mentation Processes Such as Excessive Mind Wandering, Rumination, and Mindfulness Mediate the Relationship Between ADHD Symptoms and Anxiety and Depression in Adults with ADHD," *European Psychiatry* 66, Suppl. 1 (March 2023): S113-S114, https://doi.org/10.1192/j.eurpsy.2023.309.

11. Gregory N. Bratman et al., "Nature Experience Reduces Rumination and Subgenual Prefrontal Cortex Activation," *Proceedings of the National Academy of Sciences of the United States of America* 112, no. 28 (June 29, 2015): 8567–8572, https://doi.org/10.1073/pnas.1510459112.

12. Hutson and Hutson, "Neuroinclusive Workplaces," 0549.

13. Ibid.

14. Gabriela Gonçalves et al., "Restorative Effects of Biophilic Workplace and Nature Exposure during Working Time: A Systematic Review," *International Journal of Environmental Research and Public Health* 20, no. 21 (2023): 6986, https://doi.org/10.3390/ijerph20216986.

15. University of Exeter, "Why Plants in the Office Make Us More Productive," *University of Exeter News Archive*, accessed September 30, 2024, https://news-archive.exeter.ac.uk/featurednews/title_409094_en.html.

16. Jennifer Whitehead, "*Ways Biophilic Design Promotes Human Health and Well-Being,*" University of Central Arkansas Art and Design, March 30, 2021, https://uca.edu/art/2021/03/30/ways-biophilic-design-promotes-human-health-and-well-being/.

17. Michael Kent and Stefano Schiavon, "Evaluation of the Effect of Landscape Distance Seen in Window Views on Visual Satisfaction," *Building and Environment* 183 (2020): 107160, https://doi.org/10.1016/j.buildenv.2020.107160.

18. Lara S. Franco, Danielle F. Shanahan, and Richard A. Fuller, "A Review of the Benefits of Nature Experiences: More Than Meets the Eye," *International Journal of Environmental Research and Public Health* 14, no. 8 (August 2017): 864, https://doi.org/10.3390/ijerph14080864.

19. Marcia P. Jimenez et al., "Associations Between Nature Exposure and Health: A Review of the Evidence," *International Journal of Environmental Research and Public Health* 18, no. 9 (2021): 4790, https://doi.org/10.3390/ijerph18094790.

20. Xindi Zhang et al., "Waterscapes for Promoting Mental Health in the General Population," *International Journal of Environmental Research and*

Public Health 18, no. 22 (November 2021): 11792, https://doi.org/ 10.3390/ijerph182211792.

21. Judith Goris et al., "The Relation Between Preference for Predictability and Autistic Traits," *Autism Research* 13, no. 7 (July 2020): 1144-1154, https://doi.org/10.1002/aur.2244.

22. Arthur E. Stamps III, "Some Findings on Prospect and Refuge: I," *Perceptual and Motor Skills* 106, no. 1 (February 2008): 147-162, https:// doi.org/10.2466/pms.106.1.147-162.

23. U.S. Department of Health and Human Services, "Workplace Mental Health & Well-Being," *Office of the Surgeon General*, accessed August 29, 2024, https://hhs.gov/surgeongeneral/priorities/workplace-well-being/index.html.

24. Ron Friedman, "Why Our Cubicles Make Us Miserable," *Psychology Today*, April 13, 2015, https://psychologytoday.com/intl/blog/glue/201504/why-our-cubicles-make-us-miserable.

25. Sirpa Lusa et al., "Employee Satisfaction With Working Space and Its Association With Well-Being—A Cross-Sectional Study in a Multi-Space Office," *Frontiers in Public Health* 7 (2019): 358, https://doi.org/ 10.3389/fpubh.2019.00358.

26. Alison J. Xu and Aparna A. Labroo, "Incandescent Affect: Turning on the Hot Emotional System with Bright Light," *Journal of Consumer Psychology* 24, no. 2 (April 2014): 207-216, https://doi.org/10.1016/ j.jcps.2013.12.007.

27. Gloria Mark, "*Speaking of Psychology: Why Our Attention Spans Are Shrinking*," American Psychological Association, February 2023, https:// www.apa.org/news/podcasts/speaking-of-psychology/attention-spans.

28. Dimitri van der Linden, Mattie Tops, and Arnold B. Bakker, "Go with the Flow: A Neuroscientific View on Being Fully Engaged," *European Journal of Neuroscience* 53, no. 4 (February 2021): 947-963, https://doi .org/10.1111/ejn.15014.

29. Ibid.

30. Mary Czerwinski, Paul Johns, and Shamsi T. Iqbal, "The Cost of Email Use in the Workplace: Lower Productivity and Higher Stress," published May 1, 2016, accessed September 30, 2024, https://semanticscholar

.org/paper/The-Cost-of-Email-Use-in-the-Workplace%3A-Lower-and-Czerwinski-Johns/67b8260b4779107173d073abed9ec09ac5b5f40f.

31. Microsoft, "Will AI Fix Work?" *Work Trend Index Annual Report*, Microsoft, May 9, 2023, https://microsoft.com/en-us/worklab/work-trend-index/will-ai-fix-work.

32. Microsoft. "Too Many Meetings? Here's How AI Could Change That," *Microsoft WorkLab*, accessed July 7, 2024, https://microsoft.com/en-us/worklab/how-ai-could-change-having-too-many-meetings.

33. Gloria Mark, Daniela Gudith, and Ulrich Klocke, "The Cost of Interrupted Work: More Speed and Stress," in *Proceedings of the 2008 Conference on Human Factors in Computing Systems, CHI 2008*, Florence, Italy, April 5-10, 2008, https://researchgate.net/publication/221518077_The_cost_of_interrupted_work_More_speed_and_stress.

34. Vincent Hoofs et al., "Task Switching in Autism: An EEG Study on Intentions and Actions," *Neuropsychologia* 117 (August 2018): 398-407, https://doi.org/10.1016/j.neuropsychologia.2018.07.008.

35. Athina Ioannou, "Mindfulness and Technostress in the Workplace: A Qualitative Approach," *Frontiers in Psychology* 14 (2023): 1252187, https://doi.org/10.3389/fpsyg.2023.1252187.

36. Gloria Mark, Daniela Gudith, and Ulrich Klocke, "The Cost of Interrupted Work: More Speed and Stress," *CHI '08: Proceedings of the SIGCHI Conference on Human Factors in Computing Systems* (April 2008): 107-110, https://ics.uci.edu/~gmark/chi08-mark.pdf.

37. Darla Rothman, "A Tsunami of Learners Called Generation Z," *Continuing Education at WVU*, accessed September 30, 2024, https://ce.wvu.edu/media/15624/needs-different_learning_styles.pdf.

38. Ethan Bernstein, Jesse Shore, and David Lazer, "How Intermittent Breaks in Interaction Improve Collective Intelligence," *Proceedings of the National Academy of Sciences* 115, no. 35 (2018): 8734-8739, https://doi.org/10.1073/pnas.1802407115.

39. Felicitas Biwer et al., "Understanding Effort Regulation: Comparing 'Pomodoro' Breaks and Self-Regulated Breaks," *British Journal of Educational Psychology* 93, Suppl 2 (August 2023): 353-367, https://doi.org/10.1111/bjep.12593.

40. Libby Sander, "'Disastrous Experiment': Real Reason Behind Hated Return to Work Push," *News.com.au*, June 8, 2023, https://www.news .com.au/finance/work/at-work/disastrous-experiment-real-reason-behind-hated-return-to-work-push/news-story/6f377ea396388a531d e6cedf89936fe5.

Chapter 10

1. U.S. Department of Justice, Civil Rights Division, "Americans with Disabilities Act of 1990, As Amended," ADA.gov, accessed August 1, 2024, https://www.ada.gov/law-and-regs/ada/.
2. U.S. Department of Justice, Civil Rights Division, "Introduction to the Americans with Disabilities Act," ADA.gov, accessed September 24, 2024, https://www.ada.gov/topics/intro-to-ada/.
3. Government Equalities Office and Equality and Human Rights Commission, "Equality Act 2010: Guidance," GOV.UK, published February 27, 2013, last updated June 16, 2015, https://www.gov.uk/guidance/equality-act-2010-guidance.
4. Rosemarie Rossetti, "The Seven Principles of Universal Design," *Action Magazine*, December 2006, https://udll.com/media-room/articles/the-seven-principles-of-universal-design/.
5. Nancy Doyle, "Is There a Neurodiversity Backlash?" *Forbes*, May 23, 2024, https://www.forbes.com/sites/drnancydoyle/2024/05/23/is-there-a-neurodiversity-backlash.
6. Interaction Design Foundation, "Inclusive Design," accessed September 30, 2024, https://www.interaction-design.org/literature/topics/inclusive-design.
7. Ludmila N. Praslova, "An Intersectional Approach to Inclusion at Work," *Harvard Business Review*, June 21, 2022, https://hbr.org/2022/06/an-intersectional-approach-to-inclusion-at-work.
8. Kimberle Crenshaw, "Demarginalizing the Intersection of Race and Sex: A Black Feminist Critique of Antidiscrimination Doctrine, Feminist Theory and Antiracist Politics," University of Chicago Legal Forum 1989, no. 1 (1989): 139-167, http://chicagounbound.uchicago .edu/uclf/vol1989/iss1/8.

Chapter 11

1. David Pearl, *Will There Be Donuts?: Start a Business Revolution One Meeting at a Time* (New York: HarperCollins Publishers, 2013).
2. David Robson, "Dunbar's Number: Why We Can Only Maintain 150 Relationships," *BBC Future*, October 9, 2019, accessed September 25, 2024, https://www.bbc.com/future/article/20191001-dunbars-number-why-we-can-only-maintain-150-relationships.
3. S. Colenberg and Mathilda du Preez, "Developing a Community-Supporting Office Layout for Academics: A Case Study," in *Proceedings of the 23rd EuroFM Research Symposium*, edited by Rikka Kyro and Tuuli Jylha, 2024, pp. 202-208.
4. Nicolas Fay, Simon Garrod, and Jean Carletta, "Group Discussion as Interactive Dialogue or as Serial Monologue: The Influence of Group Size," *Psychological Science* 11, no. 6 (2000): 481-486, https://doi.org/10.1111/1467-9280.00292.
5. Hannah Critchlow, *Joined-Up Thinking: The Science of Collective Intelligence and Its Power to Change Our World* (London: Hodder & Stoughton, 2022), accessed September 30, 2024, https://hannahcritchlow.com/books.

Chapter 12

1. Addi P. L. van Bergen et al., "The Association Between Social Exclusion or Inclusion and Health in EU and OECD Countries: A Systematic Review," *European Journal of Public Health* 29, no. 3 (June 2019): 575–582, published online August 6, 2018, https://doi.org/10.1093/eurpub/cky143.
2. Mike Oliver, "The Social Model of Disability: Thirty Years On," *Disability & Society* 28, no. 7 (2013): 1024–1026, https://doi.org/10.1080/09687599.2013.818773.
3. Office of Developmental Primary Care, "Medical and Social Models of Disability," University of California, San Francisco, accessed September 30, 2024, https://odpc.ucsf.edu/clinical/patient-centered-care/medical-and-social-models-of-disability/.
4. Ibid.

5. U.S. Equal Employment Opportunity Commission, "Enforcement Guidance on Reasonable Accommodation and Undue Hardship under the ADA," accessed September 30, 2024, https://www.eeoc.gov/laws/guidance/enforcement-guidance-reasonable-accommodation-and-undue-hardship-under-ada/.

6. Job Accommodation Network, "Costs and Benefits of Accommodation," *AskJAN.org*, last updated April 5, 2024, accessed September 4, 2024, https://askjan.org/topics/costs.cfm.

7. Katie Navarra, "The Real Costs of Recruitment," *SHRM.org*, April 11, 2022, https://www.shrm.org/topics-tools/news/talent-acquisition/real-costs-recruitment.

Chapter 13

1. Kerstin Sailer, "Opinion: Covid Will Force Us to Reimagine the Office. Let's Get It Right This Time," *UCL News*, August 4, 2020, https://ucl.ac.uk/news/2020/aug/opinion-covid-will-force-us-reimagine-office-lets-get-it-right-time/.

2. Erik Veldhoen, *The Art of Working* (The Hague: Academic Service, 2004), 228 pages.

3. Belinda Lanks, "Cozy in Your Cubicle? An Office Design Alternative May Improve Efficiency," *Bloomberg*, September 18, 2014, https://www.bloomberg.com/news/articles/2014-09-18/activity-based-working-office-design-for-better-efficiency.

4. Kay Sargent, "Moving Beyond Open Plan Spaces," *Work Design Magazine*, September 28, 2017, https://workdesign.com/2017/09/moving-beyond-open-plan-spaces/.

5. Ibid.

6. Andrew Mawson, "Is the One-Size-Fits-All Workplace History?" *Forbes*, February 29, 2024, https://forbes.com/sites/amawson/2024/02/29/is-the-one-size-fits-all-workplace-history/.

7. Tom Randall, "The Smartest Building in the World: Inside the Connected Future of Architecture," *Bloomberg Businessweek*, September 23, 2015, https://bloomberg.com/features/2015-the-edge-the-worlds-greenest-building/.

Chapter 14

1. Cristina M. Giannantonio and Amy E. Hurley-Hanson, *"Preface and Introduction to Generation A: Research on Autism in the Workplace,"* (Bingley, UK: Emerald Publishing Limited, 2022), https://digitalcommons .chapman.edu/business_books/12/.

2. Trades Union Congress, "Changing the World of Work for Good," accessed October 31, 2024, https://www.tuc.org.uk.

3. Emily H. Jones et al., "Rule Learning in Autism: The Role of Reward Type and Social Context," *Developmental Neuropsychology* 38, no. 1 (2013): 58–77, https://doi.org/10.1080/87565641.2012.727049.

4. National Institute of Mental Health, "Attention-Deficit/Hyperactivity Disorder," NIMH, accessed October 1, 2024, https://nimh.nih.gov/ health/topics/attention-deficit-hyperactivity-disorder-adhd.

5. Katy Hall, LinkedIn post, "This list of 10 tips aims to help increase productivity for ADHDers," *LinkedIn*, accessed September 5, 2024, https:// www.linkedin.com/posts/katy-hall-40b79214_womeninconstruction- neurodiversity-adhd-ugcPost-7195780327745691649-Mt8Y.

6. City & Guilds Foundation, "Championing and Supporting Neurodiversity in the Workplace," *City & Guilds Foundation*, accessed September 5, 2024, https://www.cityandguildsfoundation.org/what- we-offer/campaigning/neurodiversity-index.

7. City & Guilds, "Neurodivergent Employees Impacted by Lack of Training and Support in the Workplace," March 10, 2023, https:// cityandguilds.com/news/march-2023/neurodivergent-employees- impacted-by-lack-of-training-and-support-in-the-workplace/.

8. Giannantonio and Hurley-Hanson, "Preface and Introduction to *Generation A.*"

9. Understood.org, "New Survey by The Harris Poll Reveals Workplace Stigma for Neurodivergent Employees," May 16, 2024, https://under stood.org/en/press-releases/new-survey-by-the-harris-poll-reveals- workplace-stigma-for-neurodivergent.

10. Almuth McDowall, Nancy Doyle, and Meg Kiseleva, *Neurodiversity at Work 2023: Demand, Supply and a Gap Analysis* (Birkbeck University of London, 2022), accessed September 5, 2024, https://

www.berkshirehealthcare.nhs.uk/media/109514758/neurodiversity-in-business-birkbeck-university-of-london.pdf.

11. Ibid.

Chapter 15

1. World Health Organization, "*Neurological Disorders: Public Health Challenges*" (Geneva: World Health Organization, 2006), accessed September 5, 2024, https://www.who.int/publications/i/item/9789241563369.

2. Kay Sargent, "Designing for Neurodiversity and Inclusion," *Work Design Magazine*, December 6, 2019, accessed September 5, 2024, https://www.workdesign.com/2019/12/designing-for-neurodiversity-and-inclusion.

3. Nancy Doyle, "Is There a Neurodiversity Backlash?," *Forbes*, May 23, 2024, https://www.forbes.com/sites/drnancydoyle/2024/05/23/is-there-a-neurodiversity-backlash.

4. Brooke S. Stalev et al., "Attention-Deficit/Hyperactivity Disorder Diagnosis, Treatment, and Telehealth Use in Adults — National Center for Health Statistics Rapid Surveys System, United States, October–November 2023," *Morbidity and Mortality Weekly Report*, CDC, October 10, 2024, https://www.cdc.gov/mmwr/volumes/73/wr/mm7340a1.htm.

5. Jinan Zeidan et al., "Global Prevalence of Autism: A Systematic Review Update," *Autism Research* 15, no. 5 (May 2022): 778–790, https://doi.org/10.1002/aur.2696.

6. Ibid.

7. Elie Abdelnour, Madeline O. Jansen, and Jessica A. Gold, "ADHD Diagnostic Trends: Increased Recognition or Overdiagnosis?" *Missouri Medicine* 119, no. 5 (September-October 2022): 467–473, https://www.ncbi.nlm.nih.gov/pmc/articles/PMC9616454/.

8. Beata Tick et al., "Heritability of Autism Spectrum Disorders: A Meta-Analysis of Twin Studies," *Journal of Child Psychology and Psychiatry* 57, no. 5 (2016): 585–595, https://doi.org/10.1111/jcpp.12499.

9. Amirhossein Modabbernia, Eva Velthorst, and Abraham Reichenberg. "Environmental Risk Factors for Autism: An Evidence-Based Review of Systematic Reviews and Meta-Analyses," *Molecular Autism* 8 (March 17, 2017): 13. https://doi.org/10.1186/s13229-017-0121-4.

10. David Ireland, Dana Kai Bradford, and David Silvera-Tawil, "Research in Autism-Friendly Technology Needs to Improve to Make a Real Difference for People," *The Conversation*, June 8, 2017, https://theconversation.com/research-in-autism-friendly-technology-needs-to-improve-to-make-a-real-difference-for-people-71618.

11. Amanda Brignell et al., "Communication Interventions for Autism Spectrum Disorder in Minimally Verbal Children," *Cochrane Database of Systematic Reviews*, no. 11 (November 5, 2018), https://doi.org/10.1002/14651858.CD012324.pub2.

12. Steve I. Perlmutter, "Reaching Again: A Glimpse of the Future With Neuroprosthetics," *The Lancet* 389, no. 10081 (March 28, 2017): 1777-1778, https://www.ncbi.nlm.nih.gov/pubmed/28363481.

13. University of Bridgeport, "Artificial Intelligence: A Help or Hindrance to Neurodiverse Users," *University of Bridgeport News*, accessed October 1, 2024, https://bridgeport.edu/news/ai-impact-on-neurodiverse-users/.

14. Ray A. Smith, "The Real Reason You're Having a Hard Time Getting Things Done at the Office," *The Wall Street Journal*, April 8, 2023, https://www.wsj.com/articles/the-real-reason-youre-having-a-hard-time-getting-things-done-at-the-office-5dc138f1.

15. Peter Done, "Don't Forget the Downsides of Remote Work," *Forbes*, August 31, 2022, https://www.forbes.com/councils/forbesbusinesscouncil/2022/08/31/dont-forget-the-downsides-of-remote-work/.

16. Nancy Doyle, "Return to Work? Three Considerations for Neurodivergent Employees," *Forbes*, April 1, 2022, https://www.forbes.com/sites/drnancydoyle/2022/04/01/return-to-work-three-considerations-for-neurodivergent-employees/.

17. Skynova, "2/3 of Employees with ADHD Struggle Daily at Work," *Skynova*, accessed September 5, 2024, https://www.skynova.com/blog/adhd-in-the-workplace.

18. Andrew G. Guzick et al., "Change During Cognitive and Exposure Phases of Cognitive-Behavioral Therapy for Autistic Youth with Anxiety Disorders," *Journal of Consulting and Clinical Psychology* 90, no. 9 (September 2022): 709–714, https://doi.org/10.1037/ccp0000755.

19. Dianne M. Hezel and H. Blair Simpson, "Exposure and Response Prevention for Obsessive-Compulsive Disorder: A Review and New Directions," *Indian Journal of Psychiatry* 61, Suppl. 1 (January 2019): S85–S92, https://doi.org/10.4103/psychiatry.IndianJPsychiatry_516_18.

20. Gleb Tsipursky, "What Is Proximity Bias and How Can Managers Prevent It?" *Harvard Business Review*, October 4, 2022, https://hbr.org/2022/10/what-is-proximity-bias-and-how-can-managers-prevent-it.

21. Amanda Kavanagh, "Remote Worker? Here's Why You Might Not Get That Promotion or Bonus," *Euronews*, May 1, 2024, https://euronews.com/next/2024/05/01/remote-worker-heres-why-you-might-not-get-that-promotion-or-bonus.

22. KPMG, "KPMG 2024 CEO Outlook," accessed October 1, 2024, https://kpmg.com/xx/en/our-insights/value-creation/kpmg-global-ceo-outlook-survey-2024.html.

23. Josephine Joly, Luke Hurst, David Walsh, and Giulia Carbonaro, "Four-Day Week: Which Countries Are Embracing It and How Is It Going So Far?" *Euronews*, February 2, 2024, https://www.euronews.com/next/2024/02/02/the-four-day-week-which-countries-have-embraced-it-and-how-s-it-going-so-far.

24. Ibid.

Acknowledgments

HOK Contributors

To the HOK team that pulled this all together—Tom Polucci, Stephanie Miller, Lisa Green, and especially John Gilmore, whose dedication, guidance, and contributions were invaluable.

Thanks to my HOK colleagues who have sweated and toiled through this journey to help bring this research forward:

- Sarah Oppenhuizen, Director of Interiors, San Francisco
- Katelyn Hoffman, Senior Project Interior Designer, San Francisco
- Olivia Danielson-Veed, Senior Project Interior Designer, Chicago
- Kai Olsen, Director of Design, Interiors, Philadelphia
- Shem Sacewicz, Senior Lab Planner, London
- Steven Burgos, Director of Design, Interiors, Miami
- Caleb Salomons, Director of Design, Interiors, Calgary
- Ilma Wasty, Senior Designer, Interiors, Calgary
- Kristina Kamenar, Director of Design, Interiors, Toronto
- Nambi Gardner, Senior Consultant, Interiors, Los Angeles
- Katherine Antarikso, Project Architect, Philadelphia
- Caitlin Youngster, Architect, Philadelphia

Research Partners and Contributors

Thanks to those who have contributed valuable insights to our research and thought leadership on neuroinclusion:

- Jeffrey Saunders, Behavioural Strategy
- Nancy Doyle, Genius Within
- Mary Kate Cassidy, Allsteel
- Dr. Andrew Ibrahim, University of Michigan
- Gearoid Kearney, myAccessHub
- Helen Needham, Me.Decoded
- Will Wheeler, The Dyslexic Evolution
- Edward Edgerton, University of the West of Scotland
- Kristi Gaines, Texas Tech University
- Annemarie Lombard, Sensory Intelligence
- David Lehrer, Berkeley Center for the Built Environment
- Gail Brager, Berkeley Center for the Built Environment
- Angelita Scott, International Well Building Institute
- Kimberly Lewis, International Well Building Institute
- Rachel Hodgdon, International Well Building Institute
- Gary Clark, Science and Technology Architect, London
- Leslie Thompson, MillerKnoll
- Derrell Jackson, Tarkett
- Jenny Gardner, Advanced Research Clusters (ARC)
- Kathryn Page, Advanced Research Clusters (ARC)
- Clara Weber, ZHAW
- Erica Anesi, pba S.p.A
- Dave Bryant, One Workplace—ONEder Grant
- Carolyn Clark Beedle, One Workplace—ONEder Grant

Advocates and Influencers

We recognize the individuals who have blazed trails as contemporary advocates for diversity and inclusion, many of whom are referenced in this book. Credit goes to those who embraced their true selves or supported others in doing so, recognized the power of authenticity and dedicated themselves to assisting others.

We also acknowledge the families, caregivers, and advocates for neuro-divergents whose lives have been altered as well as they strive to address their loved ones' needs.

Many people we've encountered have influenced and advocated for our work. We extend special thanks to each, including:

- Benjamin Jensen, Landscape Design Professional, Washington, DC
- Eve Edelstein, Neuro-Architecture
- Komal Kotwal, EquiSustain
- Harsha Kotak, Women in Office Design
- Danielle "Dani" Schmitt, JLL
- Sally Augustin, Design with Science
- Nigel Oseland, Workplace Unlimited
- Jeremy Myerson, WORKTECH Academy

Spotlight Participants

Throughout this expedition, we have met many fascinating individuals and had opportunities to engage within people across the spectrum. Our journey has connected us with academics, HR professionals, psychologists, and advocates. We've also met parents who have proven to be some of the most powerful advocates we have encountered.

In the Spotlight profiles throughout this book, we acknowledge some of the most impactful individuals we have met. Each has a unique perspective and story to tell, and all have influenced our work, strengthened our resolve and dedication, and powered us forward in making spaces more inclusive:

- Angelita Scott, International Well Building Institute
- Kate Wardle, Neurodiversity in Business, Include Me Consulting
- Elizabeth Kibirige Namugenyi, International Finance Corporation
- Kristi Gaines, Texas Tech University
- Travis Hollman, Hollman/MeSpace
- Katie Gaudion, The Helen Hamlyn Centre for Design
- Annemarie Lombard, Sensory Intelligence® Consulting
- Gail Brager, Berkeley Center for the Built Environment
- Edward Edgerton, University of the West of Scotland

- Alex Hedlund, Deloitte, Neurodiversity in Business
- Sean Hoffmann, KPMG
- Erica Anesi, pba S.p.A
- Benjamin Jensen, Landscape Design Professional
- Valerie Fletcher, Institute for Human Centered Design
- Toby Mildon, Neurodiversity Consultant
- A.J. Paron, SANDOW Design Group
- Rachel Hodgdon, International Well Building Institute
- Scott Gibson, Melwood
- Tommaso Davi, Neuro-Sive

Clients

Great projects start with great clients, and we are fortunate to have many. These are clients who see opportunities where others see challenges, understand the power of place, and entrust us to work with them on addressing the most complex issues of the day. They go beyond where others are willing to go and address topics for neuroinclusion that benefit all.

In this book, we introduce you to a few who have left their mark:

- Arup: Alison Kilby and James Watts
- KPMG: Vanessa Scaglione, Sean Hoffman, and Frank Erickson
- Fidelity: Christina Zwart and Althea Kearney
- AstraZeneca: Christine White, Andy Parry, and Suzanne Kennedy

Special Recognition

Finally, I want to acknowledge Bob Canavan, who started it all by asking "How do you design space for someone with ADHD?" I hope this book answers your question.

About the Author

Kay Sargent is a practicing, licensed, and certified interior designer with 40 years of experience. She is the director of Thought Leadership, Interiors for HOK, a global design, architecture, engineering, and planning firm. With a passion for using design to transform how and where people work, she spends her days (and many nights) working with clients on workplace strategy, design, and inclusion.

"We are no longer designing the environments—we are designing the experience," Sargent says.

Based in Washington, DC, Sargent leads project teams that solve clients' business and organizational challenges related to real estate business processes, strategic planning, workplace strategy, change management, and designing for inclusion. She collaborates with organizations ranging from tech startups to Fortune 500 companies to optimize their real estate portfolios and create the most innovative, inclusive work experiences. She was selected to provide congressional subject-matter expert testimony to the U.S. House of Representatives on "Federal Real Estate Post-COVID-19: A View from the Private Sector" and has since shared her expertise with congressional committees several times.

In 2024, *Interior Design Magazine* recognized Sargent with a Lifetime of HiPness Award. She also received a Best of NeoCon Gold Award and an Innovation Award for designing the TOCCO hardware line for pba, designed to create more welcoming and inclusive environments. Sargent and her team at HOK have won multiple industry awards for their work on addressing neuroinclusion in the built environment, including:

- 2024 The European Centre for Architecture Art Design and Urban Studies & The Chicago Athenaeum: Museum of Architecture and Design—Green Good Design Sustainability Award
- 2024 European Diversity Award: Diversity in Technology Highly Commended Designing Inclusive Scientific Workplaces
- 2024 Best of NeoCon—Gold Award and Innovation Award
- 2024 NYC XDESIGN Awards Honoree
- 2024 IFPI Global Inclusion Award
- 2023 IWBI Next Frontier of Design Award
- 2023 EDRA Certificate of Research Excellence
- 2022 IFMA Distinguished Author Award for Research on Neurodiversity
- 2022 Melwood Ability Awards Inaugural Accelerator Award
- 2020 CoreNet Global Professional Excellence Award
- 2020 Frame Magazine Orgatec Challenge
- 2020 IWBI Community Award for Advancing Well-being
- 2019 Fast Company Design Innovation Award

Sargent is a member of both the American Society of Interior Designers' College of Fellows and the International Interior Design Association's College of Fellows, a select body of designers whose work has significantly influenced the profession. ASID has also honored Sargent with its highest award, naming her a "Designer of Distinction," whose body of work represents excellence in interior design.

Outside of HOK, Sargent serves on the Delos Advisory Board alongside wellness and sustainability advocates such as Leonardo DiCaprio and Deepak Chopra. She also serves on the advisory board for CoRETech/Real Comm and co-chaired the 2023 events. Sargent has served on the international board of directors for AVIXA, the Audiovisual and Integrated Experience Association; CoreNet Global; IFI, the International Federation of Interior Designers/Architects; IIDA; ASID; and NCQLP. She is chair of the ASID Foundation research task force and on the leadership team of IFMA's WE Workplace Evolutionaries and the advisory board of *Work Design Magazine*.

Sargent has authored numerous reports and articles on the workplace and has spoken at CoreNet, the International Facility Management Association, and other industry events. CoreNet and Tradeline, Inc., have both honored her as a top-rated speaker. A mentor to many, she is a founding member of the DC chapter of UPWARD, which accelerates career advancement for executive women.

About HOK

HOK (hok.com) is a collective of future-forward thinkers and designers who are driven to face the critical challenges of our time. We are dedicated to improving people's lives, serving our clients and healing the planet. Together, we cultivate a culture of design excellence at the confluence of art and science, blending the power of creative expression with a clear sense of purpose.

What We Do

HOK's approach to inclusive design is based on our experience as designers and architects. Our focus is to provide our clients with a wide range of design options for their spaces to accommodate the different needs of as many users as possible, including those who are neurodivergent. However, we also understand that some individuals will have needs that cannot be addressed through design solutions alone.

As discussed in this book, the effectiveness of our design and consulting work is significantly influenced by the feedback and implementation of policies and processes developed by those with expertise in human resources, technology solutions, and building operations. Working together, we all strive to provide options for workplaces that are more inclusive. However, it is important to note that we cannot assure any particular outcome for individual users.

Index